SALT

Maya Studies

Florida A&M University, Tallahassee
Florida Atlantic University, Boca Raton
Florida Gulf Coast University, Ft. Myers
Florida International University, Miami
Florida State University, Tallahassee
University of Central Florida, Orlando
University of Florida, Gainesville
University of North Florida, Jacksonville
University of South Florida, Tampa
University of West Florida, Pensacola

Maya Studies

This series focuses on both the ancient and the contemporary Maya peoples of Belize, Mexico, Guatemala, Honduras, and El Salvador, providing an integrated outlet for scholarship on Maya archaeology, epigraphy, ethnography, and history, and featuring cutting-edge theoretical works, methodologically sound site-reports, and tightly organized edited volumes with broader appeal.

SALT

White Gold of the Ancient Maya

Heather McKillop

University Press of Florida

Gainesville · Tallahassee · Tampa · Boca Raton
Pensacola · Orlando · Miami · Jacksonville · Ft. Myers

07 06 05 04 03 02   6 5 4 3 2 1

Library of Congress Cataloging-in-Publication Data
McKillop, Heather Irene
Salt: white gold of the ancient Maya / Heather McKillop.
p. cm.—(Maya studies)
Includes bibliographical references and index.
ISBN 0-8130-2511-7 (cloth: alk. paper)
1. Mayas—Belize—Economic conditions. 2. Salt industry and trade
—Belize. 3. Mayas—Belize—Antiquities. 4. Mayas—Commerce.
5. Belize—Antiquities. I. Title. II. Series.
F1445 .M35 2002
338.4'76644'09728209021—dc21
2002020045

The University Press of Florida is the scholarly publishing agency
for the State University System of Florida, comprising Florida A&M
University, Florida Atlantic University, Florida Gulf Coast University,
Florida International University, Florida State University, University
of Central Florida, University of Florida, University of North Florida,
University of South Florida, and University of West Florida.

University Press of Florida
15 Northwest 15th Street
Gainesville, FL 32611-2079
http://www.upf.com

To Gordon, Bob, Eleanor, and Tiger

Contents

Figures

Maps

Tables

Foreword

The Maya have fascinated scholars and lay-public alike since their ruined jungle-covered cities were brought to the world's attention by explorers in the mid nineteenth century. Today hundreds of thousands of tourists visit these once remote archaeological ruins each year and come into contact with the modern descendants of the Maya. Public interest in the archaeology of this region also is evident in the news coverage and television programming related to the Maya. At the same time, academic research on the Maya has reached an all-time high. The breadth of contemporary topics enveloped in Maya studies is quite extensive. Not only have traditional anthropological topics (archaeology, ethnography, and epigraphy) related to the Maya continued to be researched and published, but such studies have actively contributed to broader debates concerning warfare, urbanism, sustainable agriculture, culture contact, and hermeneutics. With the recent prominence of the Zapatistas and the Highland unrest in both Mexico and Guatemala, Maya studies also necessarily have become concerned with modern political developments involving nationalism, ethnic exploitation, human rights, and the role of tourism in a global economy.

Heather McKillop's *Salt* is the first volume in a new Maya Studies series that is being published by the University Press of Florida. Subsequent books in the series will focus on both the ancient and contemporary Maya peoples of Belize, Mexico, Guatemala, Honduras, and El Salvador and may include works on Maya who have moved from their original heartland to the United States and elsewhere. The goal for the series is to provide a high-quality integrated outlet for scholarly works dealing with Maya archaeology, epigraphy, ethnography, and history. While the series is expected to be largely archaeological in content, it is envisioned that ethnohistoric, hieroglyphic, ethnographic, and even modern political studies of the Maya would also be published. It is expected that some volumes might also be "commissioned" to fill necessary gaps in the series and to address topics in Maya studies for which theoretical and methodological discord exists. It is our hope that the series will focus on publishing cutting-edge theoretical works, methodologically sound site-reports, and tightly organized edited volumes with broader appeal. We are actively seeking the best book-length contributions to the series; volumes will take a variety of forms and may consist of original book-length texts, revised dissertations, translations of works only available in Spanish, edited works, or site reports. An important part of the series will be the "site report" or its equivalent (such as an ethnographic monograph). The site report has been and will continue to be a mainstay in the field of Maya studies. These detailed and well-illustrated expositions are of great utility to individuals with an interest in the Maya, and the data contained within these volumes will continue to be of use to future generations. We intend to anchor the Maya Studies series with site reports from our own excavations in the Maya area at the sites of Caracol and Santa Rita Corozal in Belize.

The current work by Heather McKillop is an excellent first volume for the new series. Salt was of great importance to the ancient Maya. It was a core resource that was both procured and traded from the coasts into the Maya interior. While the production and political control of salt has been documented both archaeologically and ethnohistorically in the northern Maya lowlands, particularly by Anthony Andrews, McKillop's research shows the long-term production of salt along the eastern Maya littoral. She documents the existence of different salt-production techniques as well as various levels of effort that were expended in salt production along the Belizean coastline. Solar evaporation was used in the more northern portions of Belize, such as Ambergris Cay; boiling was more common in the southern coastal areas near Placencia and Punta Ycacos. McKillop's work at Punta Ycacos clearly demonstrates that salt was produced for export and that this production process went beyond that necessary for the household level. An extensive artifact assemblage associated with salt production has been recovered from the Belizean coast. Unslipped ceramic pots were set upon pottery vessel supports and used to boil brine in order to extract salt. Both brine and partially processed salt were stored in red-slipped water jars. Eventually, the salt was hardened into cakes for transport. McKillop further suggests that the lack of standard lithic assemblages in the salt-production locales is suggestive of transient communities; other ceramic materials are interpreted as providing potential evidence for the existence of festivals. While McKillop favors a less centralized view of the Classic Maya political and social systems (an unresolved issue within Maya studies), her data are both relevant to and easily accommodated within more complex models.

The work contained within this tome is significant on a number of levels. It clearly demonstrates, on an archaeological level, the southern lowland Maya production of salt, meaning that there could have been a consequent lack of dependence upon northern lowland salt sources during the Late Classic Period. That salt was produced by groups of individuals that were larger than a single household supports the premise that Maya in different regions may have maintained distinct economic specializations. The extensive community-wide long-term production of chert has previously been documented in northern Belize at the site of Colha by Tom Hester and Harry Shafer. Together, these two examples serve to indicate the interrelatedness of the various Classic Maya political and economic landscapes. McKillop's work is also of relevance to other areas of archaeological interpretation. It specifically highlights the very real problems involved in predicting population numbers without considering "invisible population" from "vacant terrain" locations; Punta Ycacos and other sites along the Belize coast have been hidden by a 1 m rise in sea level. As such a rise in sea level has occurred in the recent past (witness former Maya occupation now under water within Corozal Bay or at the edges of Moho Cay), many former production and work areas may now be under water, thus skewing much of our archaeological understanding of the coastal production of salt, shells, salted fish, and other resources.

There is currently no other series dedicated to the publication of book-length works on the full spectrum of research on the ancient and modern Maya. We hope that our new Maya Studies series, inaugurated by McKillop's excellent contribution, will bring to Maya studies the much-needed forum it deserves.

Diane Z. Chase and Arlen F. Chase
Series Editors

Acknowledgments

The 1991 and 1994 fieldwork upon which this study is based was made possible by permits from the Belizean government's Department of Archaeology and the Department of Forestry, through Archaeological Commissioner Harriot Topsey, and was facilitated by the friendship and assistance of the government archaeologists. Funding for the fieldwork was generously provided by Earthwatch and its corps of volunteers, by an Arts and Sciences Summer Faculty Fellowship from Louisiana State University in 1991, and by private donations. Funding for analyses of artifacts in 1995 was provided by a Manship Summer Research Grant from Louisiana State University. The Department of Geography and Anthropology at LSU supported my research in many ways, for which I am grateful.

I appreciate the assistance of my field staff, notably Jodi Brandehoff-Pracht, Melissa Braud, Andrea (Freudenberger) Butler, Jean Carpenter, Brad Ensor, Laurie Jackson, Eric Malatesta, Mirtha Martin, Lyra Spang, Nathaniel Spang, Ted Steiner, Orlando Usher, Shelley Warrington, and Rachel Watson. I gratefully acknowledge the late Adel Chan and Osmond Chan for permission to camp and carry out research in 1991 at our base camp on Wild Cane Cay and appreciate their friendship. John Spang and Tanya Russ, owners of Frenchman's Cay, graciously allowed us to camp and carry out research at our base camp on Frenchman's Cay in 1994. I appreciate their friendship, good humor, and the insights into Maya archaeology that they shared with me. Many people helped in various ways from Punta Gorda, the point of embarkation and nearest place for provisioning for my project. I particularly would like to thank Paul and Amber Carpenter, Harry Gomez, Alistair and Edna King, Max Stout, Chet Schmidt, Jack Nightingale, Barbara Frasier, Brian and Anna Holland, Julio and Leonore Requena, Bobby Polonio, Peter and Irene Mahung, Will

Heyman, Wil Maheia, and Wallace and Felice Young. To our nearest coastal neighbor, the late Charlie Carlson, I acknowledge his friendship and discovery of one of the salt work shops, Killer Bee. Elsewhere in Belize, many people assisted, most notably Emory King Sr., the late Jean Shaw, and the late Winnel Branche.

I appreciate the assistance of my Earthwatch volunteers who assisted with the salt research, either in the lagoon or the field lab, including Anne Alexander, Linda Clark, Pat Colquette, Anne Daniels, Chris Degraffenreid, Ellen Devine, Carol Dodds, Scott Dougald, Cate Heneghan, Bill Heth, Anthony Holley, Eva Kulda, Janet Liles, Cassie Major, Joe Mares, Cecil McCurry, Kate Mitchell, Minor Myers, Heather Osborn, Beth Pope, Jack Romig, Sally Strazdins, and Gene Stroot, among others.

Mai Dinh assisted with data and photographic records during the summers of 1995 and 1996, when the artifacts were analyzed at LSU, and I appreciate her persistence and good humor. Mary Lee Eggart drew or enhanced most of the illustrations, either from my sketches or from the artifacts, and I am grateful to her for visually improving the manuscript. Farrell Jones answered many questions about GIS for the Wild Cane Cay maps. My graduate assistant, Bryan Tucker, assisted with manuscript preparation. I appreciate the assistance of Bill Fash and the curatorial staff at the Peabody Museum, Harvard University, for facilitating my study of Maya pottery in their collections. My husband, Bob Tague, assisted with statistical analyses and encouraged me in writing the book, for both of which I am grateful.

My views on salt, trade, and the coastal Maya have benefited over the years from discussions with many colleagues, most notably Elizabeth Graham, Tony Andrews, Shirley B. Mock, Joyce Marcus, Paul Healy, Arlen and Diane Chase, William V. Davidson, Barbara Voorhies, Robert Tague, Susan Kepecs, John Spang, and Tanya Russ. I appreciate the insightful comments of the reviewers of this book, Elizabeth Graham and Fred Valdez. In particular, I thank Meredith Morris-Babb, editor-in-chief at the University Press of Florida, and the series editors Arlen and Diane Chase for their enthusiasm for this book, as well as the editorial staff at the University Press of Florida for carefully preparing the manuscript for publication.

To these and other people who participated with me or supported the excitement of fieldwork, the discovery of clues among the artifacts, and discussions about ancient Maya salt, I extend my thanks. You made this project both possible and enjoyable.

1

ᒣᒣᒣᒣᒣᒣ

Salt as a Maya Trade Good

Although basic to daily human existence, salt was scarce in the southern Maya lowlands of Guatemala and Belize where the Classic period civilization developed between A.D. 300 and 900 (map 1.1). The prevailing interpretation is that salt was imported in bulk from the north coast of the Yucatan (Andrews 1983). Various researchers have argued that long-distance trade is usually restricted to limited quantities of precious goods, such as gold, copper, obsidian, and elite pottery vessels (Cowgill 1993; Tourtellot and Sabloff 1972; Wallerstein 1974). Even if we consider that long-distance trade is unusual for a bulk resource in preindustrial societies, there are exceptions. The extensive overland salt trade over the Sahara via Timbuktu used caravans of camels to transport bulk salt, and there are even cases of human porters each carrying loads of salt in Africa (Adshead 1992:20). Moreover, the ability of ancient Maya canoe traders to move cargo in coastal waters should not be underestimated. Certainly various ancient peoples living along the Mediterranean Sea developed thriving water commerce. However, recent fieldwork along the coast of Belize has documented closer sources of salt than those on the north coast of the Yucatan, calling into question the economic viability of importing northern Yucatan salt to the southern Maya lowlands during the height of the Late Classic civilization (A.D. 600–900).

The Belizean salt sources have been reported at Northern River Lagoon, Salt Creek Lagoon, San Juan and Marco Gonzalez on Ambergris Cay, Watson's Island and Placencia in the Stann Creek District, and Punta

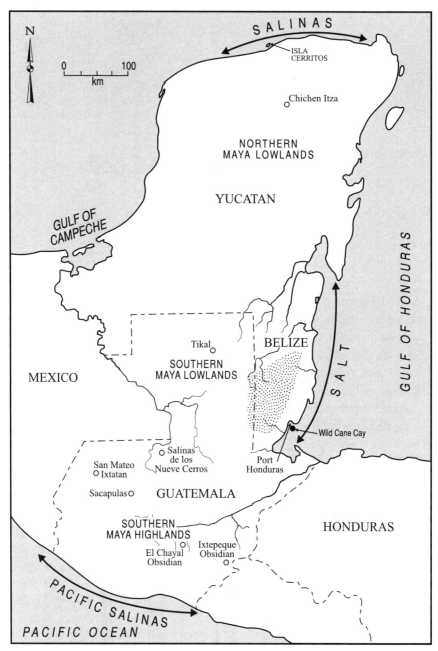

Map 1.1. Maya Area, Showing Northern Yucatan and Coastal Belize Salt Zones. By Mary Lee Eggart.

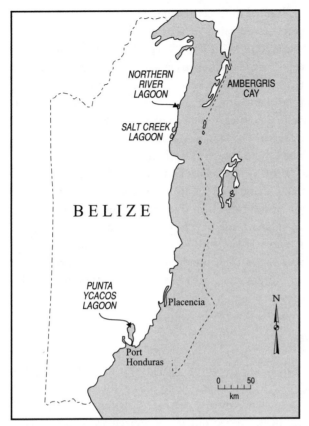

Map 1.2. Belize, Showing Ancient Salt-Production Areas. By Mary Lee Eggart.

Ycacos Lagoon (map 1.2; Braud 1996; Graham 1994; Graham and Pendergast 1989; Guderjan 1988; MacKinnon and Kepecs 1989; McKillop
1995a; Meighan and Bennyhoff 1952; Mock 1994). Could the ancient
Maya of coastal Belize have produced enough salt to meet the needs of the
Classic period Maya of the southern lowlands of Belize and Guatemala?
Alternatively, was some or most of the salt acquired from regional trade
between the coast of Belize and the interior? These questions are ad-
dressed by research in Punta Ycacos Lagoon, in the Port Honduras of
southern Belize.

The Port Honduras is a coastal bight between the modern towns of
Punta Gorda and Punta Negra in southern Belize. Punta Ycacos Lagoon is
a large, shallow lagoon system at the northern end of the Port Honduras.

Wild Cane Cay also is located in the Port Honduras, and in former times the island's inhabitants participated in coastal-inland trade as well as coastal canoe trade (McKillop 1987, 1989, 1996a, 2001). Several major rivers, including the Deep River, Golden Stream, and Middle River, as well as the smaller Seven Hills Creek, flow into the Port Honduras and, along with the Rio Grande to the south, would have provided canoe access to nearby Classic Maya inland cities, notably Lubaantun, Nim li punit, and Uxbenka. The salt works in Punta Ycacos Lagoon were discovered after fieldwork at Wild Cane Cay to investigate whether there were communities other than Wild Cane Cay in the Port Honduras and how they figured in trade. Excavation and analysis of the Punta Ycacos Lagoon salt works call for a reevaluation of long-distance trade in salt and underscore the importance of coastal-inland trade of salt and other maritime resources within the southern Maya lowlands. The Punta Ycacos salt works also provide an example of specialized, nondomestic work shop production away from the urban centers and instead located near the raw material source, in this case the sea.

Goals and Objectives

If the coastal Belize salt works produced enough salt to significantly reduce or replace long-distance salt import from the northern Yucatan coast to the southern Maya lowlands during the Late Classic period, then salt production must have been carried out in specialized work shops. This occupational specialization of salt production was arguably beyond the household level of organization: enough salt had to be produced to supply salt for inland trade as well as for local use. Since the Late Classic Maya were an advanced civilization, with evidence of occupational specialization of other tasks (Becker 1973; Foias and Bishop 1997; Fry 1980; Rands and Bishop 1980; Reents-Budet 1994, 1998; Rice 1981, 1987a; Shafer and Hester 1983), the possibility of specialized salt works along the Belize coast fits within our understanding of ancient Maya economy. Why then had previous researchers not considered salt production along the Belizean coast as a viable alternative to long-distance import of this basic daily resource?

A rise in sea level since the end of the Classic period submerged Classic Maya salt works along the coast of Belize and rendered them invisible to modern archaeological searches on dry land. Although archaeologists working along the Belize coast had mentioned the existence of submerged archaeological deposits, the impact of ancient sea-level rise on Classic Maya sites was undocumented. Sea-level rise had completely submerged the Punta Ycacos Lagoon salt work shops and hidden them from modern view. The salt work shops were discovered by underwater reconnaissance in the summer of 1991 and excavated in 1991 and 1994. Invisible in the modern landscape, the work shops were marked by artifact scatters on the seafloor. A systematic search indicated that Late Classic Maya salt work shops and communities throughout the Port Honduras were submerged by rising seas. By inference, the Late Classic landscape along the Belizean coast has been transformed by sea-level rise, effectively rendering many ancient sites invisible.

The low-lying coastal landscape of the Port Honduras incidentally provided an ideal laboratory for investigating the role of the environment in cultural change and the following issues: What was the response of the Late Classic Maya to rising seas? Were communities abandoned that were threatened by inundation? Alternatively, were preventive measures taken to ward off the rising seas, such as landfill or stone foundations to raise houses? Did anthropogenic soil buildup from centuries of human garbage keep some communities above sea level? With the modern threat of global climate warming and consequent worldwide sea-level rise submerging low-lying coastal areas, the ancient Maya responses to sea-level rise provide valuable analogues.

The artifacts recovered from excavations in Punta Ycacos Lagoon resemble pots and associated vessel supports used elsewhere to boil brine over fires to produce loose salt or salt cakes (Adshead 1992). This is a common method of salt production throughout prehistory and history in many areas of the world, including Mesoamerica (Adshead 1992; Andrews 1983; Bloch 1963; Coe and Flannery 1967; Dillon 1977; Ewald 1985; Feldman 1971; Nance 1992; Nenquin 1961; Parsons 1989; Riehm 1961). For example, most of the salt works at the 350 sites known for pre-Roman Europe used the technique of boiling a salty solution from brine springs, with ample artifactual evidence consisting of pottery sherds from salt pots, referred to as "briquetage" (Adshead 1992:4; Nenquin 1961). Known in Mesoamerica as the "sal cocida" method, it is still practiced in the highlands of Guatemala using brine from salt springs (Reina and Monaghen 1981). This method contrasts to the gathering of salt from the salt flats on the north coast of the Yucatan, in which salt—sal solar—is produced by the evaporation of seawater. Despite arguments of the greater ease of gathering salt deposited along coastlines (Andrews 1983), salt produced from the sal cocida method of boiling brine, either from the sea, salt springs, or underground salt mines, was more common prehistorically and historically elsewhere in the world (Adshead 1992). In some cases, as in sixteenth- through nineteenth-century England, salt produced by boiling brine produced most of the salt for local consumption as well as being a significant export commodity.

Another reason that Belize was not considered as a major source of dietary salt was the erroneous interpretation that there was too much rain on the Belizean coast, that salt pans were not possible in Belize, and that the northern Yucatan salt flats were more productive. Graham (1994:247) has cautiously suggested that the similarity of Coconut Walk Unslipped pottery bowl sherds from Watson's Island to salt-boiling pots at modern Sacapulas, Guatemala, indicated a similar function for the Watson's Island vessels. However, she played down the possibility of the use of Coconut Walk Unslipped bowls in salt production until more data were collected (Graham 1994:247)! Although it does rain more along the coast of Belize than on the northern Yucatan coast (and in fact, the farther south one travels in Belize, the more rain there is), rain would not have been a hindrance during the dry season. At that time it was certainly possible to boil brine in pots over fires, after the brine had been enriched in its salt content by pouring it through salt-saturated soil or evaporating it in salt pans. In fact, the sal cocida method was practiced prehistorically along the Pacific coasts of Mexico, Guatemala, and El Salvador (Andrews 1983; Coe and Flannery 1967; Nance 1992) and in historic times (Ewald 1985). The transport costs involved in moving northern Yucatan salt to the southern Maya lowlands need to be considered in any scenario calling Belizean salt inefficient.

The discovery and excavation of the Punta Ycacos salt works and the analysis of the recovered salt-production equipment call for a reevaluation of our understanding of Late Classic Maya economy and environment. The Punta Ycacos data support a new model of salt production and trade in which salt production occurred in work shops operated by independent specialists. The work shops were locally controlled near the source of the raw material (the sea), enabling the coastal Maya of southern Belize to maintain a degree of political and economic autonomy from the inland Maya at nearby large cities. The specialized production is consistent with a model of coastal-inland bulk transport of salt that significantly reduced or essentially eliminated long-distance import of salt. The development of the salt work shops is tied to population increase in the southern Maya lowlands between A.D. 600 and 800, during the Late Classic period. The high cost of bulk transport of sal solar from the north coast of the Yucatan made the Belizean sal cocida production cost efficient, despite its higher labor costs in production. Moreover, labor costs may have been incidental if work was accomplished by farmers in the nonagricultural dry season. In an ethnoarchaeological study of salt production in Mexico, Williams (1999:407) found that salt-making is carried out in the dry season when farmers are otherwise idle. The regular coastal-inland trade of salt was enhanced by the supply of ritual resources such as stingray spines from the sea to inland consumers and the integration of coastal elites into inland royal lineages by marriage.

The Coastal Maya

How important was the Belizean coast in ancient times to inland cities in the southern Maya lowlands, both as a transportation route for goods and resources from distant places and as a supplier of salt and other resources from the sea? Coastal Belizean communities were discussed by early researchers such as Vermeer (1959), Wright et al. (1959), and Craig (1966) in terms of their role in long-distance trade, but also as coastal communities integrated into regional systems focused at nearby large inland Maya cities. This dual theme has continued to permeate discussions of coastal Maya trade and has been a useful, albeit somewhat vague, framework. Only in the late twentieth century were the dynamics of specific coastal economies articulated as a result of extensive fieldwork along the Belizean coast. There were settlements along the coast of Belize from Preclassic through Postclassic times, but were these communities integrated into the larger Maya economy, or were they marginal to its development? (maps 1.3–1.5; Boxt 1989; Chase 1981; Freidel 1978; Graham 1989, 1994; Graham and Pendergast 1989; Guderjan et al. 1989; Guderjan and Garber 1995; MacKinnon 1989; McKillop 1980, 1989, 1996a; McKillop and Healy 1989). Did coastal communities figure in long-distance sea trade as occupants of trading ports? Were maritime resources such as stingray spines, conch shells, fish, and salt procured by the coastal Maya for inland trade? Alternatively, were the sites along the Belizean coast primarily fishing

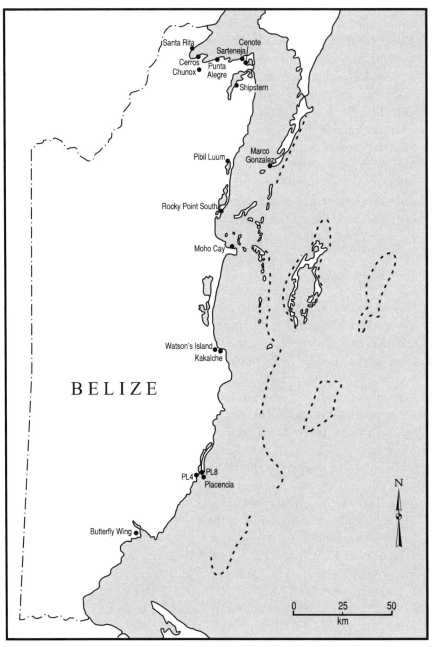

Map 1.3. Preclassic Coastal Sites in Belize. By Mary Lee Eggart.

l trade as important during the Late Preclassic period, as evidenced
 precocious display of monumental architecture and the presence of
an and finely carved jade ornaments. Similar iconography and sta-
raphernalia indicated communication among elites at Cerros and
 other emerging lowland polities. Freidel viewed the abandonment
ros at the end of the Late Preclassic period as a reflection of the
 of coastal trade.

Period Coastal Maya

tional models of Maya trade, transportation routes along the coast
 been utilized in the Late Preclassic were replaced by inland trails
rs with the rise of the Classic period cities in the interior of the
(Ball 1977; Freidel 1979; Sabloff 1977; Thompson 1970). How-
ensive settlement of the Belizean coast during the Classic period
 that there was a continuity and even expansion of maritime
t and trade from Preclassic times (map 1.4). In fact, the coast of
 a transportation corridor for long-distance traders during the
riod: various coastal and offshore island locations, such as San
Ambergris Cay (Guderjan and Garber 1995), Moho Cay near
y (McKillop 1980, 1984; Healy et al. 1984), the Colson Point
tson's Island and Kakalche on the central coast (Graham 1994),
area sites (MacKinnon 1989), Wild Cane Cay (McKillop 1987,
Frenchman's Cay (McKillop 2001; McKillop and Winemiller
described as way stations, trading ports, or transshipment cen-
otic materials during the Classic and Postclassic periods (An-
). Many other coastal sites date to the Late Classic period (map
ted with a general population increase in the southern Maya
that time. There appears to have been limited use of the Beliz-
ring the Early Classic period (A.D. 300–600), with notable ex-
Moho Cay, Wild Cane Cay, the Colson Point sites, and Santa
, among others. Santa Rita Corozal was a large community
 in long-distance trade during the Early Classic period (Chase
986, 1989).
astal Maya of Belize obtain their obsidian from sea traders
wares along a coastal trade route during the Classic period?
tal settlers supplied with obsidian and other exotic trade
 with nearby inland regional centers, supplied from inland
 routes? Research at Wild Cane Cay indicates that obsidian
de goods were transported along the Caribbean coast of

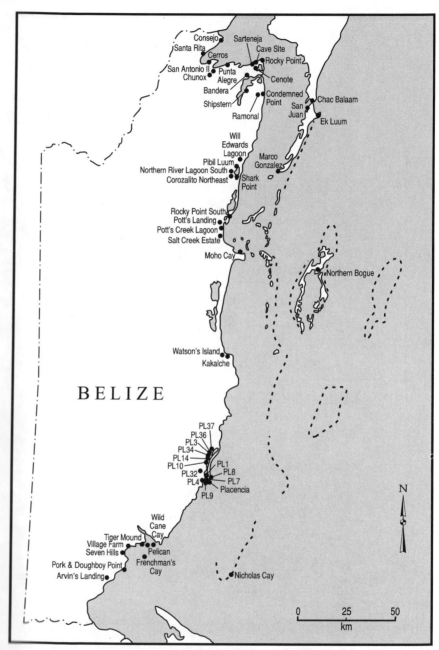

Map 1.4. Classic Period Coastal Sites in Belize. By Mary Lee Eggart.

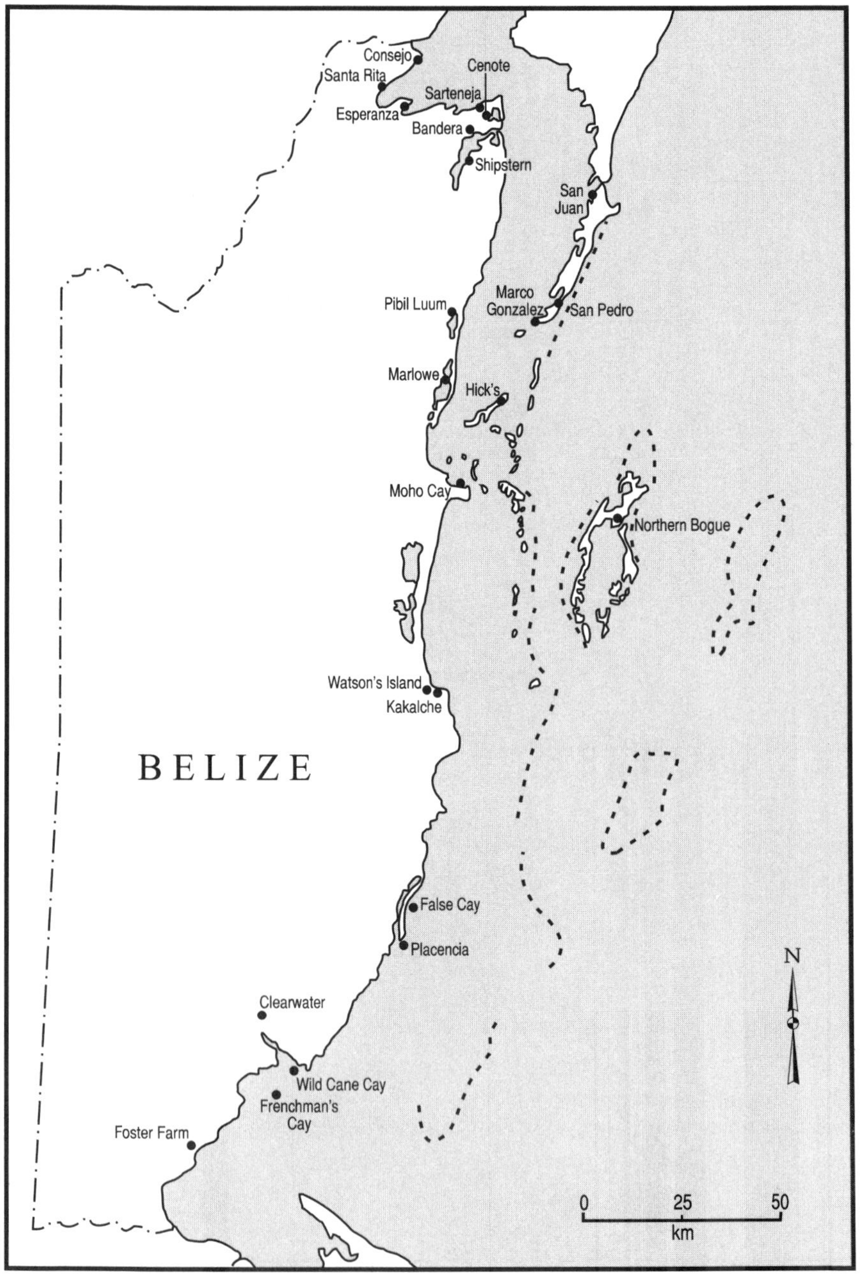
Consejo
Santa Rita
Cenote
Sarteneja
Esperanza
Bandera
Shipstern
San Juan
Pibil Luum
Marco Gonzalez
San Pedro
Marlowe
Hick's
Moho Cay
Northern Bogue
Watson's Island
Kakalche
BELIZE
False Cay
Placencia
N
Clearwater
Wild Cane Cay
Frenchman's Cay
Foster Farm
0
25
50
km

Map 1.5. Postclassic Coastal Sites in Belize. By Mary Lee Eggart.

communities that were integrated into regiona
land cities? In the latter scenario, the coastal
obtained obsidian and other trade goods by e
gional capital, and the inland Maya may even
obtain maritime resources for themselves. I
trade routes followed inland rivers and trail
Evidence from Punta Ycacos Lagoon and els
of southern Belize, as well as at other sites a
cates coastal canoe trade was active and t
Maya procured maritime resources for inla

Preclassic Coastal Maya

In addition to the Late Preclassic trading
300; Freidel 1978, 1979), a variety of coas
of Belize date to the Preclassic period (10
earliest firm evidence of Maya use of the
Preclassic Swazey pottery from Santa
kowsky and Pring 1998). Later Middle
Colson Point sites of Watson's Island a
the basis of similarity of ceramics fron
Polychrome pottery production was c
during the Protoclassic (Graham 19
discussion of the Protoclassic dates o
tery sherds from Moho Cay, locate
indicate the island site was used du
stratigraphic excavations revealed
during the early part of the Late Cl
is a shell midden on the south side
dated to the Late Preclassic and Pr
site's inhabitants extracted man
and *Isognomum alatus*) from m
mollusca in less frequency near
vessel supports and obsidian fla
source in highland Guatemala
world during the Protoclassic (

The development and impo
period is attributed to its pivo
location near two major rivers

coast
by th
obsid
tus pa
severa
of Cer
waning

Classic

In tradi
that ha
and riv
Yucatan
ever, ext
indicates
settleme
Belize w
Classic p
Juan on
Belize Ci
sites of W
Placencia-
2001), and
2001), are
ters for ex
drews 1990
1.4), associ
lowlands at
ean coast d
ceptions of
Rita Coroza
participating
and Chase 1

Did the c
plying their
Or were coa
goods by trad
transportation
and other tra

Belize during the Classic and Postclassic periods (McKillop 1987, 1989, 1996a, 2001). Transport of obsidian via the coastal route is indicated by high obsidian densities (McKillop 1989; McKillop, Winemiller, and Jones 2000), lack of conservation of scarce obsidian to make blades (McKillop 1987, 1995b), a diversity of exotic obsidian source material (McKillop et al. 1988), and a diversity of other trade goods when compared with inland areas.

Postclassic Coastal Maya

In the past, Maya sea trade has been regarded as a Postclassic period development, associated with the collapse of major inland Maya cities at the end of the Classic period and the movement of inland people to the coast (Ball 1977; Freidel 1979; Sabloff 1977; Thompson 1970). The model of Postclassic coastal settlement along the Belizean coast fits with the documented movement of people to the coast in the northern Maya lowlands, but is not appropriate for the Belizean coast, since there already were thriving coastal communities during the Classic period. Although there was evidently a reduction in the number of Postclassic sites compared to the Late Classic period, some settlements along the coast of Belize flourished during the Postclassic with the rise of Chichen Itza in the northern Maya lowlands and the associated expansion of circum-Yucatan canoe trade (Andrews 1993; map 1.5). The inventories of Pachuca green and other Mexican obsidian artifacts and Tohil Plumbate pottery at Wild Cane Cay, Frenchman's Cay, False Cay, Marlowe Cay in Salt Creek Lagoon, San Juan on northern Ambergris Cay, Marco Gonzalez on the southern tip of Ambergris Cay, and Isla Cerritos on the north coast of the Yucatan are clear evidence of circum-Yucatan coastal canoe trade at this time. There was a florescence of building at the large mainland site of Sarteneja during the Early Postclassic period, attributed to the community's role as a strategic port on Chetumal Bay (Boxt 1989).

The wealth of the Maya on Wild Cane Cay is shown by stone architecture made from coral rock and limestone slabs, brought to the island from the sea and the mainland rivers, respectively. Burials associated with building renovation contain a variety of imported pottery, gold, and obsidian (McKillop 2001). The Maya on Wild Cane Cay had reoriented their economic and political ties away from the nearby inland cities of Lubaantun, Nim li punit, Uxbenka, and Pusilha in southern Belize that were abandoned at the end of the Classic period. Instead, these coastal Maya became integral players in long-distance coastal trade around the

Yucatan. Coastal-inland trade in southern Belize was terminated for lack of inland consumers.

Various other coastal sites have been reported in northern Belize that date at least in part to the Postclassic period (map 1.5). Santa Rita Corozal stands out as a large Late Postclassic coastal settlement with extensive and varied trading ties within and beyond the Maya area (Chase 1982; Chase and Chase 1986, 1989).

Coastal-Inland Trade

The Belizean coast sometimes has been viewed simply as a transportation route supplying the southern Maya lowlands with salt, obsidian, and other exotic resources from the southern Maya highlands, northern Maya lowlands, and beyond (Rathje 1971; Rathje et al. 1978). However, the fact that the sea itself was a source of ritual paraphernalia (McKillop 1996a; Maxwell 2000), food (Lange 1971), ritual symbols (Chase and Chase 1989; McKillop 1996a; Miller 1977; Schele and Miller 1986), and salt (MacKinnon and Kepecs 1989; Valdez and Mock 1991; McKillop 1995a) underscores the importance of coastal-inland trade. While not ignoring the importance of long-distance sea trade, the extent of coastal-inland trade to the ancient Maya economy has been underestimated. This emphasis on long-distance trade can be attributed to a focus on obsidian, which can be chemically identified to its highland sources. Examination of the value of the sea in dietary and ritual spheres broadens the value of coastal economies to the emergence and development of the Classic Maya and points to the importance of trade within the Maya lowlands (Graham 1987; McKillop 1996a). Trading ports such as Wild Cane Cay served as entrepôts on the Maya sea trade route, supplying nearby inland cities with exotics as well as coastal resources. These included stingray spines (McKillop 1980:figure 6; Schele and Miller 1986:figure IV.1; Maxwell 2000), manatee bones for carvings (McKillop 1984, 1985), conch shells (notably *Turbinella angulata* used as trumpets in royal ceremonies—Coe 1978:Plate 5, 1982:Plate 63; Dochstader 1964), seafood, and salt.

Ancient Maya Salt Production

In an exhaustive survey of historic and prehistoric Maya salt-making locations, Andrews (1983) identified the salt flats along the northern coast of the Yucatan as the most likely origin for salt for the Maya lowlands from the Preclassic (1000 B.C.) to the arrival of the Spaniards in the sixteenth century. From field and archival studies, Andrews reported a variety of techniques used to produce salt in the Maya area, both historically and prehistorically. Building on others' research, notably that of Blom (1932) and Roys (1943), Andrews identified two main methods of salt production, namely, collection of salt (sal solar) from salt beds and production of salt (sal cocida) by boiling brine in pots over fires. Importantly, Andrews observed that seawater was rarely boiled without preprocessing it in order to increase the salinity. Preprocessing was carried out by solar evaporation in a variety of shallow pans or by pouring seawater or salty water from salt springs through salt-saturated soil in wooden boxes or old canoes with holes made in the bottom. This salt-saturated brine was then boiled in large jars or bowls, sometimes with many vessels held over the fire, as at Sacapulas, and other times with a single large pot. Despite a reputation in the Maya area as an inefficient method of producing salt compared to sal solar, the sal cocida method has a long history of use in the Maya area and beyond, both in Mesoamerica and elsewhere. Andrews (1983) documented the use of sal cocida at interior locations such as Sacapulas, San Mateo Ixtatan, and Salinas de los Nueve Cerros (Dillon 1977), as well as along the Pacific coast, where sal cocida was the method of choice for obtaining salt in historic times. This was evidently the case prehistorically as well (Coe and Flannery 1967; Nance 1992). At the time of Andrews' survey, the existence of ancient salt works submerged by sea-level rise along the coast of Belize was unknown. Therefore, evidence for the brine-boiling method was virtually unknown in the southern Maya lowlands.

Andrews (1983) presented a model for long-distance import of salt in bulk to feed the southern lowland Maya. The proximity of historic and prehistoric settlements of various ages, together with the occurrence of trading ports, such as Isla Cerritos, indicated ancient settlement along the northern coast and that part of that settlement was related to long-distance trade. The implication was that salt was produced for long-distance trade to feed the inland Maya—both those in the northern lowlands and others farther away in the southern lowlands. Andrews (1983:133) regarded the salt trade as important in the rise of Classic Maya society. However, he stopped short of Rathje's (1971) contention that the restricted natural occurrence of salt on the northern Yucatan coast and its import to the southern Maya lowlands was a major stimulus to the development of Classic Maya civilization by forcing the Maya to organize themselves to import critical resources. Other researchers have pointed to the management of the salt beds along the northern Yucatan coast as a stimulus for the rise of northern Yucatan cities (Ball 1977, 1978). Marcus (1991:526), however, questions the prime mover status of Maya salt.

A compelling argument for importing salt to the southern lowlands has been the human biological need for salt and its alleged shortage in the vicinity. Although the amount of salt needed for basic daily human existence depends on several factors, this material is a biological necessity (Guyton 1987; Mannino 1995; Neumann 1977). Sodium chloride is one of the major mineral components of the body. Lack of salt causes dehydration, pain and weakness in the joints and limbs, and ultimately delirium and death. Salt is essential to maintain blood pressure and for functioning of the kidneys. Salt is the main component of the intercellular system of the body. In a healthy adult, the body strives to maintain a steady amount of salt in the intercellular system, by excreting excess salt through the kidneys and by hoarding salt under situations of reduced intake or increased physical activity. Salt need increases in situations where the body loses salt, notably during high levels of physical activity and in hot and humid environments. Individual body size and metabolism also factor in salt need (Guyton 1987; Mannino 1995; Neumann 1977).

Complicating the estimates of salt need is the acquired appetite for salt common in many cultures. Saltiness is one of the four tastes perceived by the tongue (Guyton 1987; Mannino 1995). Salt enhances the flavor of food, and since feasting was such an important dimension of royal Maya rituals, as depicted on painted pictorial pots and on public carved monuments, we might expect salt would have been a desirable condiment for the royal Maya. Certainly salt would have improved the flavor of tamales and cereals featured in serving vessels on Maya art. The use of salt to enhance the flavor of food in elite feasts has a documented parallel in the Celtic civilization (Adshead 1992:8). With salt undoubtedly used to preserve food among the ancient Maya as well as its place as a biological necessity for the human body, the Maya may have simultaneously acquired a taste for salt. The acquired taste for salt may have been quite high, but difficult to quantify.

Excluding the amount of salt desired by the Late Classic Maya of the southern lowlands, determining the amount of salt they required biologically depends on population estimates and the average per capita salt need, both of which are controversial. Published accounts of salt need for farmers in tropical settings vary from 8 to 30 g per day (Adshead 1992; Andrews 1983:9), although Marcus (1984) suggests that Andrews' estimates are too high, since they include modern salt appetite. Adshead (1992:141) points out that the modern diet includes mass-produced, prepared foods that characteristically contain salt or one of its derivatives, monosodium glutamate (Adshead 1992:141). He suggests a maximum of 5 lbs. per capita per annum for ancient societies, which translates to 6 g per person per day. Andrews (1983:10) used the 8 to 30 g statistics, along with population estimates for the Classic Maya, to calculate their salt needs. He estimated that 45,000 Maya lived at Tikal at the height of the Late Classic period (A.D. 600–900), requiring some 131.4 tons of salt per year, assuming 8 g a day per person. For the estimated 5 million people in the Maya lowlands at that time, an estimated 14,600 tons of salt would have been needed a year. Since Andrews' study, additional population estimates for urban and rural areas have been made, indicating there was significant population during the Late Classic period (Culbert and Rice 1990; Rice and Culbert 1990). A peak population of 13,275 for Tikal, 92,000 within a 10 km radius of the city, and some 425,000 in the Tikal polity (Rice and Culbert 1990:21–22), underscores the high population and substantial need for dietary salt. Clearly, there was a substantial demand for salt on a daily basis regardless of the exact population figures for Tikal or elsewhere in the southern Maya lowlands (Harrison 1999; Rice and Culbert 1990) or estimates of salt need versus salt appetite. Adshead (1992) found that per capita salt intake was lower among hunter-gatherers than among farmers and that it increased over time historically. He also found that the level of salt intake varied in relation to the amount of sugar in the diet. Since both salt and honey were available to the Classic Maya, the use of honey may have reduced salt intake.

Some researchers have disagreed with Andrews' long-distance salt trade model, arguing that enough salt was available within the interior of the southern Maya lowlands for the Classic period Maya living in that area. In this alternative model, some salt was obtained by burning palm trees and by eating meat. Meat and the ashes from burned palms contain salt (Andrews 1983:20, 1984:827; Gann 1918:22; Marcus 1984; McKillop 1994a, 1996b; Pohl 1976). Additional salt was produced at the inland salt spring of Salinas de los Nueve Cerros, located at the southern periphery of the southern lowlands, on the Chixoy or Salinas River (Dillon 1977). The site had Preclassic through Classic period occupation and has extensive evidence of sal cocida salt-making. This site was certainly more accessible to the southern Maya lowlanders than were the salt flats on the northern Yucatan coast. This second model provides for local production and regional exchange within the southern Maya lowlands and is in sharp contrast to Andrews' model of long-distance bulk import of salt. However, was the salt that was available within the southern Maya lowlands from local salt springs such as Salinas de los Nueve Cerros, from burning palm trees, and from eating meat sufficient to meet the lowland Maya salt needs?

Marcus (1984, 1991) contends that sufficient quantities of salt were available within the southern Maya lowlands to obviate the need for long-distance import. Dillon (1977) compares the potential production at Salinas de los Nueve Cerros with the high levels of salt produced historically in the Maya highlands at the salt springs in Sacapulas and San Mateo Ixtatan. Others disagree. Andrews (1983) believes that only small quantities of salt were available from inland salt springs, from burning native palm trees, and from meat consumption and that these sources were insufficient to have met the needs of the Classic period Maya of the southern Maya lowlands. These issues are unresolved. However, since native palms were used for a variety of other uses, notably as a source of fronds for thatch and fruits for food (McKillop 1996b), the destruction of enough trees to produce salt for the lowland Maya seems unlikely, unless only some fronds were burned. Similarly, the lowland Maya are believed not to have eaten much meat, but rather to have consumed corn and other plants for the most part, so that the small amounts of salt in meat might not have contributed much to the daily need for salt (McKillop 1984).

The quantity of salt produced by boiling may have been limited by the availability of fuel (Baker 1999; Mock 1994:56; Parsons 1989). The large-scale clearance of the rainforest for agriculture to meet the dietary needs of the large Late Classic lowland Maya population certainly meant fewer trees were available for fueling fires.

Even discounting a major contribution from palm ash and meat, could the inland salt springs have provided sufficient quantities of salt for the local Maya? Part of the argument in favor of the import of northern Yucatan salt is the existence of the vast salt flats and the ease of collecting the salt, in contrast to the labor-intensive nature of producing salt from inland salt springs. This argument of low labor costs in itself may not be satisfactory, since salt may have been produced during the agricultural off-season by Maya who were otherwise not working. Graham (1994:315–317) suggests that Watson's Island and Kakalche were work stations used by farmers who actually lived inland and who came to the coast for part-time extraction and processing of maritime resources. Therefore, labor may not have been more costly. By way of contrast, transporting salt in bulk from the northern Yucatan would have incurred substantial costs.

Since salt itself is not preserved, researchers must of necessity build salt trade models based on the remains of salt production and the distribution of other goods that either accompanied salt or were exchanged for salt. Of course, these models assume that salt was traded. In an overview of worldwide salt production in ancient and historic times, Adshead (1992:4) notes that "salt leaves evidence fairly abundant for its production, and scarce for its consumption." In reference to the hundreds of salt sites in pre-Roman Europe, Adshead (1992:4) reports that "though a variety of techniques were used, the most frequent, giving rise to the characteristic briquetage, or shards and ashes of salt sites, was artificial evaporation of brine . . . in pottery vessels over fires."

Marcus (1991) asks for evidence, not only of salt production, but of its distribution and consumption in ancient times. Andrews (1983:1–2) notes the lack of visibility of salt itself in the archaeological record in the Maya area, pointing out that there is no evidence for containers used to transport salt in the Maya area. Goods that may have been traded in exchange for salt have provided fuel for models of Maya salt trade (Andrews 1983). Simmons and Brem (1979) account for the distribution of ash-tempered ceramics in the northern lowlands as resulting from trade of northern Yucatan salt. Canbalam is suggested as the coastal port of Chunchucmil, whose existence was arguably underwritten by its control of salt production and distribution in the northwest Yucatan (Dahlin 2000; Dahlin et al. 1998). However, the Fine Orange, Fine Gray, and Tohil Plumbate pottery, as well as Pachuca green obsidian from Canbalam used to demonstrate the contemporaneity of the northern Yucatan salt beds with the Late Classic in the southern lowlands, actually postdate the Belizean salt-making sites. Although sea trade has been documented from the Preclassic through the Postclassic periods, identifying specific goods exchanged for salt—or for other goods and resources—is difficult to prove. Furthermore, we cannot uncritically support ethnohistoric analogy between the sixteenth-century Maya of the northern lowlands, with whom the Spaniards interacted and demanded tribute—including salt—and the Late Classic Maya of the southern lowlands.

Arguments over the production of salt within the southern Maya lowlands versus long-distance import of this basic commodity intensified with the discovery of salt-making sites in the Placencia area of the central coast of Belize by MacKinnon and Kepecs (1989). They offered a modification of Andrews' model, in which all southern lowland salt was supplied from the north coast of the Yucatan. In MacKinnon and Kepecs' model, the everyday needs of the common folk were met by the Belizean coastal salt, but the northern Yucatecan salt, being of higher quality, was preferred by all, and certainly acquired by the wealthy by long-distance trade. Part of their argument was based on replication studies in which brine was boiled in pots over fires, with the ensuing salt being flavored by brine and dark in color. They noted the contrast with the fine white salt from the northern Yucatan salt flats. However, modern ethnographic studies of salt produced by the boiling method in the Maya highlands indicate, by way of contrast, that the dark salt is equally desirable and in fact sometimes preferred (Andrews 1983; Reina and Monaghen 1981). The extensive production and export of salt from boiling brine in England and elsewhere in historic times indicates sal cocida was normally considered quite palatable.

In a fourth model of Maya salt trade, researchers working at Northern River Lagoon suggest that salt produced on the Belizean coast was used to salt-dry fish for inland trade (Valdez and Mock 1991). However, following Lange's (1971) provocative paper on the use of marine fish as a protein supplement for the inland Maya, researchers have identified only small quantities of marine fish bones at inland sites in the southern lowlands (Carr 1986; Emery 1999:table 3.4; Graham 1991:328; McKillop 1984, 1985, 1996a; Wing 1975, 1977). Fish bones from inland sites indicate that seafood was imported to near-coastal settlements such as Altun Ha, Dzibilchaltun, and Lubaantun (map 1.6). The recovery at Colson Point of *Euthynnus* spp. (little tuna) vertebrae, split dorsal-ventrally as if the fish had been splayed for drying or smoking, led Graham (1994:261) to suggest that sea fishes were prepared for inland trade. Certainly some marine fishes were traded inland, even to distant inland cities such as Lamanai (Coyston et al. 1999; White and Schwarcz 1989) and Tikal (Rice 1978), but the bulk of the inland meat diet was evidently from nearby fauna (Emery 1999; McKillop 1984, 1985; Pohl 1976). The limited evidence of seafood consumption at distant inland communities such as Tikal, Tipu, or Lamanai indicates that seafood was restricted to small amounts for the elite. The Maya at distant inland communities exploited locally available land and riverine animals. The view that distance was an important criterion in resource selection is substantiated by the evidence of reliance on marine fauna at offshore islands such as Moho Cay (McKillop 1984), Cozumel (Hamblin 1980), Cancun (Andrews et al. 1975), and Wild Cane Cay. Com-

Map 1.6. Maya Area, Showing Sites Mentioned in the Text. By Mary Lee Eggart.

munities located on the mainland coast, such as Cerros, included both land and marine fauna in their diet. Still, in Valdez and Mock's model, the salt produced along the Belizean coast was evidently rather limited and focused on salt-drying fish, with the bulk of human salt intake supplied from long-distance import from the northern Yucatan coast.

This previous research provides tantalizing clues about the origins and distribution of salt in the Maya lowlands and raises important questions about salt, trade, and Maya economy and society. With the discovery of salt-production along the coast of Belize, less attention has been directed to determining the importance of inland salt sources and salt from palm ash or meat. The unsolved dilemma is whether the Late Classic Maya obtained their salt from the northern Yucatan salt beds, with higher transportation costs, or from the Belizean coast, with higher production costs. Andrews (1983) points out that since labor costs are minimal for northern Yucatan salt and the quantity of Belizean salt produced is unknown, the importance of Belizean salt in supplying the Late Classic Maya of the southern lowlands is unanswered. Research in Punta Ycacos Lagoon addresses this issue by evaluating the nature of the salt industry and the more favorable landscape along the Belizean coast for salt production during the Classic period.

Research in Punta Ycacos Lagoon suggests an alternative model for salt trade during the Late Classic period: salt was produced for dietary use by the coastal Maya and for regional trade to adjacent inland cities. Punta Ycacos Lagoon provided salt for the coastal peoples at Wild Cane Cay, Frenchman's Cay, and other coastal communities in the Port Honduras region of southern Belize, as well as being traded inland to Lubaantun, Nim li punit, Pusilha, and Uxbenka, and perhaps farther inland to the Pasion and Peten regions of Guatemala (map 1.6). This model is supported by the presence of inland goods at coastal sites, and ceramic ties between the Port Honduras, Lubaantun, and the Pasion sites of Altar de Sacrificios and Seibal. Measurement of the salt-making artifacts indicates they were standardized in manufacture, suggesting that the salt cakes were produced at salt works organized for bulk production. Individual containers were not used to transport the salt cakes to inland communities, so the material evidence for their inland distribution is the inland trade goods at the salt work shops. Although the solar evaporation method of the north coast of the Yucatan was surely less labor-intensive than boiling brine in pots over fires carried out to produce salt cakes along the Belizean coast, the advantage of the latter was the proximity to nearby inland consumers. In addi-

tion, this boiling method was likely used in conjunction with solar evaporation or enrichment of the brine before it was boiled, as indicated by
ethnographic analogy and by a slag heap resulting from brine being
passed through salt-enriched soil in vats at one of the Punta Ycacos sites.
The salt production likely occurred during the dry season, when farmers
were not occupied with agriculture, so the increased labor costs associated
with salt production were only adding to the production of the coastal
economy: the salt workers were not otherwise occupied. Although salt is
produced by family units at Sacapulas today, it is possible there was a
division of labor by sex in Belizean salt production. Certainly the female
figurines from the Punta Ycacos salt works support this interpretation. By
way of contrast, Williams (1999:407) found that salt production at Lake
Cuitzco is carried out entirely by men in the agricultural off-season.
Nonetheless, in a hierarchical civilization with evidence of economic specialization, short-term work parties organized by family, gender, or otherwise for the production of salt along the Belizean coast is a viable model.

Salt Production in the Classic Maya Economy

The possibility that the Maya obtained significant quantities of salt from
the Belizean coast is in line with a view of ancient Maya economy in
which basic subsistence resources were obtained from nearby locations,
whereas long-distance trade was concentrated on the import of elite and
ceremonial materials and goods (Cowgill 1993; Drennan 1984a, 1984b;
Price 1978; Tourtellot and Sabloff 1972). Certainly Rathje's (1971; Rathje
et al. 1978) model of bulk long-distance import of basic resources of salt,
obsidian, and basalt is moot, considering the discoveries of sources or sub-
stitutes within the southern Maya lowlands, notably limestone and Maya
Mountain granite for metates, chert for cutting stone, and salt. Most models of Maya trade view basic subsistence needs as being fulfilled by production and distribution at a more geographically restricted level, within a
region dominated by a major city and often focused within even a smaller
zone in the region, as in Hammond's (1975) model of the "realm" of Lubaantun. Apart from obsidian, which was distributed to a broader spectrum of society, exotic trade goods entering the Port Honduras at Wild
Cane Cay certainly fit the model of limited quantities of exotics traded
(McKillop 1996a). Even obsidian cannot be considered a bulk, long-distance trade item. Although obsidian was commonly used at cities near
obsidian outcrops, locally available chert was more commonly used in

households within the Maya lowlands. The importance of distance is underscored by trade models in which goods were in regular household use within a supply zone around the source of the raw material or work shop (Renfrew 1975). Distribution was limited beyond the supply zone, so that the same goods often became scarce, high-status items. Despite much research indicating otherwise, long-distance transport of staple resources in Mesoamerica in general continues to be proposed (Sluyter 1993) and import of some quantities of northern Yucatan salt into the southern Maya lowlands in particular is still discussed (MacKinnon and Kepecs 1989). Salt from the Belizean coast, however, would have been much closer at hand for both coastal settlers and for the inland Maya of the southern Maya lowlands.

Classic Maya Craft Production

During the Classic period, burial vessels, carved jade objects, eccentric flints, and other highly crafted goods—some made from exotic materials—were produced by craft specialists in the service of royal households at large Maya cities (Adams 1970; Becker 1973; Reents-Budet 1994, 1998). Typical of ancient civilizations, these craft workers are often termed "attached specialists" (Costin 1991; Earle 1981). The highly crafted goods were status markers or badges of power for the elite during their lifetimes and in perpetuity in their graves. By way of contrast, some utilitarian and ceremonial goods were made outside large cities near raw material sources, such as the chert outcrops at Colha in northern Belize (Shafer and Hester 1983). Furthermore, their regional distribution was not administered by elites at major cities (Dockall and Shafer 1993; Hult and Hester 1995; McAnany 1989a; McSwain 1991; Mitchum 1991; Santone 1997). Other examples in the Maya area where production and distribution were focused outside the major lowland cities include production of everyday pottery and some serving vessels at Tikal (Fry 1980), Palenque (Rands and Bishop 1980), and the central Peten Lakes region (Rice 1987a). These goods were produced by independent specialists and had wider distribution among the general public. Their production was not controlled by the Maya at large cities. Still other goods were produced within households, including some for family use and others, produced in cottage industry style, for use by others. Janusek (1999) calls this household production "embedded production," in contrast to the work of attached or independent specialists, which occurred outside of the home. The Punta Ycacos salt works fit the model of independent specialists who had trading and other alliances with the Maya at inland Maya cities who were supplied with salt cakes. The higher labor costs for producing sal cocida compared with sal solar may be moot if salt was produced seasonally during the agricultural off-season by independent specialists. In fact, the sal cocida industry along the Belizean coast may have added to the wealth of the coastal Maya without incurring additional labor costs, if people were not otherwise "working."

The rise of the Belizean salt industry during the Late Classic period coincided with the tremendous population increase at nearby inland communities, the increasing differentiation and specialization of the economy, and in some cases, initial settlement of coastal areas. Was settlement of the Belizean coast a response to population pressure with people settling in marginal agricultural land (Ball 1977; Mock 1994:18–19), a response to the inundation of northern Yucatan salt beds (Dahlin 1983; Folan et al. 1983), or a case of opportunistic Maya developing an industry to meet the demands of the nearby inland Maya during the Late Classic period? In southern Belize, the sal cocida industry coincides with the occupation of the major inland cities of Lubaantun, Nim li punit, and Pusilha. The possibility of salt production by solar evaporation, given different environmental conditions, is also proposed for earlier times and in conjunction with the sal cocida production of the Late Classic period, for which there is so much artifactual evidence.

Salt Production and Sea-Level Rise

Arguments about the more favorable environmental conditions for obtaining salt along the northern Yucatan as opposed to the Belizean coasts during the Classic period are questioned by new data indicating that the landscape was intrinsically different. Today, there are indeed favorable conditions for sal solar production along the north coast of the Yucatan, including low rainfall, an absence of rivers, and a system of shallow barrier lagoons that create a sheltered area of concentrated salty water. The seawater is evaporated in shallow salt pans and easily collected (Andrews 1983:16; Eaton 1978). The paleoclimatological record for the Maya lowlands suggests that there was regional variability in the past. Unfortunately for archaeological interpretations of the effects of climate change on past settlement, there are contrasting interpretations of ancient climate: some researchers argue for a drier climate, perhaps even drought conditions, during the Late Classic (Curtis et al. 1996; Hodell et al. 1995). Other researchers found there was more rainfall at that time (Leyden 1987; Messenger 1990). Folan et al. (1983) proposed that there was a peak in sea level about A.D. 500 to 600 that flooded the northern Yucatan salt beds and caused the lagoons to be abandoned. This coincides with the beginning of the sal cocida industry in the Port Honduras. However, it was also the time of initial inland settlement at nearby cities whose inhabitants desired and biologically needed salt.

What was the interplay of cultural and environmental factors in the rise and demise of the salt industry in Punta Ycacos Lagoon? The fact that the sal cocida work shops in Punta Ycacos Lagoon are currently inundated underscores the major environmental changes that have occurred in the area since the Classic period. In some other areas, such as Cape Cod and the coast of England, the inundation of coastal salt works by sea-level rise resulted in the shift in location of the salt works and their continued operation. Certainly Belize has a steadily accreting coastline, evident both on the mainland and the offshore islands, in addition to loss of land by a rise in sea level. I will argue that cultural rather than environmental changes were responsible for the abandonment of the Port Honduras salt works, owing to the drop in inland demand with the abandonment of nearby Late Classic Maya cities.

The Port Honduras Archaeological Project

The Punta Ycacos salt-making sites were discovered in the course of a multiyear project in the Port Honduras investigating sea trade. The Port Honduras study area extends from the coastal plain to the barrier reef between the modern towns of Punta Gorda and Punta Negra in southern Belize (map 1.7). Punta Ycacos Lagoon was declared Paynes Creek National Park in 1994 by the government of Belize. In 2000, the Port Honduras was declared the Port Honduras Marine Reserve. The first phase of the archaeological project was aimed at identifying the characteristics of the ancient trading port on Wild Cane Cay and determining the timing and extent of the islanders' participation in sea trade (McKillop 1987, 1989, 2001). Several lines of evidence indicated use of the island as a Classic through Postclassic trading port: the density of obsidian in middens and on the island's surface indicates unusual access to this exotic resource for

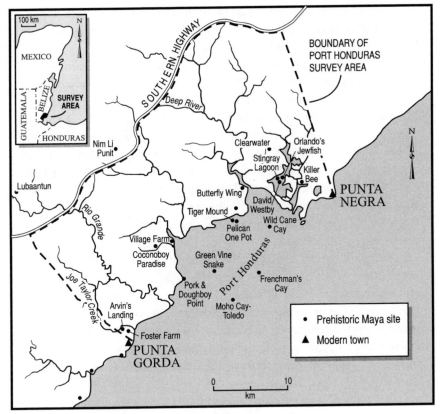

Map 1.7. Port Honduras Research Area. By Mary Lee Eggart.

the island's relatively small size and location away from lowland Maya cities (McKillop 1989; McKillop, Winemiller, and Jones 2000). The diversity of obsidian sources represented at the site, including obsidian from six known locations in the volcanic highlands of Mexico, Guatemala, and Honduras, indicates coastal trade of Mexican obsidian from the north and trade of highland Maya obsidian from the south (McKillop et al. 1988). The diversity of other exotic resources and artifacts that arrived at the port from various directions underscores the variety of exotics to which the Wild Cane Cay Maya had access. These items include Tohil Plumbate pottery from Pacific Guatemala (McKillop and Healy 1989, cover), copper from Honduras, gold from lower Central America, basalt from the Guatemalan highlands, and Tulum Red pottery from farther north, among other items. The island's location on a historically known coastal trade route, its relatively protected location in the coastal bight of Port Honduras, its natural harbor, and river-mouth location were supporting evidence for the island's role in waterborne trade.

The second phase of the project, between 1988 and 1997, examined the integration of long-distance trade and the coastal economy of southern Belize by regional survey and excavation (McKillop 1994b, 1996a, 2001; McKillop and Herrmann 2000; McKillop and Winemiller 2001). Although there was clear evidence of long-distance trade at Wild Cane Cay, the role of the island—and by extension, of trading ports elsewhere—in the coastal economy was unknown. Were trade goods that arrived at Wild Cane Cay distributed within the local region? Or was local exchange for the common Maya distinct from elite trade of valuables that were destined for the wealthy at lowland cites? A study of the relationship between long-distance and local trade in south coastal Belize required knowledge of the distribution and dating of settlements and their access to obsidian and other trade goods relative to Wild Cane Cay. The discovery and excavation of some 30 coastal sites indicated Wild Cane Cay and Frenchman's Cay were nodes for long-distance import and inland trade of goods and resources. However, both exotic and inland trade goods reached smaller communities as well, indicating access to trade goods was determined by wealth and not narrowly defined by an elite/commoner dichotomy.

The discovery of salt-making sites in Punta Ycacos Lagoon underscores the role of regional trade between the coast and nearby inland cities. Previously, limited quantities of valuable marine goods were known to have been traded inland. Arguments for bulk inland trade of seafood (Lange 1971) have not been supported (White and Schwarcz 1989; McKillop 1985). Not only was salt a bulk subsistence item for coastal-inland trade, but it may have solidified the economic power of coastal trading ports by providing a regular exchange item to the arrival of periodic long-distance importers. Was coastal-inland trade pivotal to Classic Maya trading ports? Regular inland shipments of salt would have contributed to the viability of small-scale island trading ports like Wild Cane Cay and Frenchman's Cay if they controlled local salt economic production and distribution in addition to import of exotic resources via the coast and exchange of other resources between the coast and interior.

2

The Punta Ycacos Salt Works

A New Source of Salt for the Late Classic Maya

Three sites in Punta Ycacos Lagoon, submerged by a rise in sea level, were hidden from modern view until they were discovered by underwater reconnaissance in 1991 (figures 2.1–2.3). They are Stingray Lagoon, located 300 m in the middle of Punta Ycacos Lagoon, David Westby, located 172 m offshore, and Orlando's Jewfish, located some 50 m offshore in the lagoon (map 2.1). The sites were located by the surface presence of artifacts on the seafloor, during boat survey done by looking over the side of the boat and jumping into the water when artifacts were spotted (figures 2.4–2.5). A fourth inundated site, Killer Bee Site, was discovered in the adjacent mangroves.

Stingray Lagoon Site

Fieldwork at Stingray Lagoon site in 1991 included transit-mapping of artifact clusters on the seafloor, as well as excavations (figure 2.6). Terrestrial archaeology techniques were used in the excavations, since the site is only about 1 m below the water's surface (figures 2.7–2.9). The site area was identified by the distribution of artifacts on hard, compacted sediment, covered by a layer of loose silt. The silt extended off the site area, where the lagoon floor was silt with unconsolidated mangrove mud below.

Fig. 2.1. Oblique Air View of Punta Ycacos Lagoon from the North. This view shows two routes through the mangroves from the main channel to the southern section of the lagoon, where salt works were discovered. Photo by H. McKillop.

Fig. 2.2. Oblique Air View of Punta Ycacos Lagoon from the Northwest. This view shows the barrier bar in the background with the Port Honduras beyond. Photo by H. McKillop.

Fig. 2.3. Mangroves along Punta Ycacos Lagoon Shoreline.

Fig. 2.4. Salt Artifacts on the Seafloor in Punta Ycacos Lagoon. Photo by H. McKillop.

Left: Fig. 2.5. Reconnaissance in Punta Ycacos Lagoon. Photo by H. McKillop.

Below: Fig. 2.6. Mapping the Location of Artifact Clusters on the Seafloor at Stingray Lagoon with a Transit and a Snorkler. Photo by Carol Dodd. Reprinted from *Latin American Antiquity* 6 (1995): 219, Figure 5.

Fig. 2.7. Screening Excavated Sediment from Stingray Lagoon. Photo by H. Mc-Killop.

Fig. 2.8. Excavating at Stingray Lagoon.

Fig. 2.9. Excavating at Stingray Lagoon.

A wooden stake was placed near the center of the site as identified by the distribution of artifacts (map 2.2). The stake was used as a datum marker for mapping. A seine net was placed around the perimeter of the excavation to keep out stingrays, which were attracted to the turbidity created by our work (figures 2.10–2.12). Nineteen artifact clusters were located by snorkeling at the water's surface, without stirring the silt, which reduced visibility. The artifact clusters were locations of dense concentrations of artifacts that rose above the silt. Once located by snorkeling, each cluster's location was recorded using the transit, stadia rod, and metric tape. Artifacts were collected from each cluster to identify activity areas.

A 2 × 2 m excavation grid composed of red mangrove poles, held in place by mangrove stakes, was established with the datum in the center. Since mangrove wood sinks, the grid frame was easily secured and relocated in the low-visibility conditions of the underwater site. The excavation, called Unit 1, was divided into four subunits, each measuring 1 × 1 m. Each subunit was excavated to a depth of 10 cm using shovels. Excavation depths were recorded from the water's surface using a tape measure. The sediment was from mangrove mud, which stayed in the shovel as the blade was removed from the water to empty the contents into an excavation screen placed nearby in the lagoon. The artifacts and charcoal recov-

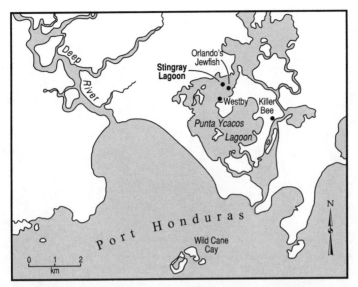

Map 2.1. Ancient Salt Works in Punta Ycacos Lagoon. By Mary Lee Eggart.

Fig. 2.10. Seine Net by Research Vessel at Stingray Lagoon. Photo by H. McKillop.

Fig. 2.11. Setting Up Seine Net at Stingray Lagoon. Photo by H. McKillop.

Fig. 2.12. Setting Up Seine Net. Photo by H. McKillop.

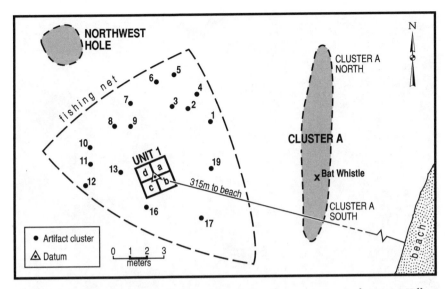

Map 2.2. Stingray Lagoon Site. By Mary Lee Eggart from transit map by H. McKillop. Reprinted from *Latin American Antiquity* 6 (1995): 220, Figure 6.

ered from screening through quarter-inch mesh were placed in 100 lb. plastic rice sacks, with several sacks of material recovered from each sub-unit (figure 2.13). The contents were subsequently exported to Louisiana State University, where they were sorted and analyzed in 1995 and 1996 and then returned to the Belizean Department of Archaeology in 1997, along with the material from the other salt work shops.

The site's surface was 90 cm from the water's surface, making the ground surface of the site 1 m below current sea level. Southern Belize is a microtidal environment, and the tidal variation in the lagoon was minimal. Bathymetry of the lagoon was estimated to be uniformly 1 m, based on transit measurements each 10 m from the datum point at Stingray Lagoon site to the north shore, 315 m away (figure 2.14).

Because of good preservation of plant remains and little evidence of postdepositional site trampling, Stingray Lagoon was interpreted as an activity area that had been submerged by a sea-level rise soon after the place was abandoned. Underwater visibility was minimal owing to the stirred-up silt, so we did not attempt to expose artifacts in situ in the excavations. The screened material included large sherds and partial vessels, thousands of fragments of fired clay, and charcoal. Much of the charcoal

Fig. 2.13. Artifacts in Excavation Screen. Photo by H. McKillop.

was congealed together with fired clay into layers that varied between 5 and 10 cm in thickness. The congealed pieces were interpreted as the remains of fire hearths. The large size of the pottery sherds contrasted with the small size of sherds from dry-land sites in the vicinity and indicated little postdepositional site trampling.

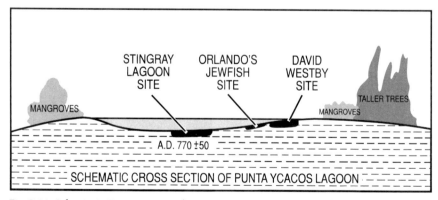

Fig. 2.14. Schematic Cross-section of Punta Ycacos Lagoon. Drawn by Mary Lee Eggart.

David Westby Site

The David Westby site was discovered by a Placencia fisherman, David Westby, who helped relocate the site in 1991. The site is 172 m from shore and 27 cm below the water surface. The site is evident from the distribution of artifacts on the lagoon floor. Artifacts were collected in 1991 and 1994 to compare with those from Stingray Lagoon.

Shovel tests were carried out in 1991 to estimate the depth of the cultural deposits and the nature of the lagoon sediments associated with the site (map 2.3, figure 2.15). The shovel tests were excavated by arbitrary 20 cm levels until a sediment change was discovered, at which point a new level was begun. The sediment was screened through quarter-inch hardware cloth in excavation screens placed near the excavations in the lagoon. The matrix of the site consisted of an upper layer of mangrove peat, with sand below. Relatively few artifacts were recovered, compared with their high density at Stingray Lagoon. In tests 2 through 5, the artifacts were in the mangrove peat layer, extending to a maximum depth of 40 cm in shovel test 5 and 20 cm in tests 2 to 4. In shovel test 1, artifacts were

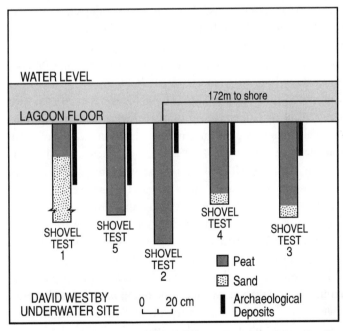

Fig. 2.15. Shovel Tests at David Westby Site. Drawn by Mary Lee Eggart.

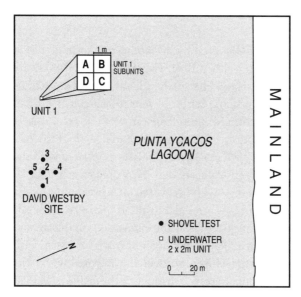

Map 2.3. David Westby Site. By Mary Lee Eggart from transit map by H. McKillop.

recovered in the mangrove peat layer, but also in the underlying sand to a depth of 40 cm. In the area of the shovel tests, the base of the archaeological deposits is 67 cm below modern sea level.

An excavation was carried out in 1994 under the supervision of Melissa Braud (1996) as part of her M.A. thesis research, along with Earthwatch volunteers and the author (figure 2.16). The goals were to compare the site with nearby Stingray Lagoon, in terms of artifact inventory, site function, and sea-level change. A 2 × 2 m unit was placed in an area of high-surface-artifact density. Two subunits, A and D, each measuring 1 × 1 m, were excavated in arbitrary 10 cm levels by shovels into screens in the lagoon. Measurements were taken from the water surface. Maximum depth of the excavation was 20 cm below the lagoon floor. The base of the archaeological deposits is 47 cm below modern sea level in the area of unit. The matrix of the site was firm mangrove peat, which stayed on the shovel as it was used to excavate the sediment into the screens. Ceramics and charcoal were recovered in abundance and placed in 100 lb. rice sacks for later sorting. The excavations were completed in one day, with a crew of two shovelers, four screeners, and the author. The excavations were recorded, videotaped, and photographed (figures 2.17–2.18).

Fig. 2.16. Excavating at David Westby. Photo by H. McKillop.

Fig. 2.17. Underwater Excavation Grid at David Westby. Photo by H. McKillop.

Fig. 2.18. Field Crew by Research Vessel *Adel 2*. Photo by H. McKillop.

Orlando's Jewfish Site

Orlando's Jewfish is located some 50 m offshore in Punta Ycacos Lagoon. The site was discovered by Orlando Usher and the author during a fishing break while on boat survey in 1991. While wading in the shallow water and pursuing a jewfish in its underground burrow, we discovered artifacts underfoot. A surface collection made at that time prompted a return to excavate in 1994 in order to compare the site with Stingray Lagoon.

Two excavation units were placed where artifacts had been noticed on the lagoon floor (map 2.4). Unit 1 was placed near the 1991 site discovery location. No artifacts were found during excavation. Unit 2 was then set out 45 m offshore; artifacts were found on the lagoon floor therein. Two subunits, A and C, were excavated by arbitrary 10 cm levels to a maximum depth of 30 cm, using the mangrove pole grid from Stingray Lagoon to mark the unit's location (figure 2.19). The sediment was shoveled into screens, with the screened material stored in 100 lb. rice sacks (figures 2.20–2.22). The matrix was mangrove peat (figure 2.23). The recovered material was similar to that at David Westby and Stingray Lagoon, with amorphous clay lumps, pottery sherds, and quantities of charcoal. Excava-

Above: Fig. 2.19. Measuring Excavation Grid at Orlando's Jewfish Site. Photo by H. McKillop.

Left: Fig. 2.20. Excavating at Orlando's Jewfish. Photo by H. McKillop.

Above: Fig. 2.21. A Shovelful of Lagoon Sediment from Orlando's Jewfish. Photo by H. McKillop.

Left: Fig. 2.22. Screening at Orlando's Jewfish. Photo by H. McKillop.

Right: Fig. 2.23. Sorting Organic Remains from Orlando's Jewfish. Photo by H. McKillop.

Below: Map 2.4. Orlando's Jewfish Site. By Mary Lee Eggart from transit map by H. McKillop.

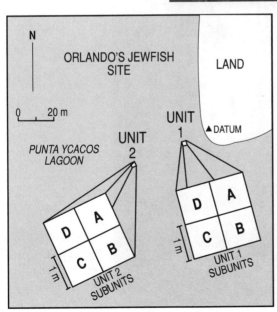

tions were completed in one day, with a team consisting of two shovelers, two screens operated by three screeners each, and the author. The excavations were videotaped.

Killer Bee Site

The site was reported to me by the late Charlie Carlson of New Haven, Port Honduras, who took me to visit it in 1988. With only a small collection of nondiagnostic sherds from the 1988 surface collection, Killer Bee was revisited in 1991 to map and excavate the site to better understand its age, function, and current water-logged condition.

Killer Bee is located along the northern channel of Punta Ycacos Lagoon in a mangrove forest abutting a broadleaf forest (figure 2.24). The

Fig. 2.24. Mangrove Forest at Killer Bee Site. Photo by H. McKillop.

Fig. 2.25. Low Earthen Mound at Killer Bee. Photo by H. McKillop.

site consists of a low earthen mound with a distribution of ceramics on the surrounding mangrove soil, which is free of vegetation (figure 2.25). Excavations were carried out to recover datable artifacts and to discover the nature of the site and its relation to sea level (map 2.5). A 1 × 1 m unit on the mound yielded only a few nondiagnostic artifacts. A shovel test was excavated in the off-mound area 12 m west of the mound where abundant ceramics were noticed on the ground surface (figure 2.26). The shovel test was excavated by arbitrary 20 cm levels to a maximum depth of 80 cm, with ceramics from all levels. The 60–80 cm level contained many large sherds, in contrast to the small bits from higher levels. The water table was reached at 40 cm depth. Excavations of the shovel test were inter-

Fig. 2.26. Examining a Shovel Test at Killer Bee.

rupted by the arrival of a jaguar. The transit-mapping and mound excavation were interrupted by the arrival of a swarm of killer bees, which ended our work at the site.

Discussion

The Punta Ycacos sites were interpreted as special-purpose activity areas, each consisting of abundant ceramics of similar form and fabrication, along with charcoal and pieces of fired clay. Hearths at Stingray Lagoon consisted of charcoal with sherds and fired clay. By ethnographic analogy, the artifacts were interpreted as the remains of pots placed over fires to boil brine to produce salt. At Stingray Lagoon, the charcoal was congealed and consolidated into lenses between 5 and 10 cm in thickness, with fired clay and pottery sherds embedded within it. Although charcoal was abundant at Orlando's Jewfish and David Westby, congealed charcoal lenses were not discovered at those sites. Relatively few ceramics or charcoal fragments were recovered from Killer Bee, where preservation of organic remains was poor compared to the underwater sites.

Although some measures were undoubtedly taken to increase the salinity of seawater before brine was boiled, the only evidence of such measures was from Killer Bee site. The earthen mound at Killer Bee may be a slag heap from the salt-making process, in which salt water was poured through large vats or old canoes with holes made in the bottom. The containers were filled with salt-saturated soil to produce salt-enriched brine for boiling into salt cakes (Andrews 1983; Reina and Monaghen 1981). There is no evidence of slag heaps at the other Punta Ycacos sites. However, any slag heaps that might have been present would have been deflated by wave action or currents. Similarly, there are no traces of other measures at Killer Bee or the sites now in Punta Ycacos Lagoon that may

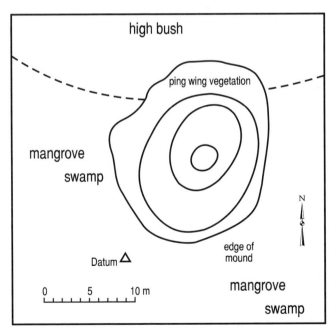

Map 2.5. Killer Bee Site. By Mary Lee Eggart from transit map by H. McKillop.

have been used to increase the salt content of the brine, such as seasonal solar evaporation in ponds documented elsewhere during historic times (Andrews 1983). Even today during the dry season, the lagoon waters are saltier than seawater. However, in other areas where the boiling method is used to produce salt, the water is first salt-enriched by pouring it through salty soil in vats or canoes with holes or by evaporation in enclosures (Andrews 1983).

The Punta Ycacos salt work shops were single-component sites. The large size of the pottery sherds contrasts to the smaller size of sherds at other Port Honduras sites. This is interpreted as a lack of postdepositional site trampling and indicates the sea rose to submerge the sites soon after they were abandoned.

3

ллллл

Salt-Production Equipment

By analogy with the modern Maya in the highlands of Guatemala and elsewhere, the assemblages of artifacts at the Punta Ycacos Lagoon sites were interpreted as evidence of salt production, in which brine was boiled in a dozen or more pots over fires to produce salt cakes (figure 3.1; Adshead 1992; Andrews 1983; Bloch 1963; Coe and Flannery 1967; Dillon 1977; Ewald 1985; Nance 1992; Nenquin 1961; Parsons 1989; Reina and Monaghen 1981; Riehm 1961). This sal cocida method was a good strategy in the Port Honduras region, where the short, unpredictable dry season was not ideally suited to solar evaporation. The slag heap at Killer Bee site indicated that the seawater was preprocessed by pouring it through salt-saturated soil to produce a salt-enriched brine for boiling. Although this procedure was likely carried out at the other sites, any evidence of it has probably been obliterated by inundation. Salt was produced in the form of hard cakes suitable for storage or transport without additional individual containers, although some loose salt for local use within the Port Honduras region may also have been made. Ethnographic analogy indicated that the production of salt cakes involves more cooking to harden the salt into a solid mass and may have involved breaking the containers in which the brine was boiled. In addition to preprocessing the salt water and boiling the brine, other activities included the manufacture of the salt boiling vessels and vessel supports from local clays and sand temper.

Fig. 3.1. Schematic Illustration of Brine-Boiling Jars. Drawn by Mary Lee Eggart. Reprinted from *Latin American Antiquity* 6 (1995): 225, Figure 10.

Analysis of the artifacts from the Punta Ycacos Lagoon sites indicated that a specific and limited activity was carried out. In fact, the sites were work shops for salt production by people who lived elsewhere. Similar artifact assemblages were recovered from the four salt work shops. Most of the artifacts were the same type of jar and bowl pottery sherds and their vessel supports associated with abundant charcoal, corroborating the interpretation that a specific and limited activity was carried out at the work shops. The most striking feature of the artifact assemblages was the lack of diversity of ceramic types and the abundance of sherds from similar large, utilitarian vessels. In addition to the sherds from brine-boiling vessels, sherds from two types of water jars suitable for storing brine were recovered. A few ceramics, including sherds from fine-ware serving bowls, clay whistles, and boat models, were recovered and interpreted as the remains of rituals associated with salt production, as practiced by the modern Maya. There were few other stone or clay artifacts and no animal bone remains at the Punta Ycacos sites, in contrast to other Port Honduras Maya settlements, such as the nearby trading port of Wild Cane Cay. In sum, there were no signs of settlement at the work shops.

Radiocarbon and ceramic analyses indicate the salt work shops were single-component sites dating to the Late Classic. A radiocarbon date from Stingray Lagoon of A.D. 770 ± 50 years was obtained from wood charcoal from the fire hearth at the work shop. Interpreting the date at two standard deviations provided a 95 percent probability that the true age of the fire hearth and the salt production was some time between A.D. 670 and 870. The identity of the artifacts at the four sites indicates that they were contemporaneous. Similar ceramic types were recovered from Lubaantun in southern Belize and Altar de Sacrificios and Seibal in the adjacent Pasion region of Guatemala, also supporting the assignment of the Punta Ycacos Lagoon salt work shops in the latter part of the Late Classic, comparable to Tepeu 2 and 3 in the Uaxactun ceramic sequence (Adams 1971; Hammond 1975; Sabloff 1975; Smith 1955).

Methods: Type-Variety Classification and Attribute Analysis

Two types of analyses were carried out on the artifacts to provide information on chronology and variability, respectively, in salt production. In the first analysis, the artifacts were classified into types based on shared characteristics. For the ceramics, the type-variety system of Maya ceramic classification was used. According to this classification system, the pottery sherds were grouped according to similarities in decoration and surface finish, which have been found to be sensitive to chronological changes in the Maya area. The type-variety classification was useful in helping to assign an age to the work shops, for describing the ceramics, and for making comparisons with ceramics from other Maya sites, both within the Port Honduras region and beyond. The format and terminology followed Sabloff's (1975) analysis of the ceramics from Seibal. Type names used in the present study refer to ceramics from the Port Honduras region, with names from geographic locations in the coastal zone of the Toledo District. Comparisons were made with the artifacts from other salt work shops along the Belizean coast and, for chronological purposes, with other Maya sites. Ceramic collections from the Maya area at the Peabody Museum, Harvard University, were examined and compared with type specimens from the Punta Ycacos and other Port Honduras area sites.

In the second artifact analysis, a variety of observations and measurements were taken on each pottery sherd and on the vessel supports. This attribute analysis provided a description of variability within types and was also used to examine the nature of the salt-production activities at the work shops and the postdepositional inundated setting of three of the work shops. Some variables were used to describe the ceramic types as part of the type-variety descriptions (vessel part, form, rim and lip shape, surface finish, slip, decoration, motif, diameter, thickness, and temper).

Some variables were used to describe the nature of the salt production, in terms of the vessels used and variability among the work shops (vessel form, diameter, thickness, and temper). The diameter of the salt pots and their supports indicated that the vessels were standardized in their manufacture, contributing to an interpretation that the salt production at Punta Ycacos Lagoon was specialized beyond the household. The ceramic assemblages at each site were characterized in terms of richness (number of types) and evenness (number of sherds per type), indicating a limited range of activities were carried out and that settlement occurred elsewhere. The percentage of rim circumference, sherd and vessel-support weights, and lengths of the vessel-support fragments were used to describe the size of the artifacts, whose relative largeness was attributed to a lack of postdepositional site trampling and a rapid sea-level rise that submerged the salt work shops soon after their Late Classic period use. A variety of characteristics were examined that suggest that the boiling pots were not ideally suited as cooking vessels. However, the local availability of clay and sand temper as well as the short life expectancy of the pots used in the boiling process are factors that evidently superseded ideal traits such as durability.

Type-Variety Classification

There were four ceramic types identified among the pottery sherds from the salt work shops, including two unslipped and two slipped types. These and many other types were identified at other Port Honduras sites dating to the Late Classic (McKillop 2000). The low diversity of ceramic types is quite unusual for Maya sites, including other sites in the Port Honduras region and further supports an interpretation of a limited activity at the work shops. In fact, the ceramics do not include the usual array of vessel forms and types typically found at Maya communities (figure 3.2 and table 3.1). Ceramic diversity also is low at Late Classic Colson Point and at Marco Gonzalez (Graham, personal communication, 2001).

Punta Ycacos Unslipped: Punta Ycacos

Type: Punta Ycacos Unslipped.
Variety: Punta Ycacos Variety.
When Established as a Type and/or Variety: In the present study. The description was based on 412 sherds, 1 complete vessel support, 616 ves-

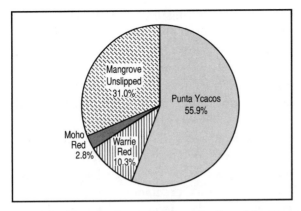

Fig. 3.2. Pottery Sherds per Type as a Measure of the Evenness of the Ceramic Assemblages at the Salt Work Shops. By Mary Lee Eggart from sketch by H. McKillop.

sel-support fragments, 20 spacers, 33 sockets, 1 base, 42 spacer, socket, or base fragments, and 68.67 kg (35,722 items) of fragmentary salt-making artifacts from the Stingray Lagoon, Orlando's Jewfish, Killer Bee, and David Westby sites.

Ceramic Group: Punta Ycacos.

Ware: Uaxactun Unslipped.

Ceramic Complex: Golden Stream.

Ceramic Sphere Affiliation: Tepeu; Boca; Tepejilote/Boca; Spanish Lookout.

Description:

Principal Identifying Characteristics:

1. unslipped surface

Table 3.1. Vessel Forms for Pottery Types from the Salt Work Shops

	Pottery Type				
Vessel Form	Punta Ycacos Unslipped	Warrie Red	Moho Red	Mangrove Unslipped	Total
Plate	1	—	—	—	1
Dish	9	—	1	—	10
Bowl	24	18	21	5	68
Jar	182	61	—	54	297
Unknown	196	2	—	154	352
Total	412	81	22	213	728

2. coarse paste with sand temper showing throughout the surface

3. jars with out-curved necks and direct or exterior folded rims

4. bowls with out-curved sides and direct rim

Paste, Temper, and Firing: The paste was coarse with sand temper. Occasional large pebble inclusions were present. The color of the paste included sherds with black, dark gray, light gray, brown, red, and tan, with the first two predominating. The thick jar rims often had black cores, whereas the body area of the same sherd was gray, brown, or red. The pottery was not well-fired. The pottery sherds were more durable than the spacers, sockets, bases, and cylinders, which easily fell apart. The jars often broke at the neck, either leaving a short, thick rim, or exfoliating the exterior part of the vessel and leaving the interior part attached to the rim. Some sherds showed clay that was poorly mixed and layered in cross-section.

Surface Finish and Decoration: Both the interiors and exteriors of the vessels were unslipped (figures 3.3–3.8). The surfaces were rough and pit-

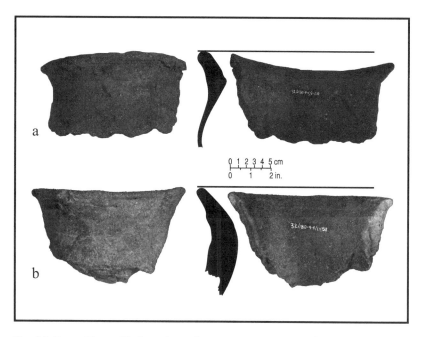

Fig. 3.3. Punta Ycacos Unslipped Jars from Stingray Lagoon. The exterior is to the left of the profile, and the interior is to the right. Photos by H. McKillop; profiles by H. McKillop and Mary Lee Eggart.

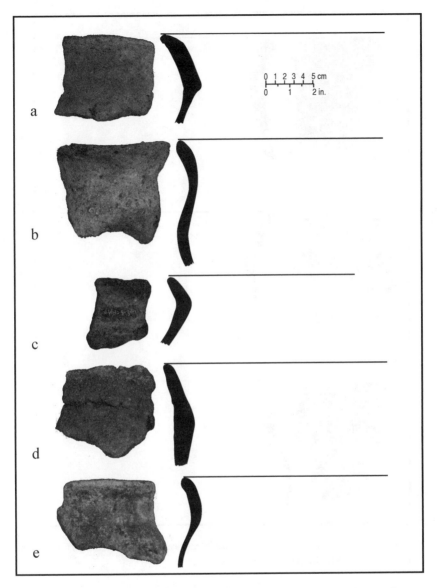

Fig. 3.4. Punta Ycacos Unslipped Jars from Stingray Lagoon. Photos by H. McKillop;
profiles by H. McKillop and Mary Lee Eggart.

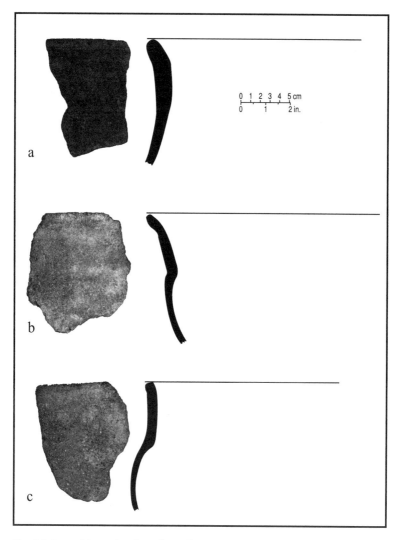

Fig. 3.5. Punta Ycacos Unslipped Jars from Stingray Lagoon. Photos by H. McKillop; profiles by H. McKillop and Mary Lee Eggart.

ted due to the high density of sand temper. The interiors of the vessels were smooth, whereas the exteriors were generally rough and uneven, although a few were smooth. Several sherds were striated. The surface finish may have been altered by immersion in salt water, since the pottery from the land site of Killer Bee was smoother. The underwater sites had pottery that was discolored a dark gray, whereas the Killer Bee pottery was reddish pink in color. Occasionally vessels were burnt on the exterior. *Form:* Vessel shapes included jars with restricted orifices as well as open bowls, a few dishes similar to the bowls, and one plate (table 3.2). Most of the vessels were jars. A variety of wall shapes were represented, although two quite similar jar forms were most common: jars with in-curved sides and out-curved neck and jars with in-curved sides and vertical neck, both of which had direct or exterior folded rims and round lips (tables 3.3–3.4). Average jar rim diameter was 22 cm. Bases were probably round, since no flat or concave sherds were recovered. The jars were thickest at the neck (up to 3.5 cm thick), rapidly tapering in the vessel body and toward the lip. Variation in vessel thickness is quite common for modern Maya pots (see, for example, Reina and Hill 1978). Average jar thickness for the Punta Ycacos jars was 1.6 cm, with a range from 0.7 to 3.6 cm (figure 3.9).

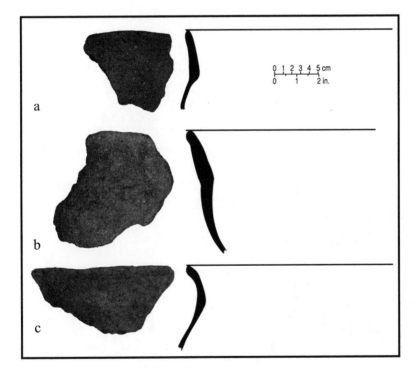

Fig. 3.6. Punta Ycacos Unslipped Jars from Stingray Lagoon. Photos by H. McKillop; profiles by H. McKillop and Mary Lee Eggart.

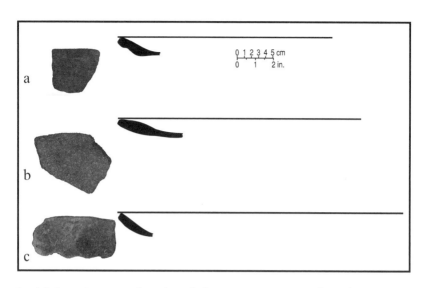

Fig. 3.7. Punta Ycacos Unslipped Bowls from Stingray Lagoon. Photos by H. McKillop; profiles by H. McKillop and Mary Lee Eggart.

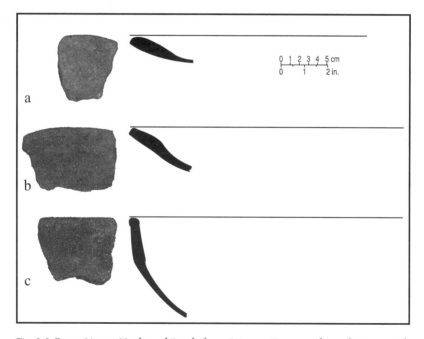

Fig. 3.8. Punta Ycacos Unslipped Bowls from Stingray Lagoon. Photos by H. McKillop; profiles by H. McKillop and Mary Lee Eggart.

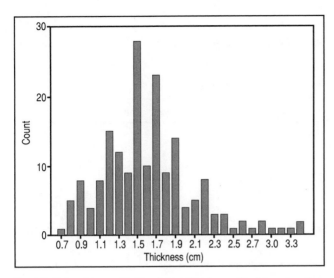

Fig. 3.9. Punta Ycacos Unslipped Jar Thickness. By Mary Lee Eggart from sketch by H. McKillop.

Table 3.2. Wall Shape for Punta Ycacos Unslipped Vessels from Salt Work Shops

	Vessel Form					
Wall Shape	Plate	Dish	Bowl	Jar	Unknown	Total
Vertical	—	—	1	—	—	1
Flared	—	1	5	—	—	6
Out-curved	—	3	1	—	—	4
Round	—	4	11	1	—	16
Slightly in-curved	—	—	3	—	—	3
Markedly in-curved, restricted orifice	—	—	1	1	—	2
In-curved sides, vertical neck	—	—	—	58	—	58
In-curved sides, out-flared neck	—	—	—	4	—	4
In-curved sides, out-curved neck	—	—	—	85	—	85
Vertical neck	—	—	—	8	—	8
Z-angle	—	1	—	—	—	1
Miniature incense burner	—	—	—	1	—	1
Unknown	1	—	1	13	196	211
Total	1	9	23	171	196	400

Table 3.3. Lip and Rim Form for Punta Ycacos Jars with In-Curved Sides and Out-Curved Neck

| | **Lip Form** | | | | |
Rim Form	Round	Pointed	Square	Unknown	Total
Direct	23	3	6	—	32
Exterior thickened	2	—	—	—	2
Exterior folded	15	—	—	—	15
Out-flared everted	7	—	—	—	7
Unknown	—	—	1	2	3
Total	47	3	7	2	59

Bowls and dishes had round sides, and most had direct rims and round or squared lips (tables 3.5–3.6). Base shape was unknown, but probably round, since no flat or concave body sherds were recovered. Compared with the jars, the bowls and dishes of this type were relatively thin, averaging 1.4 and 1.2 cm in thickness, respectively, although one bowl sherd was 3.1 cm in thickness.

The vessels were supported over fires by solid clay cylinder vessel supports. There were likely three cylinder supports used per pot, as was the custom with other Maya pottery. The recovery of a complete cylinder measuring 26.5 cm in length provides an indication of the height the vessels were supported over the fire (figure 3.10). The cylinder vessel supports were remarkably similar in diameter and cross-section shape, most being oval (figures 3.11–3.14). The cylinders had a flat base at one end where the vessel rested on the ground. The recovery of a cylinder in a base from Stingray Lagoon indicated the vessel supports were angled. The intact cylinder base shows the angle at which the cylinder was set (figure 3.15). At the other end of the cylinder, there was a socket to support the vessel over the fire (figures 3.16–3.18). Also recovered were disc-shaped spacers with concave surfaces to separate jars placed together over a fire (figures 3.19–3.20). They were made from poorly mixed clay and included pieces of charcoal. Fourteen spacers, 8 sockets, and 16 spacers or sockets were from Stingray Lagoon. Five items from Orlando's Jewfish and 14 from David Westby were either spacers or sockets.

Fired clay lumps, found in abundance at the salt work shops, were interpreted as unrecognizable fragments of the jars, bowls, vessel supports, and spacers that had accumulated after discard—either during vessel manu-

Table 3.4. Lip and Rim Form for Punta Ycacos Jars with In-Curved Sides and Vertical Neck

	Lip Form						
Rim Form	Round	Pointed	Square	Beveled In	Beveled Out	Unknown	Total
Direct	15	3	1	1	1	—	21
Exterior thickened	2	—	—	—	—	—	2
Exterior folded	19	1	2	—	—	—	22
Out-flared everted	4	—	1	—	—	—	5
Unknown	—	—	—	—	—	1	1
Total	40	4	4	1	1	1	51

facture or after use in the brine boiling itself. At Stingray Lagoon site, quantities of fired clay were found embedded in a fire-hardened charcoal lens about 5–10 cm in thickness. Elsewhere at Stingray Lagoon and at the other sites, fired clay lumps were intermixed with abundant charcoal— evidently the remains of the salt works fires. Some of the fired clay un- doubtedly represents breakage during manufacture of the vessels them- selves prior to boiling the brine, but they were not distinguishable from other discards. The recovery of broken salt pots was expected, since the slag from previous day's work accumulated in the fire hearths and the work shop. In some cases it was possible to determine the artifact type from which the fired clay lump derived. However, identification was rare.

Table 3.5. Rim Form for Punta Ycacos Unslipped for Salt Work Shops

	Vessel Form					
Rim Form	Plate	Dish	Bowl	Jar	Unknown	Total
Direct	1	8	22	84	6	121
Exterior thickened	—	—	—	5	—	5
Square	—	1	—	1	—	2
Exterior folded	—	—	1	51	1	53
Horizontal everted	—	—	—	2	—	2
Outflared everted	—	—	—	18	—	18
Unknown	—	—	1	8	189	198
Total	1	9	24	169	196	399

Table 3.6. Lip Forms for Punta Ycacos Unslipped for Salt Work Shops

	Vessel Form					
Lip Form	Plate	Dish	Bowl	Jar	Unknown	Total
Round	1	5	10	132	7	155
Pointed	—	1	5	10	2	18
Square	—	2	6	16	—	24
Beveled in	—	—	—	1	—	1
Beveled out	—	1	2	1	—	4
Grooved	—	—	—	1	—	1
Unknown	—	—	1	8	187	196
Total	1	9	24	169	196	399

Generally, the material was the same coarse, sand-tempered ware as Punta Ycacos Unslipped and was assumed to represent sherds and other fragments from the salt-making pots and their supports. In order to quantify the amount of fired clay lumps and their size, weights and counts were made.

The greatest quantity of fired clay was found at Stingray Lagoon, where the fires were so intense that some of the clay slag became imbedded with the charcoal in the fire pits. Excluding this clay, the counts and weights were still higher than they were for the other work shops (figure 3.21; Appendix 2). At Orlando's Jewfish, most of the slag was from the first 10 cm of excavation. The mound at Killer Bee, interpreted as a slag heap from concentrating the salinity of sea water by pouring the brine

Fig. 3.10. Complete Punta Ycacos Vessel Support. Photo by H. McKillop. Reprinted from *Latin American Antiquity* 6 (1995): 226, Figure 11.

Fig. 3.11. Punta Ycacos Vessel-Support Fragments from Stingray Lagoon. Photo by H. McKillop.

Fig. 3.12. Punta Ycacos Vessel-Support Fragments from David Westby. Photo by H. McKillop.

Fig. 3.13. Punta Ycacos Vessel Supports from Stingray Lagoon. Photo by H. McKillop.

Fig. 3.14. Punta Ycacos Vessel-Support Fragments from Killer Bee. Photo by H. McKillop.

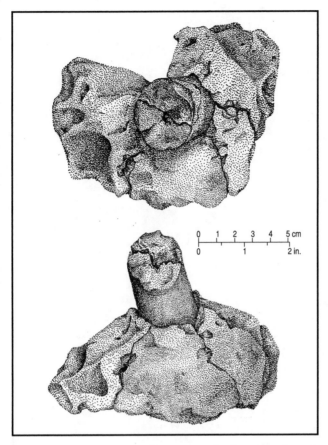

Fig. 3.15. Punta Ycacos Vessel Support with Intact Base from Stingray Lagoon. By Mary Lee Eggart. Reprinted from *Latin American Antiquity* 6 (1995): 224, Figure 9b.

through salt-enriched soil before the boiling process, contained fired clay in all levels, as did the shovel test. The recovery of fired clay, as well as other artifacts, to the base of the excavations at 80 cm depth in the shovel test at Killer Bee indicated this work shop had the thickest deposits. The high weight for Unit 1d at David Westby was attributed to the recovery of a few large items. Significant quantities of fired clay, both by count and by weight, were recovered from the salt work shops.

Intrasite Locations and Contexts: Jars, bowls, spacers, sockets, and cylinders were recovered from underwater excavations at Stingray Lagoon in a workshop area evidenced by congealed charcoal and clay. These artifacts were also recovered from underwater excavations at Orlando's Jew-

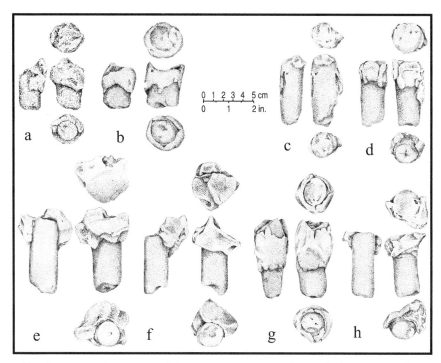

Fig. 3.16. Punta Ycacos Vessel-Support Fragments with Attached Base or Socket Fragments from Killer Bee. Drawing by Mary Lee Eggart.

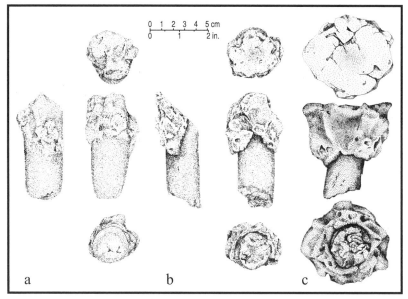

Fig. 3.17. Punta Ycacos Vessel-Support Fragments with Attached Base or Socket Fragments from Stingray Lagoon. Drawing by Mary Lee Eggart.

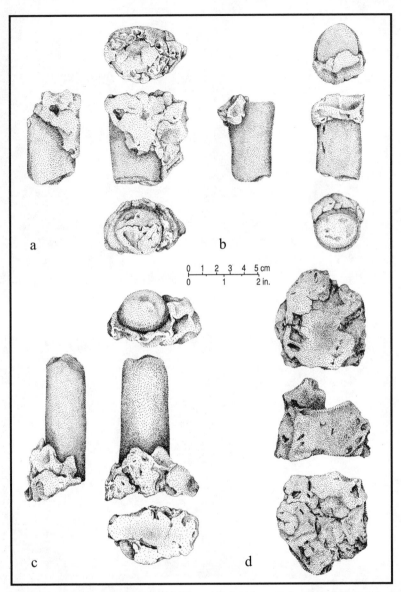

Fig. 3.18. Punta Ycacos Vessel-Support Fragments from Orlando's Jewfish (*a* and *c*) and Killer Bee (*b*) and a Spacer from Stingray Lagoon (*d*). Drawing by Mary Lee Eggart.

Fig. 3.19. Punta Ycacos Unslipped Spacer from Orlando's Jewfish. Photo by H. McKillop.

Fig. 3.20. Punta Ycacos Unslipped Spacer from Stingray Lagoon. Photo by H. McKillop.

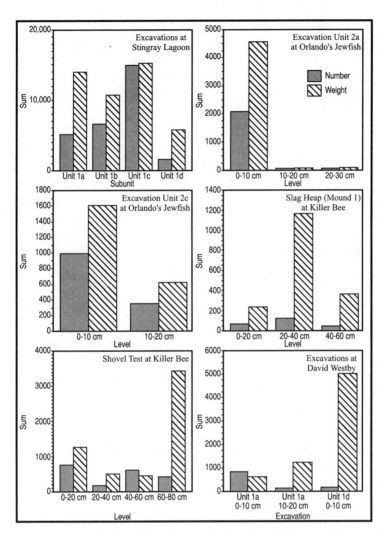

Fig. 3.21. Counts and Weights of Fired Clay. By H. McKillop and Mary Lee Eggart.

fish and David Westby and at the land site of Killer Bee, in areas interpreted as the debris from salt production. Underwater surface recoveries were mapped at Stingray Lagoon and collected from the other three salt-making sites.

Sand-tempered jars and bowls were recovered at other sites in the area where they were multipurpose vessels. The specific thickened-neck jar form was specific to the salt-making sites.

Intersite Locations and Contexts: Similar jar forms were recovered in the Placencia salt-making sites (MacKinnon 1989). Solid clay cylinders have been recovered from coastal Maya sites, including Moho Cay (McKillop 1980), Northern River Lagoon site (Mock 1994), Placencia area (MacKinnon 1989), and Potts Creek Lagoon. The spacers and sockets were recovered from Placencia area.

Cultural Significance: Punta Ycacos Unslipped included pottery vessels and associated artifacts involved in the production of salt by boiling brine in pots held over fires supported by solid clay cylinders embedded in clay bases at the lower end and clay sockets at the top end where they supported the vessel. Disc-shaped solid clay spacers with concave surfaces were used to separate jars held over the fire. Significant quantities of amorphous clay lumps that were interpreted as remnants of salt-making artifacts were recovered from the congealed fire-pit area at Stingray Lagoon site and from the other salt-production sites. The cylinders were recovered from a number of other sites in the south-coastal Belize area, but not in any quantity, suggesting that salt-making was carried out at these other sites on a sporadic, household basis. Sand-tempered bowls recovered from other sites may have served other utilitarian purposes in addition to salt-making.

Mangrove Unslipped: Mangrove Variety

Type: Mangrove Unslipped.
Variety: Mangrove Variety.
When Established as a Type and/or Variety: In the present study. The present description was based on 213 sherds.
Ceramic Group: Mangrove Unslipped.
Ware: Uaxactun Unslipped.
Ceramic Complex: Golden Stream.
Ceramic Sphere Affiliation: Tepeu; Boca; Tepejilote/Boca; Spanish Lookout.
Description:
Principal Identifying Characteristics:
    1. unslipped surface
    2. medium paste with calcite temper or pore holes visible on surface
    3. jars with out-curved or straight necks, direct or out-flared, everted rims, and square or round lips
Paste, Temper, Firing: The paste was coarse with calcite, although the temper is leached from most of the pottery from the underwater sites. The

color of the paste included black, light and dark gray, tan, red, and brown. Few of the Mangrove Unslipped ceramics from the salt sites reacted to a 5 percent solution of hydrochloric acid, although some had white specks visible on the surface that resembled calcium carbonate temper flecks. The vessels were not completely fired, since many had black or dark gray cores.

Surface Finish and Decoration: Both the exteriors and interiors of the vessels were unslipped. The surfaces were smooth, although there was extensive pitting on the vessel sherds from the underwater sites (figures 3.22–3.24). Occasionally, vessels were burnt on the exterior. Several body sherds were striated, with parallel score marks on the exterior. Three body sherds had an impressed fillet that may have been located around the shoulder of jars. The fillet was not appliqué like the one on some bowls of other types in the Port Honduras region. Some of the jars were discolored back or gray from immersion in salt water. A few sherds were fire-blackened. One sherd had a rectangular stamp, and another had vertical gouged lines below the neck.

Form: This type included jars and bowls (table 3.7). Most jars had incurved sides with an out-curved neck, with either a direct rim or an out-

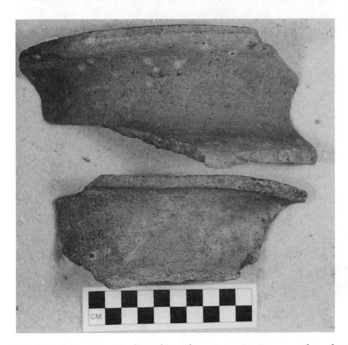

Fig. 3.22. Mangrove Unslipped Jars from Stingray Lagoon. Photo by H. McKillop.

Fig. 3.23. Mangrove Unslipped Jar from Stingray Lagoon. Photo by H. McKillop.

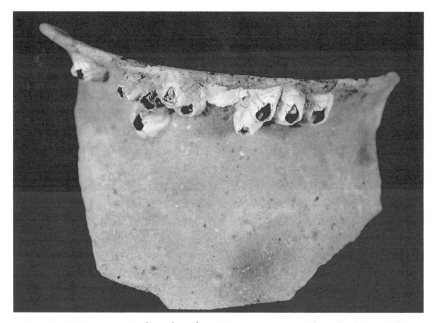

Fig. 3.24. Mangrove Unslipped Jar from Stingray Lagoon. Photo by H. McKillop.

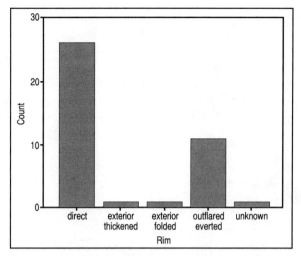

Fig. 3.25. Mangrove Unslipped Rim Forms for Jars with In-Curved Sides and Out-Curved Necks. By Mary Lee Eggart and H. McKillop.

flared, everted rim (figure 3.25). Most jar lips were round or square and were associated with direct or out-flared everted rims (table 3.8). Some of the out-flared, everted rims with square lips were depressed and flattened on the interior, with a slight interior break between the neck and rim and a few of the lips had a slight depression, almost a groove. Two of the square-lipped sherds had an incised line below the lip on the exterior, with a slight thickening on the exterior rim. Vessel diameters averaged 24

Table 3.7. Wall Shape for Mangrove Unslipped Vessels from Salt Work Shops

	Vessel Form			
Wall Shape	Bowl	Jar	Unknown	Total
Out-curved	1	1	—	2
Round	1	—	1	2
Markedly in-curved, restricted orifice	1	—	—	1
In-curved sides, vertical neck	—	4	—	4
In-curved sides, outflared neck	1	3	—	4
In-curved sides, out-curved neck	—	43	—	43
Vertical neck	—	1	—	1
Unknown	1	2	153	156
Total	5	54	154	213

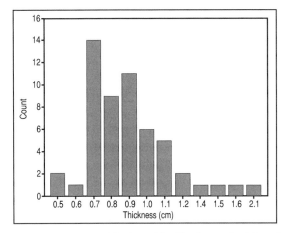

Fig. 3.26. Mangrove Unslipped Jar Thickness. By Mary Lee Eggart and H. McKillop.

cm. The necks varied in height from 3 to 3.5 cm. Jar rims averaged 0.7 cm in thickness (figure 3.26). The thickness tapered in the body to 0.4 cm on rim sherds. Base shape was unknown, since no complete vessels were recovered. Bases were assumed to be round, since no flattened or concave body sherds were found.

Intrasite Locations and Contexts: The jars were recovered from Late Classic (Tepeu 2–3) contexts at Stingray Lagoon, Killer Bee, Orlando's Jewfish, and David Westby sites on the seafloor.

Intersite Locations and Contexts: Mangrove Unslipped resembles unslipped jars recovered from other Late Classic sites, notably Cambio Unslipped from Seibal (Sabloff 1975:153–55) and Uaxactun (Smith 1955). At Uaxactun, Cambio Unslipped occurs throughout the Late Classic (Tepeu 1–3). At Seibal, the complete vessels were recovered from Bayal deposits

Table 3.8. Lip and Rim Forms for Mangrove Unslipped Jars with In-Curved Sides and Out-Curved Neck

Rim Form	Lip Form				
	Round	Pointed	Square	Unknown	Total
Direct	12	4	13	—	29
Exterior thickened	1	—	—	—	1
Exterior folded	1	—	—	—	1
Out-flared everted	4	4	3	—	11
Unknown	—	—	—	1	1
Total	18	8	16	1	43

associated with Fine paste sherds. The few striated body sherds in this collection (< 10 sherds) may resemble Encanto Striated at Seibal or Altar, but the absence of rims and small number of body sherds indicated there was no reason to isolate them from Mangrove Unslipped.

Cultural Significance: Mangrove Unslipped were the main unslipped, utilitarian ceramics in use. At the salt-making sites, the type would have been suitable for storing brine to pour into the salt-making vessels. Water jars were used in the sal cocida method of salt production in Sacapulas, Guatemala, to pour brine into the vessels while they were over the fire, as well as to store the salt before it was formed into salt cakes. There were two types of water jars recovered from the Punta Ycacos salt-making sites. Mangrove Unslipped jars were large, unslipped jars of local manufacture. Warrie Red jars were smaller, red-slipped jars, often with unit-stamped decoration.

Warrie Red: Warrie Variety

Type: Warrie Red.
Variety: Warrie Variety.
When Established as a Type and/or Variety: In the present study. The present description was based on 81 sherds from the Stingray Lagoon, Orlando's Jewfish, and Killer Bee sites.
Ceramic Group: Warrie Red.
Ware: Peten Gloss.
Ceramic Complex: Golden Stream.
Ceramic Sphere Affiliation: Tepeu; Boca; Tepejilote/Boca.
Description:
Principal Identifying Characteristics:

1. red slip, often weathered or discolored gray or black
2. jar with neck and out-curving to out-flaring rim and direct lip, or bowl or dish with out-curving to out-flaring sides and basal break or ridge
3. medium to fine paste without notable visible inclusions, except on eroded sherds
4. on some vessels, unit-stamped or other impressed or incised decorations on the shoulder of jars or exterior incised decoration on some bowls

Paste, Temper, Firing: The paste was similar to that for Mangrove Unslipped, of which this was the slipped development. The paste was black, tan, gray, or red. For the bowls and dishes, the paste color varied from black or gray to tan, red, beige, or light brown. There was a clear difference between the exterior surface and the core, suggesting an incomplete firing of the ceramic material. Temper was calcium carbonate, with some examples of sand temper.

Surface Finish and Decoration: The exterior of jars and their interior necks showed traces of slip. The slip had been discolored to a dark gray from immersion in salt water. The slip easily eroded, leaving a smooth exterior surface. Some of the sherds had impressed or incised decoration on the shoulder area of jars. There were several unit-stamped designs that

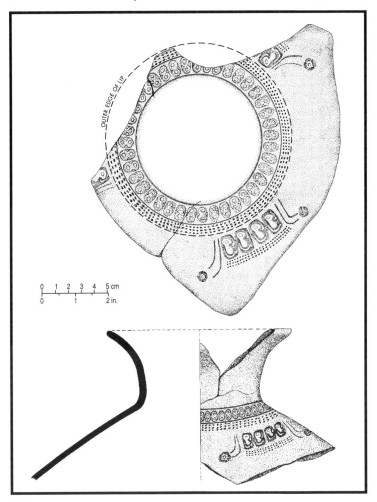

Fig. 3.27. Unit-Stamped Decoration on Warrie Red Jar from Stingray Lagoon. Drawn by Mary Lee Eggart.

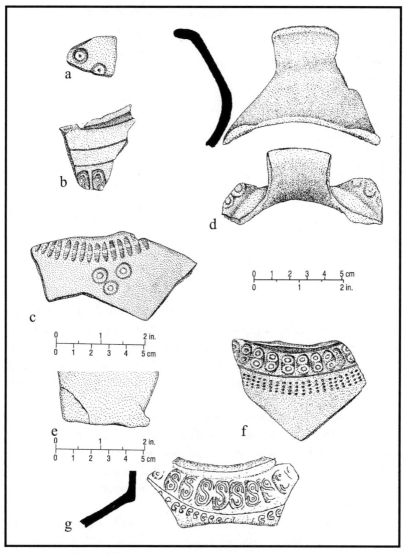

Fig. 3.28. Unit-Stamped Decoration on Warrie Red Jars from Stingray Lagoon (*a–f*) and Wild Cane Cay (*g*). Drawing by Mary Lee Eggart.

were impressed in a circumferential band on jar shoulders (table 3.9; figures 3.27–3.29). A circumferential band of comb-stamping also was used, sometimes in association with unit-stamping, either above or below the unit-stamped design. The unit-stamped designs included curvilinear motifs of monkeys, **S** shapes, and circles with dots inside. In comb-stamping,

Table 3.9. Motifs on Warrie Red Vessels from the Salt Work Shops

Motif	Frequency	Percentage
None	58	71.6
Unit-stamped circle, comb and monkey	1	1.2
Gouge-incised vertical line	1	1.2
Unit-stamped comb and circle	3	3.7
Unit-stamped S	3	3.7
Unit-stamped circle	2	2.5
Unit-stamped comb	6	7.4
Incised lines	4	4.9
Unclear unit-stamped design	1	2.5
No data	2	2.5
Total	81	100.0

a fine-toothed comb was used to make a line of conical pits of round to oval shapes vertically on the vessel in a band around the shoulder. One sherd with a complete rim, neck, and shoulder from Stingray Lagoon had a circumferential band of S shapes immediately below the neck on the shoulder, with comb-stamping below. Below the comb-stamping, there were three groups of five monkey stamps arranged around the vessel, each with incised decoration radiating from the unit-stamping. One example of radiate-incision, in which short, straight incised lines from the top of the vessel with a point dragged downwards, was recovered from Wild Cane Cay. In addition to the impressed decoration, one or two circumferential incised lines were used, sometimes above and/or below the impressed decoration.

The surfaces of bowls and dishes were eroded, with traces of red slip on the exterior sides and interior sides and base of bowl or dish sherds. The slip was discolored from immersion in salt water to a dull reddish brown, silver gray, or black color. The ceramics were hard and durable. Two rim sherds were dishes or bowls with out-flaring sides and a circumferential incised line below the lip on the exterior of the vessel. One of these rims also had a circumferential incised line midway along the vessel exterior. Surface finish, when visible, was glossy.

Form: Two vessel forms were present: a necked jar and a bowl or dish with out-curving to out-flaring sides and basal break or ridge. Jars had a vertical-

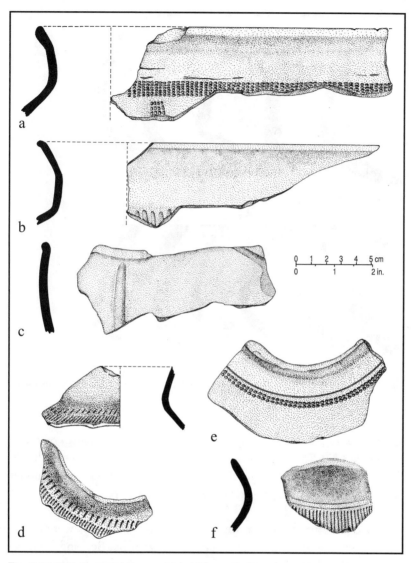

Fig. 3.29. Unit-Stamped Decoration on Warrie Red Jars from Stingray Lagoon (*a–c, e*) and Orlando's Jewfish (*d, f*). Drawing by Mary Lee Eggart.

to-out-flaring neck with an out-curving or direct rim (figure 3.30). A minor form, represented by two large rim sherds, was the spouted vessel (figure 3.31). The lips were round or pointed. Large rim sherds were recovered from Stingray Lagoon site, including one sherd with 100 percent of the rim and neck and part of the shoulder of the vessel. The dishes or bowls

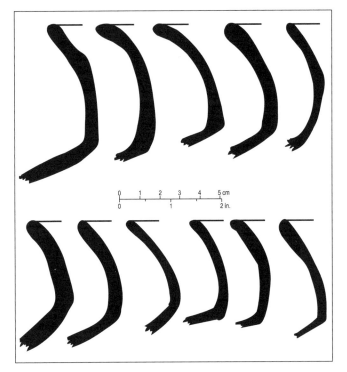

Fig. 3.30. Warrie Red Jar Rim Profiles from Stingray Lagoon. Drawing by H. McKillop and Mary Lee Eggart.

had out-flaring or out-curving sides, direct rim, and beveled-in or round lip (figure 3.32). There was a basal angle or basal ridge on five rim sherds. There was a variety of vessel thicknesses, but the vessels were thinner than Mangrove Unslipped or Punta Ycacos Unslipped vessels (figures 3.33–3.34).

Intrasite Locations and Contexts: Warrie Red jar sherds were recovered from the seafloor at Stingray Lagoon, from Killer Bee, and from the surface at Wild Cane Cay. The bowl and dish sherds were recovered from underwater-surface (seafloor) locations at Stingray Lagoon and Orlando's Jewfish.

Intersite Locations and Contexts: Warrie Red was similar to Remate Red at Lubaantun and Tinaja Red at Seibal and Altar de Sacrificios and shared their characteristics of an eroded red slip, necked jars, and impressed, especially "unit-stamped" decoration. The unit-stamped designs from Stingray Lagoon were more similar to the monkey and S and dot motifs from Lubaantun than the abstract motifs from Seibal or Altar de Sacrificios, which lack monkey or S and dot motifs (Adams 1971; Hammond 1975; Sabloff 1975).

Unit-stamped pottery is also known from cave sites in the Maya Mountains region, including Rio Frio Cave (Pendergast 1970), Actun

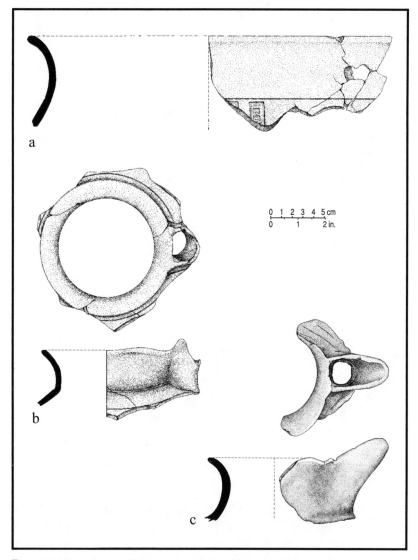

Fig. 3.31. Unit-Stamped Mangrove Unslipped Jar and Warrie Red Spouted Jars from Stingray Lagoon. Drawing by Mary Lee Eggart.

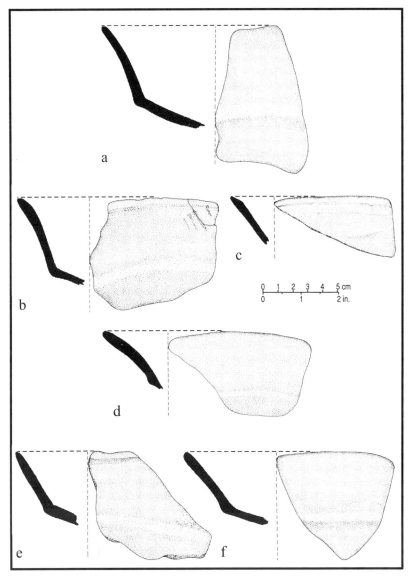

Fig. 3.32. Warrie Red Bowls. Drawing by Mary Lee Eggart.

Balam (Pendergast 1969a), and Eduardo Quiroz Cave (Pendergast 1971), as well from Mountain Cow (Kidder 1954:figure 7d), Poptun (Kidder 1954:figure 7), Tikal, Barton Ramie, Lake Peten Itza (Adams 1971:47–48, figure 59), and Aguateca (Ian Graham in Hammond 1975:305). Hammond (1975:305) suggests that there may have been two main areas of

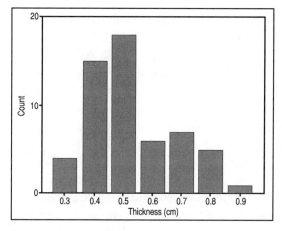

Fig. 3.33. Warrie Red Jar Thickness. By H. McKillop.

production/use of unit-stamping, including the Pasion region of Seibal, Altar de Sacrificios, and other sites on the west, and the eastern sites of the Upper Belize Valley, Mountain Pine Ridge to Lubaantun area. The current study bears out Hammond's interpretation, since the south-coastal Belize material resembles the Lubaantun motifs rather than those from Seibal and Altar de Sacrificios.

Similar vessels at other sites are dated to the Late to Terminal Classic in the Maya lowlands. Spouted vessels were not reported from Lubaantun, Seibal, or Altar de Sacrificios. Sidrys (1983) places spouted vessels from northern Belize in the Terminal Classic. Hammond placed Remate Red in

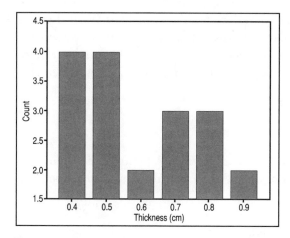

Fig. 3.34. Warrie Red Bowl Thickness. By Mary Lee Eggart and H. McKillop.

Tepeu 2–3 at Lubaantun, whereas Adams restricted Tinaja Red to Tepeu 3. Sabloff placed Tinaja Red in the Late Classic. The radiocarbon date of A.D. 770 ± 50 years from Stingray Lagoon placed the Warrie Red material in Tepeu 2–3, contemporary with Lubaantun. Red-slipped dishes and bowls with basal breaks or basal angles were common at Late Classic sites in the Maya lowlands. Hammond (1975:314–15: figure 113a) reported a red-slipped, tripod bowl form from Lubaantun that he placed within the Remate Group. Similar red bowls at Uaxactun and Seibal were placed within the Tinaja Red type (Sabloff 1975; Smith and Gifford 1966:145, 172). The presence of a basal break or basal angle on several of the rim sherds more closely resembled, in form, Hammond's Louisville Polychrome, but it was not possible to discern whether or not the Stingray Lagoon and Orlando's Jewfish examples were polychrome or monochrome.

Cultural Significance: Warrie Red was the major monochrome-slipped pottery at Stingray Lagoon site and was present at Orlando's Jewfish, Killer Bee, Wild Cane Cay, and Frenchman's Cay. Warrie Red likely was traded to the Port Honduras region, and the vessels were similar to unit-stamped vessel types from inland sites in southern Belize and Guatemala. The jar form was smaller and more gracile than the Mangrove Unslipped jars. The two spouted jars clearly indicated a pouring function to the vessels, but even the out-flared to out-curved necks of the other Warrie Red jars were a suitable form for pouring. Warrie Red jars may have been used, along with their unslipped Mangrove Unslipped counterparts, to store brine for processing salt at Stingray Lagoon. While suitable for storing and pouring brine into the salt pots at the work shops, Warrie Red jars may also have been used in salt rituals at the work shops, since it was not recovered from the Stingray Lagoon excavations and the vessels are much nicer than the brine-boiling pots or the Mangrove Unslipped water jars.

Moho Red: Moho Variety

Type: Moho Red.
Variety: Moho.
When Established as a Type and/or Variety: In the present study. The present description was based on 22 sherds from Stingray Lagoon and Orlando's Jewfish.
Ceramic Group: Moho Red.
Ware: British Honduras Volcanic Ash.

Ceramic Complex: Golden Stream.
Ceramic Sphere Affiliation: Tepeu; Boca; Tepejilote/Boca.
Description:
Principal Identifying Characteristics:
   1. red slip, which erodes easily
   2. fine yellow paste, which erodes easily
   3. bowls or dishes with tripod supports and basal angle or ridge on the
   exterior

Paste, Temper, Firing: Moho Red vessels had a fine yellow paste that felt chalky and scraped off easily with a fingernail into a fine powder. The core was uniform in color and texture throughout the cross-section of the sherd. There was no reaction to a 5 percent solution of hydrochloric acid on a fresh break.

Surface Finish and Decoration: The surfaces were hard, but all examples were eroded showing the paste. Five rim sherds had incised decoration on the exterior wall, including an oblique, incised line (presumably several if the vessels were complete) framed within a panel of incised lines below the rim and above the basal break or basal angle (figures 3.35–3.36). The oblique line ran left to right on four of the sherds, but right to left on the other. One sherd had oblique fluting from left to right on the exterior wall, with oblique incised lines on the flute ridges.

Form: Rim sherds included bowls or dishes with basal breaks or basal angles, and tripod supports (with only the attachment spot remaining on the vessel bottom). Rims were direct with round or beveled-in lips, and the walls were thinner than the Punta Ycacos or Mangrove Unslipped vessels (figure 3.37).

Intrasite Locations and Contexts: All the rims were recovered from Stingray Lagoon, with body sherds also from Orlando's Jewfish site. Moho Red was the rare, fine-ware ceramic at these work shops.

Intersite Locations and Contexts: Moho Red resembled Belize Red from Lubaantun, particularly the volcanic-ash-tempered tripod bowls, which included examples with incised lines, including a circumferential line below the rim and above the basal angle. Hammond (1975:312) placed Belize Red in the Late Classic associated with Remate Red. Belize Red was established as a type at Barton Ramie in the Belize Valley, where it was placed in the Spanish Lookout, Tepeu 3 phase of the Late Classic (Gifford 1976). A few sherds of Belize Red at Seibal were placed in the Tinaja Red type (Sabloff 1975). Hammond (1975:312) suggested that Belize Red was

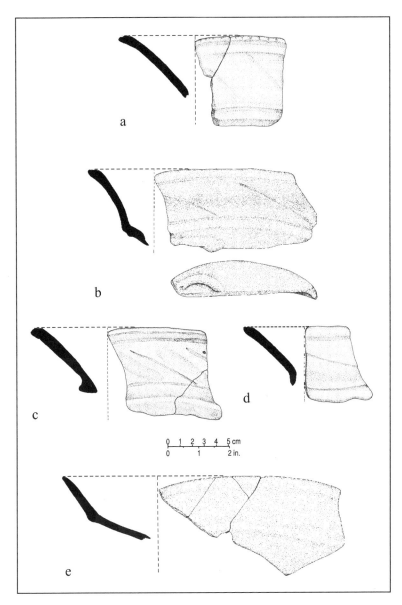

Fig. 3.35. Moho Red Bowls from Stingray Lagoon. Drawn by Mary Lee Eggart.

Fig. 3.36. Moho Red Bowls from Stingray Lagoon. Photo by H. McKillop.

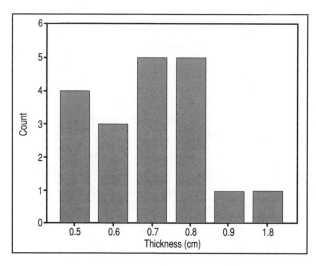

Fig. 3.37. Moho Red Bowl Thickness. By Mary Lee Eggart and H. McKillop.

a trade ware from the Belize Valley at Lubaantun, where 150 sherds were recovered, whereas there were more than 23,000 Belize Red sherds at Barton Ramie. Elsewhere in the Port Honduras region, Moho Red was found at Frenchman's Cay (McKillop 2000).

Cultural Significance: The tripod bowls or dishes of Moho Red formed part of the monochrome gloss-ware pottery in the Late Classic in the Port Honduras region, complementing the jars of Tinaja Red. The exotic origin of the volcanic ash temper and the tripod bowl or dish form of the slipped vessels indicated that these vessels were not everyday ware and were not part of the brine-boiling process. Instead, they were serving vessels likely used in rituals associated with salt production.

Salt Production

Two levels of craft production were associated with the salt-making sites, namely, the manufacture of pottery vessels and associated clay artifacts and the use of these vessels in boiling brine. The production of the Punta Ycacos brine-boiling ceramics arguably occurred either on-site or nearby. Both clay and sand temper were available locally. A clay source was identified on the west shore of the lagoon near a natural spring by the late Charlie Carlson of New Haven and reported to me. Quartz sand was washed down the Deep River and Freshwater Creek from the Maya Mountains. Since the vessels were poorly made and friable—with coiling visible both in jar necks and solid cylinder cross-sections—it was unlikely these objects were transported far from their place of manufacture. The abundance of fired clay lumps mixed with the charcoal in the fire pits indicated discard of used salt pots and their associated vessel supports, but may also have included the remains of wasters from production of the vessels themselves. The other ceramic types were not likely produced at the salt work shops. The Mangrove Unslipped jars were likely made in the Port Honduras region as water jars for various communities. The Warrie Red and Moho Red vessels were traded from outside the region.

Suitability of Vessels for Boiling Brine

How suitable were the salt-making artifacts for that purpose? The salt-making artifacts included Punta Ycacos Unslipped jars, bowls, and associated vessel supports used to boil the brine. In addition, there were Mangrove Unslipped and Warrie Red water jars used to store brine and pour it into the pots while they were over the fire. The water jars may also have been used to store the granular salt before it was hardened into salt cakes. Optimal vessels for boiling brine might have included those with durable and impermeable walls that would have transmitted heat from the fire, not allowed salt to seep through the vessel walls, and resisted breakage from repeated heating and cooling. Several characteristics of the vessels were observed to evaluate their suitability for boiling brine, including the kind and size of the temper, the amount of mixing of the clay, the surface treatment (Rice 1987b:232), vessel shape, vessel porosity, and vessel hardness. Durable vessels might have had clay that was well-mixed and with the temper also well-mixed in with the clay, so the vessel would have conducted heat evenly (Rye 1976). Impermeability could have been enhanced by burnishing the exterior of vessels and by mixing the clay and temper well so that the size, shape, and number of pores in the paste—the porosity—was low (Riehm 1961:183–84; Rice 1987b:231). Some temper, such as quartz sand, has high thermal expansion properties, so would have been less well suited than other materials, such as crushed limestone, for repeated heating and cooling (Rye 1976).

The Punta Ycacos Unslipped jars appeared poorly suited for boiling brine, unless their short-term use and local manufacture and use are considered. Sand temper was used exclusively, so it might have increased breakage rates during repeated heating and cooling. The sand was poorly mixed with the clay. In fact, the clay itself was poorly mixed. The same was evident for the clay cylinder vessel supports and for the sockets and spacers. The poor mixing of the clay and temper would have contributed to breakage rates during heating and would also have produced high porosity. The porosity would have led to seepage of brine through the vessel walls during boiling. The jars and bowls were friable, with low hardness. Vessel thickness varied from a thin lip, thickening at the vessel neck and then gradually thinning toward the vessel body. The vessels often split longitudinally at the neck—the thickest part of the jars, where the poor mixing of the clay affected durability. The rough exterior surfaces of the jars and bowls, with temper visibly extruding from the vessel surface, may have improved the absorption of heat from the fire, as argued by Charlton (1969:75) for salt vessels in central Mexico. The underwater matrix of the sites meant that the pottery was uniformly discolored gray and that they were impregnated with salt in the pores. Any evidence of surface finish, such as burnishing (which might have reduced evaporation through porous vessel walls) was not evident. Jars were clearly suitable vessel forms for containing liquids, although open bowls, such as used at Sacapulas today, may have facilitated repeated filling of containers with brine while the pots were over the fires.

The apparent poor selection of vessels for boiling brine was explained by their short-term use and local manufacture. Woods (1981) noted that locally available materials were usually used for tempering utilitarian cooking vessels, even if the temper was quartz. In the case of the Punta Ycacos Unslipped ceramics, the locally available material was evidently used, despite its less than optimal suitability. More disturbing was the high porosity. Adding cornmeal to the vessel before the brine was added, as at Sacapulas (Reina and Monaghen 1981), may have enhanced the impermeability of the jars, so that vessel porosity was not a problem. Clearly, the Punta Ycacos Unslipped pottery was not intended for transport or for long-term use. The thick jar necks may have been well suited to lifting the vessels on and off the fires, regardless of the long-term durability of the vessel. The fact that the vessels had a short life span was unimportant, since clay and temper were readily available and the vessels were used locally and for a short and specific task. When a vessel broke, its sherds could have been added to the fire and helped retain heat. Despite the short life span, the jars could presumably have been used more than once. Some may have lasted the short salt-production season each year; the others ended up in the fire. The clay cylinders had a similarly short life span and a similar fate.

Other Artifactual Evidence of Salt-Production Activities

Although most of the artifacts were the remains of pottery vessels used in brine boiling itself, there were a few artifacts that may have been associated with other aspects of the salt-making process. The recovery of a mano and metate from the seafloor at Stingray Lagoon was not surprising, since the use of corn in modern brine-boiling has been documented (Reina and Monaghen 1981). The metate was a turtleback shape and was made from Maya Mountain granite. The mano was round in cross-section and also made from granite. At Sacapulas, brine was concentrated by pouring it through salt-enriched soil in vats or boats. The salinity of the resulting brine was tested by means of small balls of ground, moist corn flour, which, when dropped into the brine, either sunk or floated, depending on the salinity (Reina and Monaghen 1981). The corn balls' ceasing to float in the brine indicated that the brine was ready for boiling; it also indicated that the salt content of the soil was essentially depleted. Together with the slag heap at Killer Bee, the mano and metate from Stingray Lagoon suggested that indeed the salinity of the already salt-enriched lagoon water was increased by pouring the water through salty soil. A corn solution may likewise have been put into the boiling pots to seal the wall surface before beginning the brine-boiling process, as was done at Sacapulas. Moreover, at Sacapulas, corn was later added to the boiling brine to make the salt finer-grained, which also may have been done at the Punta Ycacos salt work shops. While corn was not recovered from the salt work shops, corncobs dating to the Classic period were recovered from middens at the nearby settlement on Wild Cane Cay (McKillop 1994a). Lime deposits on the interior of Coconut Walk unslipped pottery sherds from Watson's Island (Graham 1994:figure 5.7d) may have resulted from the use of corn solution to seal the pots before brine was boiled.

A pottery stamp recovered from the seafloor at Orlando's Jewfish Site may have been used to mark ownership on salt cakes (figure 3.38), as was the case with cylinder seals in the ancient Near East. Alternatively, ownership marks may have been made on textiles or baskets used to transport the Punta Ycacos salt cakes. The salt stamp was sand-tempered, so it may have been locally manufactured. The impressions were on all surfaces. The interesting motifs on the clay stamp included a mat sign on one side and tau signs on the other side—symbols of rulership, power, and ownership among the Maya that provide tantalizing clues to the ancient use of this object.

Boats were necessary for transportation to and from the lagoon salt work shops, and old boats that were no longer seaworthy may also have been used in the brine-concentration process before the boiling began, if holes were made in the bottom of the boats. Two fragmentary boat models provide clues about the shape of the ancient Maya boats used by the Punta Ycacos salt workers (figure 3.38). Fragmentary boat models were recovered from excavations at Orlando's Jewfish and from the seafloor at Stingray Lagoon. In size and form the salt work shop canoe models resemble Classic-period boat models made from carved manatee rib bones from Moho Cay (figure 3.38; McKillop 1984:figure 4) and Altun Ha (Pendergast 1979:figure 46b). A similarly shaped clay boat model was found at the Dixon site on Roatan in the Bay Islands, Honduras (Strong 1935). Other depictions of similar boats are known from Tikal, where bones

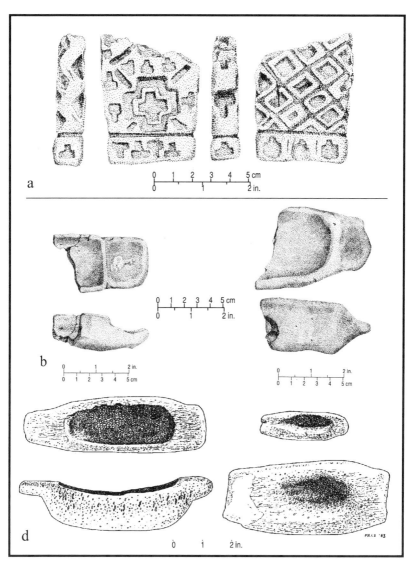

Fig. 3.38. Pottery Stamp from Orlando's Jewfish (*a*) and Clay Boat Models from Stingray Lagoon (*b*), Orlando's Jewfish (*c*) and Moho Cay–Belize City (*d*). Drawings *a*–*c* by Mary Lee Eggart; drawing *d* by Cathy Mills. Drawing *d* reprinted from *World Archaeology* 16 (1985): 343, Figure 4.

were incised with mythical figures in canoes in Burial 116 in Temple 1 (Trik 1963:figures 3a, 4–7) and from a painted mural from Chichen Itza (Thompson 1951:figure 1). Boats were depicted on a carved wooden lintel from Piedras Negras, recording a Yaxchilan emissary's trip downstream to attend a ruler's accession to the throne (Marcus 1983:figure 9).

A reliable supply of wood was critical to the Punta Ycacos salt production. Wood was needed to fuel fires both for baking the pots and for boiling the brine to produce salt cakes. Abundant charcoal was recovered from Stingray Lagoon, David Westby, and Orlando's Jewfish, with limited quantities from Killer Bee. Cross-sectioning of charcoal from Stingray Lagoon (Baker 1999) revealed a diversity of woods, including red mangroves (*Rhizophora mangle*). A wide variety of species is available in the area today, particularly south of the lagoon, with pine and palmetto palms available on the pine savannah to the north (Wright et al. 1959). Dry pine is good for kindling, whereas mangrove is a hardwood that provides an enduring hot fire and source of charcoal.

Salt Rituals at the Work Shops

Rituals at the beginning of each salt-production season, as well as daily ritual performed by each salt work crew, were part of salt production at Sacapulas and elsewhere (Andrews 1983; Reina and Monaghen 1981). The rituals included music, food, incense-burning, fireworks, and dancing. The recovery of whistles, incense burners or candeleros, and fineware serving bowls at the Punta Ycacos work shops may reflect a similar ritual dimension to salt production there. Three mold-made figurine whistles and a mold-made bat-head effigy whistle were recovered from Stingray Lagoon (figure 3.39–3.40). One figurine whistle depicts an individual holding flowers in one hand. Another figurine shows elaborate clothing and a necklace having a pendant in the form of an animal head—perhaps that of a bat or monkey. Two other figurine whistles are fragmentary, with only the bases remaining, so the depictions are unknown. It is interesting that the clothing depicted on the figurines indicates that the figures are female. Perhaps this implies that the work parties were composed of females, suggesting salt production, like weaving, was a female occupation. The figurine whistles resemble those from Lubaantun, where they may have been made. In addition to whistle fragments from Wild Cane Cay and Frenchman's Cay, many whistles were found at the mainland site of Village Farm in the Port Honduras region (McKillop 2000).

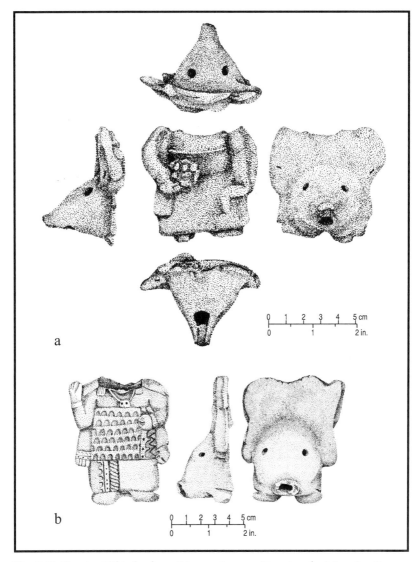

Fig. 3.39. Figurine Whistles from Stingray Lagoon. Drawings by Mary Lee Eggart. Drawing *a* reprinted from *Latin American Antiquity* 6 (1995): 223, Figure 8.

The bat-head whistle has no other counterparts in the Port Honduras or southern Belize regions.

A miniature tripod candelero was recovered from the Stingray Lagoon seafloor, and a miniature, flat-based candelero was recovered from the seafloor at David Westby (figure 3.41). The candeleros were sand-tempered and resembled others from Wild Cane Cay, Frenchman's Cay, and Moho Cay near Belize City, where they were plentiful (McKillop 1980). A tripod and two legless candeleros were found at Watson's Island (Graham 1994:figure 5.7a–c). A modeled clay object in the shape of the head of a

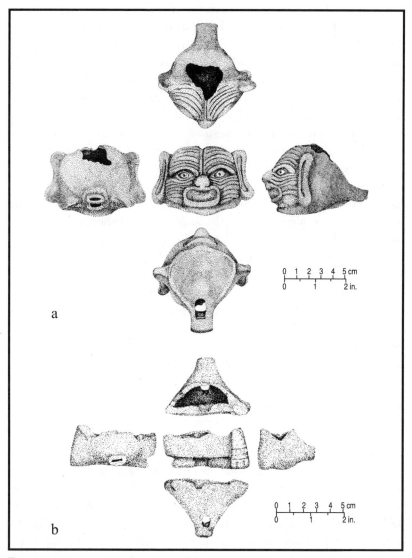

Fig. 3.40. Figurine Whistle and Bat Effigy Whistle from Stingray Lagoon. Drawings by Mary Lee Eggart. Drawing *a* reprinted from *Latin American Antiquity* 6 (1995): 222, Figure 7.

dog or gibnut (paca) was surface-collected from Stingray Lagoon (figure 3.41).

Other Activities at the Salt Work Shops

Absent from the artifact inventories were the ubiquitous remains of food and domestic activity regularly found at contemporary sites in south-coastal Belize. Apart from a coyol palm fruit (endocarp from *Acrocomia mexicana*) from Orlando's Jewfish, the botanical remains consisted only of abundant charcoal. The chipped-stone tools, which included an obsidian blade and a chert bifacial point, and the ground-stone tools, which included two axe fragments and a pumice disk, are not the repertoire of a settlement's stone tool needs. The stone tools may have been lost or used for meal preparation or snacks for the salt workers. One complete ground-stone axe was recovered from Orlando's Jewfish (figure 3.42). A fragmentary ground-stone axe was found at Stingray Lagoon (figure 3.42). A partially perforated pumice disk was recovered from Stingray Lagoon (figure 3.42). Pumice was plentiful along the coast and the offshore cays of Belize, where it washes ashore. The pumice evidently was washed down the Motagua River from volcanic areas of highland Guatemala and northward along the Belizean coast and cays. One obsidian blade fragment from Orlando's Jewfish was visually sourced to El Chayal. One bifacial chert lanceolate point from Orlando's Jewfish (figure 3.42) was discolored black from immersion in the salt water. One flake, one piece of debitage, and two chunks of chert, all showing flaking, were recovered from Stingray Lagoon and Orlando's Jewfish sites (figure 3.42).

Variability among the Salt Work Shops

Similar types of ceramics were recovered from the four salt-making sites, although more material was found at Stingray Lagoon related to the larger size of the excavations and more extensive program of surface collection. Comparison of the ceramic assemblages from the four sites was made by tabulating the number of items in each type (table 3.10; figure 3.43). There were differences among the four sites in terms of richness (number of types) and evenness (number of sherds in each type). In comparison to other Port Honduras–area sites, the richness was low for each of the salt work shops, suggesting a specific activity. At Frenchman's Cay, a contemporaneous island settlement in the Port Honduras, more than two dozen ceramic types were identified in the foundations and floors of Great White Lucine, Spondylus, and Crown Conch Mounds (McKillop 2000). In terms of evenness, most of the sherds were from the Punta Ycacos salt vessels, so the ceramic assemblages were characterized as uneven. Apart from a single miniature incense burner, all activity was fo-

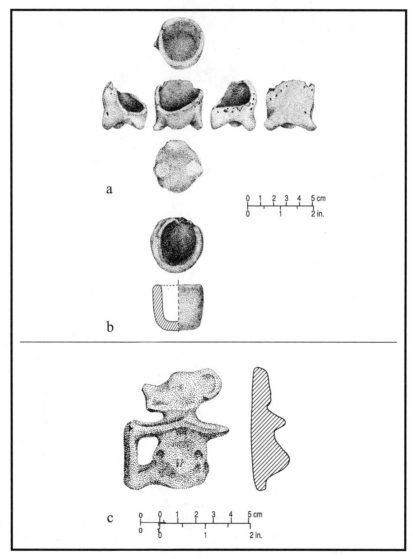

Fig. 3.41. Miniature Incense Burners from Stingray Lagoon (*a*) and David Westby (*b*) and Animal Effigy from Stingray Lagoon (*c*). Drawings by Mary Lee Eggart.

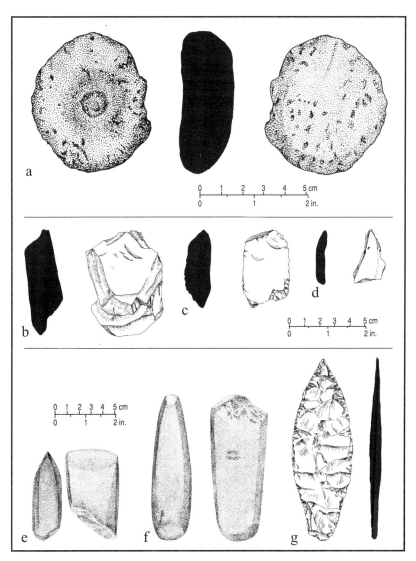

Fig. 3.42. Stone Tools. Shown are partially perforated pumice disk from Orlando's Jewfish (*a*), chert chunk from Orlando's Jewfish (*b*), chert flakes from Stingray Lagoon (*c–d*), ground-stone axe fragment from Stingray Lagoon (*e*), ground-stone axe from Orlando's Jewfish (*f*), chert biface from Orlando's Jewfish (*g*). Drawings by Mary Lee Eggart.

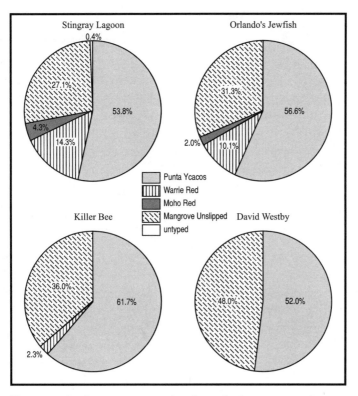

Fig. 3.43. Sherds per Type at Each Salt Work Shop. Drawing by H. McKillop and Mary Lee Eggart.

Table 3.10. Comparison of the Richness (# of Types) and Evenness (# of Sherds per Type) of Ceramic Assemblages at the Different Salt Work Shops in Punta Ycacos Lagoon

Site	Punta Ycacos Unslipped	Mangrove Unslipped	Warrie Red	Moho Red
Stingray	248	125	66	20
Westby	26	24	0	0
Orlando's	56	31	10	4
Killer Bee	108	63	4	0

Table 3.11. Wall Shapes for Punta Ycacos Vessels from Stingray Lagoon

	Vessel Form					
Wall Shape	Plate	Dish	Bowl	Jar	Unknown	Total
Vertical	—	—	1	—	—	1
Flared	—	1	3	—	—	4
Out-curved	—	3	1	—	—	4
Round	—	4	7	1	—	12
Slightly in-curved	—	—	2	—	—	2
Markedly in-curved, restricted orifice	—	—	1	—	—	1
In-curved sides, vertical neck	—	—	—	51	—	51
Incurved sides, out-flared neck	—	—	—	3	—	3
In-curved sides, outcurved neck	—	—	—	60	—	60
Vertical neck	—	—	—	8	—	8
Z-angle (dishes)	—	1	—	—	—	1
Miniature incense burner	—	—	—	1	—	1
Unknown	1	—	1	10	78	90
Total	1	9	16	134	78	238

cused on salt production at David Westby, with the Punta Ycacos salt pots and Mangrove Unslipped water jars. By way of contrast, nearby Stingray Lagoon and Orlando's Jewfish work shops included the non-salt-making Moho Red and Warrie Red serving vessels, as well as other artifacts, as a minor part of their ceramic inventories. Perhaps this inclusion indicated rituals relating to salt-making were carried out at Stingray Lagoon and Orlando's Jewfish work shops and that David Westby was a subsidiary work shop. Similarly, the work shop at Killer Bee may have been affiliated with a nearby, unlocated larger work shop.

Examination of intratype variability in a number of attributes indicated that the salt-making equipment and hence the salt production was remarkably uniform at the four salt work shops. The typical Punta Ycacos Unslipped jar at Stingray Lagoon had in-curved sides and an out-curved or vertical neck, with a direct or exterior folded rim and round lip (tables

Table 3.12. Comparison of Lip and Rim Form for Punta Ycacos Unslipped Jars with In-Curved Sides and Out-Curved Neck from Stingray Lagoon

	Lip Form				
Rim Form	Round	Pointed	Square	Unknown	Total
Direct	23	3	6	—	32
Exterior thickened	2	—	—	—	2
Exterior folded	15	—	—	—	15
Out-flared everted	7	—	—	—	7
Unknown	—	—	1	2	3
Total	47	3	7	2	59

3.11–3.13). Out-curved and vertical neck forms were equally popular. Jars with out-curved necks were more common at Orlando's Jewfish than were those with vertical necks (tables 3.14–3.16). Direct or exterior folded rims with round lips were the most common at Orlando's as at Stingray. At Killer Bee, all six measurable Punta Ycacos Unslipped jars had in-curved sides with out-curved neck, direct rim and round lip.

Table 3.13. Comparison of Lip and Rim Form for Punta Ycacos Unslipped Jars with In-Curved Sides and Vertical Neck from Stingray Lagoon

	Lip Form						
Rim Form	Round	Pointed	Square	Beveled In	Beveled Out	Unknown	Total
Direct	15	3	1	1	1	—	21
Exterior thickened	2	—	—	—	—	—	2
Exterior folded	19	1	2	—	—	—	22
Out-flared everted	4	—	1	—	—	—	5
Unknown	—	—	—	—	—	1	1
Total	40	4	4	1	1	1	51

Table 3.14. Wall Shapes for Punta Ycacos Vessels from Orlando's Jewfish

| | Vessel Form | | | |
Wall	Bowl	Jar	Unknown	Total
Flared	2	—	—	2
Round	3	—	—	3
Slightly in-curved	1	—	—	1
Markedly in-curved, restricted orifice	—	1	—	1
Incurved sides, vertical neck	—	7	—	7
In-curved sides, out-curved neck	—	19	—	19
Unknown	—	3	20	23
Total	6	30	20	56

Activity Areas at Stingray Lagoon

Activity areas were evident at the Stingray Lagoon work shop, which was possible to examine, since material was mapped and collected from specific areas on the seafloor, in contrast to the general surface collections carried out at the other work shops. The spatial distribution of ceramics from the different pottery types was examined by location, either at different places on the seafloor or from the excavations. Unprovenienced ceramics and other artifacts from the general surface collection were excluded from the analysis. Two activity areas were evident: the excavation and sur-

Table 3.15. Comparison of Lip and Rim Form for Punta Ycacos Unslipped Jars with In-Curved Sides and Out-Curved Neck from Orlando's Jewfish Site

| | Lip Form | | | |
Rim Form	Round	Pointed	Square	Total
Direct	7	2	1	10
Exterior thickened	—	—	1	1
Exterior folded	6	—	—	6
Horizontal everted	2	—	—	2
Total	15	2	2	19

Table 3.16. Comparison of Lip and Rim Form for Punta Ycacos Unslipped Jars with In-Curved Sides and Vertical Neck from Orlando's Jewfish Site

	Lip Form			
Rim Form	Round	Square	Grooved	Total
Direct	2	—	—	2
Square	1	—	—	1
Beveled in	2	1	1	4
Total	5	1	1	7

rounding area were a focus of salt production, whereas the area designated Cluster A (including Cluster A north and south) included the remains of ritual activities and salt production. The excavation and surrounding area was interpreted as a primary location for salt production owing to the presence of a fire-hardened layer of charcoal and salt-production debris. On the other hand, Cluster A included the remains of activities that took place in that area or discards gathered from elsewhere. Excavation might provide clues, such as fire hearths, about the nature of the activity and its primary or secondary context. Ritual offerings and feasting in the Cluster A area were evident from the musical instruments—including two figurine whistles and a bat whistle—the miniature incense burner, and the fine-ware serving bowl fragments of Warrie Red and Moho Red, as well as the clay dog ornament, boat model, and ground-stone celt. None of these artifacts was recovered from the excavations or from the surface clusters around the excavations (table 3.17; figure 3.44).

The distribution of brine-boiling equipment—the remains of the Punta Ycacos Unslipped vessels and their supports and the Mangrove Unslipped water jars—was widespread throughout the site, indicating significant salt production took place at the Stingray Lagoon work shop (figure 3.45). Similarly, the Punta Ycacos Unslipped vessel supports were recovered from the excavation and surrounding area as well as from Cluster A (figure 3.46). However, the spatial patterning of jar sherds showed all Warrie Red jar sherds except one were recovered from Cluster A (figure 3.47). Although the Warrie Red jars—including those with unit-stamped decoration—were suitable as jars for storing brine, along with the Mangrove Unslipped jars, the concentration of the Warrie Red jar sherds with the remains of ritual activities and away from the excavation

Table 3.17. Spatial Patterning of Pottery Types at Stingray Lagoon

Location	Punta Ycacos	Warrie Red	Moho Red	Mangrove Unslipped	Total
Cluster A	35	16	5	20	76
Cluster A South	24	13	3	7	47
Cluster A North	92	27	11	61	191
Northwest Hole	6	3	1	7	17
Southwest Corner	1	—	—	—	1
Cluster 2	1	—	—	—	1
Cluster 3	2	—	—	—	2
Cluster 6	—	—	—	1	1
Cluster 7	1	—	—	2	3
Cluster 8	3	1	—	—	4
Cluster 17	2	—	—	2	4
Cluster 18	2	—	—	—	2
Cluster 19	1	—	—	—	1
Unit 1b	14	—	—	6	20
Unit 1c	14	—	—	—	14
Unit 1d	19	—	—	8	27
Totals	217	60	20	114	411

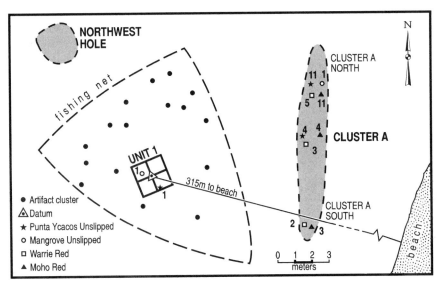

Fig. 3.44. Spatial Distribution of Bowls at Stingray Lagoon.

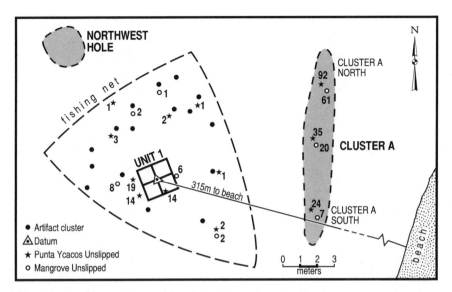

Fig. 3.45. Spatial Distribution of Unslipped Pottery at Stingray Lagoon.

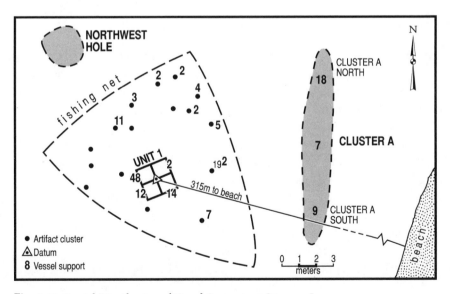

Fig. 3.46. Spatial Distribution of Vessel Supports at Stingray Lagoon.

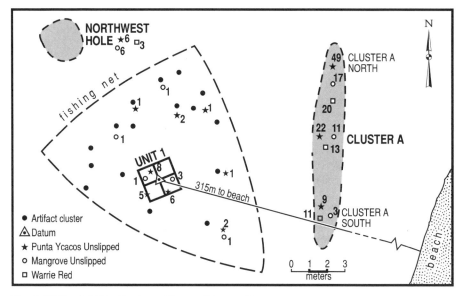

Fig. 3.47. Spatial Distribution of Jars at Stingray Lagoon.

area suggested Warrie Red was also used in ritual rather than just for storing brine.

Artifact Size and Postdepositional Site Trampling

Impressionistically, the large size of the pottery sherds at the salt work shops in general, and particularly at Stingray Lagoon, indicated a lack of postdepositional site trampling. This impression was borne out by measurements of the percentage of rim remaining on pottery sherds and the weight of pottery sherds (figures 3.48–3.49). Both Punta Ycacos and Mangrove Unslipped jars had many sherds with between 7 and 20 percent of the rim remaining, while Warrie Red sherds clustered between 15 and 45 percent and ranged to 100 percent of the rim remaining (figure 3.50). Moho Red showed no clear clustering, with a range between 3 and 17 percent of the rim remaining.

The large size of the pottery sherds at Stingray Lagoon and Orlando's Jewfish sites was in marked contrast to other Port Honduras area sites (table 3.18). A sample of 979 sherds of Bedford Unslipped from Wild Cane Cay had a maximum percentage of rim of 17 percent, which was much lower than the maximums for the Punta Ycacos Unslipped pottery from Stingray Lagoon and Orlando's Jewfish. The average sherd weight (in-

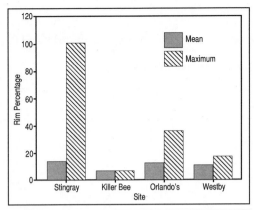

Fig. 3.48. Percentage of Rim Circumference for Pottery Sherds. By H. McKillop.

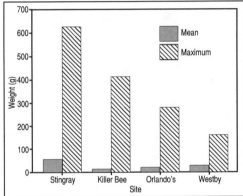

Fig. 3.49. Sherd Weights. By H. McKillop.

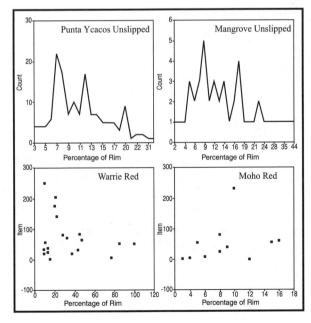

Fig. 3.50. Percentage of Rims. By H. McKillop and Mary Lee Eggart.

Table 3.18. Punta Ycacos Work Shops Ceramics: Completeness of Recovered Vessel Rims

			Percentage of Rim Circumference Recovered				
Site	Pottery Type	# Rims	Mean	Min	Max	Range	SD
Stingray	Punta Ycacos	114	12	5	32	27	5.45
Stingray	Mangrove	38	16	5	44	39	9.03
Stingray	Warrie Red	19	37	9	100	91	31.1
Stingray	Moho Red	11	9	3	16	13	4.27
Orlando's	Punta Ycacos	34	10	3	20	17	4.33
Orlando's	Mangrove	4	19	9	35	26	12.07
Orlando's	Warrie Red	1	20	20	20	0	—
David Westby	Punta Ycacos	11	10	4	16	12	3.54
Killer Bee	Punta Ycacos	1	6	6	6	0	—
Wild Cane Cay	Bedford Unslipped	979	—	—	17	—	—

Min = minimum; Max = maximum; SD = standard deviation

cluding zero values) of 15.9 g and maximum sherd weight of 93.2 g for the Bedford Unslipped sherds from Wild Cane Cay also was much lower than for the Punta Ycacos Unslipped pottery (table 3.19). The low values for Killer Bee were similar to those from Wild Cane Cay—both terrestrial sites where postdepositional soil accumulation and other factors contributed to artifact size in contrast to setting of the underwater salt work shops.

Clay cylinder vessel supports for the Punta Ycacos Unslipped vessels also were abundant and large. Only one complete cylinder was recovered, measuring 26.5 cm in length (from Stingray Lagoon), but this was not surprising considering the friable nature of the cylinders. Once again, the relatively large size of the cylinder fragments indicated a lack of postdepositional site trampling (tables 3.20–3.21). The cylinder vessel supports from the underwater sites of Stingray Lagoon and Orlando's Jewfish were larger than their counterparts at Killer Bee site, which was on land, suggesting the overlying soil also may contribute to postdepositional artifact size.

Table 3.19. Punta Ycacos Work Shops Ceramics: Weight

Weight of Sherds (g)

Site	Pottery Type	# Rims	Mean	Min	Max	SD	Sum
Stingray	Punta Ycacos	247	74.5	4.2	627.4	70.8	18,397.7
Stingray	Mangrove	121	42.7	1.2	320.8	51.52	5,165.1
Stingray	Warrie Red	61	40.0	2.7	394.7	55.47	2,437.1
Stingray	Moho Red	18	46.9	10.2	163.1	38.27	844.6
Orlando	Punta Ycacos	56	73.1	5.0	276.3	71.45	4,093.4
Orlando	Warrie Red	10	19.7	4.8	69.7	18.86	196.8
Orlando	Moho Red	2	15.5	10.4	20.6	7.21	31.0
Orlando	Mangrove	30	10.7	0.4	65.1	12.33	319.9
Killer Bee	Punta Ycacos	106	19.7	0.3	408.5	44.74	2,083.0
Killer Bee	Warrie Red	4	2.1	0.8	2.7	0.88	8.3
Killer Bee	Mangrove	62	4.4	0.4	39.4	6.0	270.6
Westby	Punta Ycacos	24	55.5	12.4	158.9	49.63	1,331.1
Westby	Mangrove	24	4.2	0.9	25.2	5.20	100.2
Wild Cane Cay	Bedford Unslipped	979	15.9	—	93.2	—	—

Min = minimum; Max = maximum; SD = standard deviation

Table 3.20. Punta Ycacos Unslipped Clay Cylinder Vessel Supports: Weight

Weight of Recovered Vessel Supports (g)

Site	# Items	Mean	Min	Max	SD	Sum
Stingray Lagoon	213	101.2	7.9	452.7	65.70	21,562.9
Orlando's Jewfish	182	91.8	7.0	352.2	60.98	16,701.3
David Westby	141	78.6	9.3	274.4	55.44	11,081.5
Killer Bee	81	65.8	9.3	263.2	44.45	5,328.0

Min = minimum; Max = maximum; SD = standard deviation; only measurable artifacts included

Table 3.21. Punta Ycacos Unslipped Clay Cylinder Vessel Supports: Length

		Length of Recovered Vessel Supports (cm)				
Site	# Items	Mean	Min	Max	SD	Sum
Stingray Lagoon	212	7.8	2.9	26.5	3.14	1,661.7
Orlando's Jewfish	182	7.2	2.4	19.0	2.64	1,307.9
David Westby	141	7.2	1.1	8.5	7.25	1,010.2
Killer Bee	81	5.7	1.9	12.4	2.24	461.0

Min = minimum; Max = maximum; SD = standard deviation

Salt Production Equipment at Other Sites along the Belizean Coast

Similar artifacts at other sites along the Belizean coast indicated brine boiling was a common and widespread method of salt production during the Late Classic. As a response to dramatically higher population density and size as compared to earlier times, salt works were established or expanded in coastal lagoons along the coast of Belize at Placencia Lagoon (MacKinnon and Kepecs 1989), at Watson's Island and elsewhere on Colson Point (Graham 1994), at Northern River Lagoon (Mock 1994; Valdez and Mock 1991), at Midwinter's and Salt Creek Lagoons (Mock 1994), on Ambergris Cay (Graham and Pendergast 1989; Guderjan 1988), and in Punta Ycacos Lagoon. Incidental salt production also occurred on offshore islands where salt pans were naturally created seasonally on the interior of the islands, such as at Moho Cay, Frenchman's Cay, Wild Cane Cay, and Ambergris Cay.

The Punta Ycacos Lagoon salt work shops were distinctive along the coast of Belize in being exclusive work shops geographically separated from Maya settlements and in their inventory of salt-making equipment. Elsewhere along the coast of Belize, salt-making was described as an activity that occurred at Maya settlements. At Northern River Lagoon, for example, salt-making artifacts were recovered in the context of household debris at the settlement. A variety of salt-making locales are described in the Placencia Lagoon area, with domestic debris indicative of settlement. The Colson Point sites were activity-specific places occupied part-time by inland Maya, but not exclusively used for salt-making (Graham 1994). Watson's Island was heavily engaged in trade and food processing of shellfish through the Late Postclassic, but because of mixed deposits from burrowing land crabs and subsequent human occupants of the site, it was

Fig. 3.51. Clay Cylinder Vessel Supports from Moho Cay. Photo by H. McKillop.

unclear if salt was produced as early as the Protoclassic or Early Classic. Both Marco Gonzalez and San Juan on Ambergris Cay were significant Maya settlements, with salt-making just one of the activities at the communities. Rather than dwelling on the uniqueness of the Punta Ycacos Lagoon salt-making work shops in their locations away from Maya settlements, it may be that it was expedient to live nearby in more favorable settings. It was fortunate archaeologically, however, to be able to examine the material remains of the salt-making activities in isolation and to see this activity in a single time period.

Salt production by the brine-boiling method occurred along the coast of Belize and on Ambergris Cay during the Late Classic period using a variety of techniques. Only in the south at the Placencia Lagoon and Punta Ycacos Lagoon sites were restricted-orifice jars, spacers, and sockets reported. Friable open platters, termed Coconut Walk Unslipped, reported from Watson's Island (Graham 1994), San Juan and Marco Gonzalez on Ambergris Cay (Graham and Pendergast 1989; Guderjan 1988; Valdez et al. 1995) and at Northern River Lagoon (Mock 1994) were identified with salt-making as well. Graham (1994) first described Coconut Walk Unslipped at Watson's Island in the Stann Creek District, and states there is

Fig. 3.52. Clay Cylinder Vessel Support from Late Classic Period Burial 5 at Moho Cay, near Belize City. Photo by H. McKillop.

no doubt they were used to make salt cakes (Graham, personal communication, 2001). Not surprisingly, then, sockets and spacers were only reported at the southern sites. Solid cylinder vessel supports were reported from Moho Cay (figure 3.51; McKillop 1980), including one from a Late Classic burial (figure 3.52), Northern River Lagoon, Placencia, and the Punta Ycacos Lagoon sites, but not from Ambergris Cay or Watson's Island. The Coconut Walk ceramics were open or round-sided bowls with friable and thin walls that did not resemble the Punta Ycacos Unslipped jars or bowls, which were thicker and more durable, and of course the jars are a different shape. The evaporative properties of an open bowl form contrasted to the lack of spillage of liquids by using jars.

The limited array of stone tools or food remains and the abundance of salt-making artifacts indicated there was virtually no habitation at the Punta Ycacos sites. Furthermore, there were no burials, which would be expected at a settlement. The sites were work stations for the production of salt by people who lived elsewhere. The specialized, single-activity nature of the Punta Ycacos salt industry contrasted with other sites along the Belizean coast, where salt-making was carried out as one activity of many at Maya communities.

4

ЛЛЛЛЛ

The Organization of Salt Production

Occupational Specialization among the Late Classic Maya

Craft production, often correlated with complex societies, has been difficult to identify archaeologically for the Classic Maya (Adams 1970; Becker 1973; Foias and Bishop 1997; Fry 1980; McKillop 1995a; Rice 1987a; Shafer and Hester 1983). The tangible products of artisans' work are visible in the form of stuccoed and painted masks on temples, Codex-style painted pottery vessels, images of elaborate clothing, and architectural adornment depicted on Maya stelae, as well as pottery vessels, stone tools, and other items (Adams 1970; Becker 1973; Joyce 2000; Reents-Budet 1994). What was the organization of labor required to produce these goods? The change from a domestic mode of production in relatively egalitarian societies, in which most of the goods and services are produced and acquired by each household, to a more complex mode of production, in which there is specialization beyond the household, is characteristic of stratified societies like the Classic Maya (Brumfiel and Earle 1987; Fried 1967; Sahlins 1972; Service 1975). Certainly the variety of highly crafted goods as well as the various skilled services that must have been a part of Classic Maya society—such as construction workers (Abrams 1994), limestone quarry workers (Winemiller 1997), scribes (Fash 1991), and others (Adams 1970; Becker 1973)—demonstrates occupational specialization existed among the Classic Maya. How specialized was the Classic Maya economy in terms of craft production?

By the Late Classic period, the southern Maya lowlands was organized into competing city-states with a central capital at Tikal and other high-order capitals, notably Calakmul and Copan (Chase and Chase 1992; Marcus 1976). Each city-state dominated a hierarchy of settlements defining a region, but the extent of political and economic control by the royal and upper-class Maya in the cities within the region is unclear. Trade and communication among elites between and within regions were maintained and renegotiated by royal marriages and other alliances and by military campaigns (Culbert 1991; Freidel 1992; Reents-Budet et al. 2000; Schele and Mathews 1991). The military defeat of Tikal by Caracol is a testimony of the fragility and ephemeral power of Late Classic Maya city-states. The alliances required ceremonies with feasting and gifts, with well-crafted pottery vessels and other material displays of wealth, power, and status.

Relatively few craft workers were needed to supply the limited number and variety of highly crafted goods acquired by Maya royalty at lowland cities, goods that were recovered in their graves or depicted on pottery vessels and carved monuments, such as fancy headdresses and clothing, carved jades, and Codex-style painted pots. By way of contrast, the bulk of Maya craft production was geared to making utilitarian and ceremonial goods that were less highly crafted. This included polychrome pottery that had a wide distribution within elite Maya society and utilitarian stone tools, ceramics, salt, clothing, and other goods (such as imported obsidian) that had distribution to the Maya populace. Although some research has focused on the production of utilitarian goods and extraction of natural resources (Foias and Bishop 1997; Fry 1980; Rands and Bishop 1980; Rice 1987a; Shafer and Hester 1983), the extent of this craft production and its geopolitical importance in Classic Maya society is less well understood than the production and distribution of the limited number of highly crafted goods for Maya royalty or the import of obsidian and other exotics from beyond the Maya lowlands.

The Organization of Craft Production

Understanding the importance of craft production in Late Classic Maya society requires examining the organization of production. This includes determining production locations, the scale and intensity of production, the relationship between producers and consumers, and the relationships between political power and production. In terms of the location of production, was production in the city centers, in the suburbs, in outlying communities, or near naturally occurring resources? Was production part of household activities, attached to households in "cottage industries," or spatially separated in work shops?

In terms of the relationships between political power and craft production, was production controlled by the state, as in "administered craft specialization" (Brumfiel and Earle 1987); was it part of household production, as in "socially embedded household production" (Janusek 1999), "high-intensity domestic manufacture" (Feinman 1999), or "concentrated intensified urban craft production (Charlton et al. 2000:261); or was it carried out by "independent specialists" who were not under the direct administrative control of an urban elite (Foias and Bishop 1997)? If the production of craft goods was spatially segregated from the urban elite, how did they maintain access to desired goods? Were the scale (size of the production facilities) and intensity of production (amount of goods produced, part- or full-time) limited in extent (Fash 1991; Mallory 1986), or were there large production locales where goods were mass-produced (Shafer and Hester 1983, 1986)? Answers to these questions about the location of production, the relationships between producers, consumers, and political leaders, and the scale and intensity of craft production have important implications for understanding the extent to which the Classic Maya economy was under the central control of the urban rulers, the vertical and horizontal alliances that may have been established for the urban elite to maintain access to goods from nearby and afar, and the incorporation of communities of various sizes into the macroeconomy.

Even among the more politically centralized, empire-building Aztec, much of the economy, in particular craft production, may not have been state controlled and much of the distribution may have been carried out through market exchange (Charlton et al. 2000; Smith 1990). Of course, some researchers argue instead for a significant role of Aztec cities in managing craft production and distribution (Sanders and Santley 1983, for example). Still other researchers consider Aztec craft production was not extensive (Brumfiel 1987).

Clearly, some of the most highly crafted Maya goods were made by artisans attached to royal households in urban settings (Fash 1991; Adams 1970; Becker 1973; Reents-Budet 1994, 1998). Attached specialists were sponsored by Maya royalty in urban centers to produce the finest carved jades, elite ceramics, and other highly crafted goods depicted on carved monuments and painted pots and found in royal burials (Adams 1970;

Becker 1973; Reents-Budet 1994, 1998). Reents-Budet and Bishop identified separate schools of style among Late Classic painted pottery vessels
by analysis of vessel style and chemical composition of vessel paste
(Reents-Budet 1994). Some vessels were identifiable to individual artists,
with a few vessels even signed by the painter (Reents-Budet 1994:figure
2.20). The high level of artistic skill indicates there were specialized painters in royal court work shops who were painting vessels made by other
specialists. Some painters of elite painted pottery even depicted themselves in scenes with Maya royalty, attesting to the importance and high
rank of these artisans in Late Classic Maya society (Reents-Budet 1994).

Elite painted pots and other highly crafted items were used in royal
rituals and public feasts and were given as gifts to establish, maintain, and
solidify relationships among Maya royalty in other polities and with
lesser lords within a polity (Leventhal 1990; Marcus 1995; Reents-Budet
1994; Schele and Miller 1986). Furthermore, the public display and burial
of highly crafted and nonlocal items by Maya royalty reminded the general public of their lower status and provided symbols of status enhance-
ment to emulate. Elite items used in royal rituals and feasts are depicted
on painted pottery and on carved monuments, sometimes accompanied by
hieroglyphic inscriptions describing the ritual or feast (Coe 1978, 1982;
Reents-Budet 1994, 1998; Schele and Miller 1986). The nonlocal origin of
some highly crafted goods in graves suggests they were gifts in public
relations. A good example is the Quetzal Vase, found in a royal burial at
Copan, but in the style of ceramics from Altun Ha (Longyear 1952:41–42;
Reents-Budet 1994:338–39, Plate 57). The final resting place for many
highly crafted goods was as offerings to accompany royalty and other
nobles after death in their graves. For example, the largest carved jade
item in the Maya lowlands, a head of Kinich Ahau, the sun god, was buried
in a temple at Altun Ha, Belize (Pendergast 1969b).

Not even the most royal Maya used exclusively highly crafted pottery
vessels, but instead used a variety of vessels and other craft goods in their
ceremonies. Where were these less highly crafted pots made? Depictions
of goods used in royal Maya rituals and feasts show both highly crafted
and more utilitarian items. For example, as depicted on Maya pots, vessels
with food served at regal meetings often included a vase for chocolate, a
jar with an alcoholic beverage made from corn, a bowl with cereal, and a
plate with a solid food such as tamales (Reents-Budet 1994:85–86; Taube
1989; Palka 1997:figure 8). They often were not matched sets, nor were
they all fancy ceramics. One elite painted vessel depicts a scene of three

Maya lords and food, in which there is a utilitarian jar with three fancier painted pots (Reents-Budet 1994:figure 3.4). The jar is unslipped. The hieroglyph on one side that may identify the vessel contents appears placed for the viewer of the painted scene instead of being on the depicted vessel itself. In the same scene, there is a plain, red-slipped bowl or dish that may contain cornbread or tamales. The accompanying vase and bowl are fancier, each being slipped red and white with a band of hieroglyphs.

Quantities of polychrome pottery were made for lower-tier elite and nonelite members of Maya society (Reents-Budet 1994:66). There are qualitative differences between highly crafted elite painted pots, including Codex-style and other vases with hieroglyphs (Coe 1978, 1982) and many other polychrome vessels. Clearly some of the Saxche and Palmar Orange polychromes of the Late Classic at Seibal, Altar de Sacrificios, and even at smaller communities such as Moho Cay, the Classic Maya island trading port located in the mouth of the Belize River, are finely made, but represent less artistic skill and care. These pots may have had more diverse production locales and a wider distribution geographically and socially than Codex-style and other high-quality royal Maya ceramics. In fact, Rice (1987a) has argued for limited control over production of much polychrome and utilitarian pottery in the Maya lowlands during the Classic period. Similarly, Graham (1994) argued that the Protoclassic and Early Classic polychrome production in the Stann Creek District of Belize was not elite controlled and that the vessels were widely traded at all social levels of society.

In some cases, there is evidence of local copies of fine ceramics. At Buenavista del Cayo, there was a ceramic work shop producing hundreds of polychrome vessels as local copies of a trade piece from Holmul—the Buenavista vase. "They represent local ceramic production for use and distribution by the Buenavista elite to the local aristocracy (for example, the sahals or 'secondary lords' mentioned on many stone monuments). . . . The local pottery's lesser painting quality may indicate . . . The Buenavista elite were unable to command and support the work of the top artists" (Reents-Budet 1994:96–97, figure 3.25). A painted pottery vase from Moho Cay depicts a Maya personage in fancy clothing and an elaborate headdress (figure 4.1). The accompanying pseudoglyphs on the vessel attest to the importance of the display of elite pottery, suggesting the general public was illiterate but understood the significance of the format and style of elite painted pottery.

Perhaps we have difficulty finding evidence for craft production at

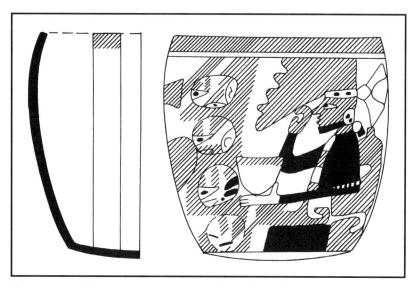

Fig. 4.1. Late Classic Polychrome Vase with Pseudoglyphs from Moho Cay, near Belize City. Vessel is 13 cm in height. Drawing by Briony Penn.

Maya cities because some of it was carried out by craft workers located outside the cities near the sources of clay, high-quality chert, salt, and other raw materials. Old characterizations of the Maya lowlands as environmentally homogeneous (Sanders and Price 1968) have been replaced with models showing the environmental diversity that exists within the Maya lowlands (Graham 1987, 1994; Sanders 1977). Studies documenting resource diversity and the localized abundance of specific resources indicate that the Maya lowlands is an area of environmental and resource heterogeneity (Graham 1987). The dichotomy between models of economic symbiosis in highland Mesoamerica and limited local trade in the Maya lowlands has been weakened. The localized abundance of Maya Mountain granite (Shipley and Graham 1987), seashells (Andrews 1969; Cobos 1989; Feldman 1974), slate, high-quality chert (Shafer and Hester 1983), clay sources, and other materials may have been a stimulus to intra- and interregional trade within the lowlands. Environmental diversity within the Maya lowlands even may have triggered localized craft production. This interpretation follows research in highland Mesoamerica, where occupational specialization arguably developed from environmental heterogeneity (Sanders and Price 1968). In that area, "economic symbiosis" developed among communities having access to different resources. Marcus (1995) suggested that local trade may have been critical for survival and even the development of the ancient Maya state, as has been argued for the Near East (Johnson 1973). However, models of economic specialization related to environmental diversity in the Maya lowlands have lagged.

The incidence and relative importance of household production in comparison to more specialized craft production outside the household among the Classic Maya have been unclear. Some goods were produced and used by individual Maya households, whereas other goods were produced by craft specialists outside the household and distributed by trade. In some cases, Classic Maya craft goods may have been produced in a cottage industry within households so that they are more difficult to identify than spatially segregated workshops. Janusek (1999:126) describes household craft workers within the Tiwanaka state in Bolivia as an example of "socially embedded household production." Similarly, Feinman (1999) describes household craft work shops for the production of shell objects at the Classic period city of Ejutla in Oaxaca. Even in the Maya lowlands, the production of tremendous quantities of chert tools at Colha occurred in workshops attached to households. We should expect variability in Maya craft production, reflecting the variety of consumers, the geographic dispersion of raw materials, and the noncentralized organization of Late Classic Maya economy.

Defining and Identifying Ancient Maya Work Shops

A work shop is a place where goods were produced for use elsewhere (Clark 1995). A work shop represents a particular kind of production activity that is associated with differentiation of the economy, economic specialization, and differential access to basic and discretionary goods and resources—characteristics of ancient civilizations. Work shops were often spatially separated from households. Of course, much production was carried out within households and was for household use.

Relatively few work shops have been identified in the Maya lowlands, and in fact, relatively few areas of production activity have been found. Work shops themselves have been identified from residues from the production process such as obsidian microdebitage (Moholy-Nagy 1990) or shell and obsidian debitage (Fash 1991:159–60) that have become embedded in floors. Pottery kilns have been found elsewhere in Mesoamerica (Arnold et al. 1993; Balkansky et al. 1997). The brine-boiling hearths at Stingray Lagoon are evidence of equipment and activity areas where production took place.

By way of contrast, much of the evidence for production, either within households or work shops, is not from the production area itself. Instead, in many cases evidence for production comes from material that has been redeposited in debitage piles, household refuse areas or middens, burials or caches, or construction fill (Moholy-Nagy 1997). This material includes debitage—production errors, wasters, and used cores in the case of lithics, or other remains from the production of stone tools, pottery vessels, or other goods—that have been moved from the original place of production activity. Other evidence of production is inferred from finished goods that, for example, required a high level of craftsmanship indicating that some kind of craft specialists existed (Adams 1970; Becker 1973). Reents-Budet et al. (2000; Reents-Budet 1998) suggest that Late Classic pottery sherds similar typologically, stylistically, and chemically from dumps adjacent to a palace at Buenavista del Cayo represent the debris from a palace work shop. Their work is intriguing, since they argue that schools of pottery making existed, in which both elite and everyday pots were made, and that this mixing of classes of pottery making was a good economic strategy to maintain production. Ethnographic and ethnohistoric studies of pottery making in Mesoamerica may help clarify the single-purpose or multiple-purpose nature of household production and work shop production, but at least some studies indicate that craft workers were specialized (Druc 2000), and that when multiple activities took place at a single work shop, the activities were related, such as spinning, carding, and weaving cotton (Clark and Houston 1998).

The presence, or even the abundance, of a certain product or finished good at a site is not necessarily an indication that a work shop dedicated to the production of that good or product was ever there. Thus, the abundant obsidian on the surface at Teotihuacan identified as obsidian work shops (Spence 1981) may actually indicate either accumulated household debris or that obsidian blades were used in the production of other items which were not preserved (Clark 1986). Similarly, the analysis of obsidian from 191 surface-collection areas, each measuring 10×10 m, on the trading port of Wild Cane Cay, indicates extensive use of obsidian blades by the great abundance of blades (McKillop et al. 2000). The dispersed and limited evidence of blade production on the surface, notably cores, production errors, and debitage, points to household manufacture and use of blades—or even "socially embedded household production"—instead of an obsidian work shop (McKillop et al. 2000).

The presence of production errors and debitage at Colha and Ejutla was used to indicate that more goods were produced than could have been used by the occupants of the households. The production was interpreted as specialized production, even though it occurred within the context of households. Stone tools were produced by craft specialists at Colha, a small community with modest architecture in northern Belize located adjacent to outcrops of high-quality chert (Shafer and Hester 1983, 1986). The production and distribution of stone tools at Colha were spatially separated from Maya elite at major lowland cities. Elite participation is evident as consumers of a limited number and variety of objects, notably eccentrics and stemmed blades. Tools were produced in household work shops at Colha, but domestic debris was not intermixed with work shop debris, indicating a separation of activities. The household location of the work shops resembles a cottage industry of perhaps Janusek's (1999) "socially embedded production" or Feinman's (1999) "high-intensity domestic manufacture." The large quantity of chert debitage, the occurrence of several workshops, and the array of tools argue for significant production of stone tools at Colha. Although Mallory (1986) suggests this production was of low intensity, Shafer and Hester (1986) point out that it was more likely mass-production, based on their calculations of the large quantity of tools produced. Certainly the distribution of Colha chert tools to a variety of communities in northern Belize, where they form the core of the stone tool assemblages, demonstrates an intensity of production beyond household or even community needs. Colha chert was distributed to Pulltrouser Swamp (McAnany 1989a), Santa Rita Corozal (Dockall and Shafer 1993), Ambergris Cay (Hult and Hester 1995), Cuello (McSwain 1991), Moho Cay (McKillop 1980, 1984), and Cerros (Mitchum 1991). Lower-grade local chert was used to make some tools at these communities. Elite chert objects from Colha were distributed beyond northern Belize but were for limited elite and ceremonial use.

The scale and intensity of production, the relations of production, and the locations of production among the Maya and in other ancient civilizations have been the focus of much discussion (Costin 1991; Feinman 1999; Janusek 1999; McAnany 1989b; Peacock 1982; Pool 1990; Rice 1981;

Santley et al. 1986; Santley and Kneebone 1993; van der Leeuw 1976). Van de Leeuw (1976), Peacock (1982), Costin (1991), and Santley et al. (1989), among others, have proposed models of craft specialization that range from part-time household production for family use that is unspecialized to full-time work shop or factory production. Both Feinman (1999) and Janusek (1999) suggest, by way of contrast, that household production of goods for use by others—specialized craft production—was more extensive and important than independent work shops in ancient Mesoamerica and Andean economies, respectively. In this regard, Feinman (1999:85) suggests that researchers have confused the scale and intensity of craft production: "Although the volume or intensity of stone tool manufacture appears unusually high, at densities clearly signaling exchange far beyond the needs of single production or domestic units, the scale most clearly associated with these production activities is not a workshop or factory but the household."

Evidence of Nondomestic Maya Work Shops

The Punta Ycacos salt works were, in contrast, nonresidential work shops. This nondomestic setting of salt production contrasts to the household setting of chert tool production at Colha—and in fact salt production elsewhere along the coast of Belize—and indicates that we should expect variability in craft specialization in ancient civilizations. Feinman's and Janusek's research shows that in some situations in ancient complex societies craft specialization was carried out within households—perhaps analogous to preindustrial "cottage industries" in Europe—but the salt works at Punta Ycacos Lagoon are examples of Late Classic Maya specialized production carried out in work shops away from home.

Distribution of Craft Goods

Studies of production and distribution of everyday goods within the Maya lowlands have been overshadowed by research on long-distance trade of prestige items. This research focus can be attributed to the ability to chemically or even visually identify obsidian and other artifacts from lowland Maya sites to distant origins and thereby facilitate the development of models of production and distribution. Notable exceptions are the chert tool production and distribution identified in northern Belize (Dockall and Shafer 1993; Hult and Hester 1995; McAnany 1989a;

McSwain 1991; Mitchum 1991; Shafer and Hester 1983), the production and distribution of utilitarian vessels near Tikal, Palenque, and in the Petexbatun area (Foias and Bishop 1997; Fry 1980; Rands and Bishop 1980; Rice 1987a), the specialized production units for salt, shellfish processing, and other activities at Watson's Island (Graham 1994), and the production of salt cakes in Punta Ycacos Lagoon (McKillop 1995a).

The long-distance exchange of highly crafted prestige goods for the Maya elite is regarded as an important indicator of the rise of social complexity—even as a stimulus to the development of civilization (Freidel 1979). By way of contrast, the exchange of less highly crafted, often bulky, utilitarian goods over short distances for the common folk has been regarded as critical to the rise of other ancient civilizations, notably in highland Mesoamerica and Mesopotamia (Johnson 1973; Marcus 1995; Sanders and Price 1968). Fundamental to these models is the understanding that long-distance bulk transport was limited in preindustrial societies lacking pack animals. Still, some researchers have suggested that bulk goods and resources such as salt were transported over long distances in ancient Mesoamerica (Rathje 1971; Rathje et al. 1978; Sluyter 1993). A closer look at the economics of salt production in Punta Ycacos Lagoon will clarify our understanding of ancient Maya craft production and distribution systems and their roles in Classic Maya society. Analysis of this salt production underscores the importance of production and distribution of utilitarian goods within the southern Maya lowlands and highlights the noncentralized nature of Classic Maya economy.

Context and Intensity of Punta Ycacos Salt Production and Distribution

The location and intensity of production are factors to be considered when evaluating the importance of craft specialization in Late Classic Maya society. The work location refers not only to the physical site at which the work was carried out, but also to the social context within which work took place. This could be within the household (Sahlins' 1972 "domestic mode of production"), as "attached specialists" for royal households (Earle 1981), as a cottage industry or "embedded production" within households (Janusek 1999), or as independent specialists in nondomestic work shops. The intensity of production refers to the quantity of goods that were produced and distributed.

The social context of production has been identified in previous chapters on the description of the salt-making sites and their artifacts as independent work shops located away from the Maya settlements where the salt workers lived. Various additional lines of evidence support the interpretation of the Punta Ycacos Lagoon salt works as operated by independent specialists. The sites lack evidence of the usual array of settlement remains found at other Port Honduras sites, including plant food and animal bone remains, domestic pottery, and burials. People were not living or being buried at the salt work shops. Moreover, the assemblage of ceramics, consisting of four ceramic types, is incomplete for a settlement and instead is focused on the single activity of salt production.

The social context of distribution includes the consumers and traders. The inland Maya at large cities were the consumers. Their badges of power were recovered at the salt work shops in the form of trade goods used in rituals that reinforced vertical ties between the lesser coastal elite and the regional elite at inland cities. The traders were the island Maya at Wild Cane Cay and Frenchman's Cay who supplied the inland Maya with long-distance coastal resources. This vertical integration of salt workers into Maya society may be extended to other independent specialists: Maya leaders in cities established ritualized trading alliances with independent craft specialists in outlying areas near raw material sources. The craft specialists obtained elite paraphernalia and, most important, the concomitant status and ceremonies. This facilitated the maintenance of the regular supply of utilitarian goods and resources from the peripheries to the cities.

In establishing a patron-client relationship, the royal Maya at lowland cities initiated and reinforced political relationships within and between Late Classic Maya polities. Political relationships among the elite are recorded by hieroglyphs and pictures on Maya monuments and painted pottery, as battles won, alliances made, and regal accessions. Records inform of hierarchical relationships, including the winner and loser in battle, the status gained by marrying a high-ranking royal woman, and the godly status of a new king, who through a vision quest temporarily becomes a Maya god (Schele and Miller 1986). Late Classic Maya society was highly structured. The elite paraphernalia at the Punta Ycacos salt works provides a glimpse of the salt workers' participation in the power and grandeur of a distant king and royal family. Little is known of the royal lineages and alliances of the urban Maya in southern Belize. Hieroglyphic records at Uxbenka, Pusilha, and Nim li punit are largely unreported, although some archaeological research has been carried out (Joyce 1929; Joyce et al. 1927, 1928; Leventhal 1990).

Scale of Salt Production

The scale of salt production will be investigated by examining the variability in the equipment used to produce the salt cakes. The assumption is that the more variable the equipment, the less specialized the activity. By way of contrast, more standardized equipment is related to routinization of activities, higher output, and mass production. The process of salt production as described in earlier chapters involves the placement of two dozen or more pots over a fire to boil brine. In addition to the pots, there were cylinder vessel supports holding the pots over the fire, clay spacers to separate the pots while over the fire, water jars to fill and periodically replenish brine while it boiled in the pots, and jars to store the loose salt before it was formed and hardened into salt cakes for transport. Other supplies include firewood, temporary storage, and boats to transport the salt. Variability of the salt-making equipment within and between salt work shops would be expected if salt was produced by families or other work parties traveling to the lagoon. The separation of the salt-making equipment from domestic debris indicates that salt was not produced within households, so we are not talking about household production or "socially embedded production" within households. More standardized salt-making equipment would be expected if the production was organized in nondomestic work shops, with workers organized by lineage, by "fictive" kin, by gender, or even by unrelated members of a village. Standardization reflects work parties, whether related by familial or lineage ties or by unrelated members of a village consistently working together. The key is consistency not blood ties.

Standardization, Variability, and Production

Various studies identifying craft specialization by standardization or by diversity measures are pertinent to the study of Maya salt production. Rice (1989) used diversity measures from biology to calculate the richness (number of pottery types) and evenness (relative number of sherds within each type) of Maya pottery from Barton Ramie, Belize. She found differences over time which she related to changes in specialization. The richness of the Late Classic Wild Cane Cay or Frenchman's Cay ceramic assemblages contrasts with the recovery of just four ceramic types from the salt work shops. The evenness of the salt ceramics is skewed, with most ceramics either salt boiling pots or water jars and relatively few other types. This contrasts with the greater evenness of ceramics from Wild Cane Cay or Frenchman's Cay, where abundant slipped and unslipped ceramics were recovered (McKillop 2000). By Rice's diversity measures, the salt site ceramic assemblages lack richness and are skewed in terms of evenness, suggesting a specialized activity.

Standardization of vessel manufacture has been used as an index of the level of production (Arnold 1991; Foias and Bishop 1997; Nance 1992). Using measurements of vessels, the more variable assemblages indicate household production, whereas the more standardized assemblages indicate more specialized activities. Statistics used to measure variability include mean and standard deviation, variance, and coefficient of variation. Vessel diameter and diameter-to-height ratios are often used to gauge variability. Ethnoarchaeological studies have cautioned that other factors can contribute to standardization in vessel form, notably custom and use of the same measuring devices to produce pottery vessels (Arnold 1991; Costin 1991). Skill in the manufacture of pottery vessels also contributes to the production of similar pots (Feinman 1999). In traditional societies, styles change slowly and the consumer expects a certain type of pottery vessel within a restricted range of attributes (Costin 1991; Brumfiel and Earle 1987). The use of molds in pottery production, as among the Moche and Chimu, and among the Maya for figurine whistles, results in standardized vessels. Importantly, Costin (1991) points out that standardization is a relative measure instead of an absolute, requiring comparison with other vessels. If we extend the discussion of standardization to a discussion of variability within an assemblage or between assemblages, then standardization of vessel form becomes interpretable within a specific cultural context. Discovery of standardized vessels can be a compelling argument, along with other lines of evidence, for craft specialization.

The Punta Ycacos Sample and Methods

Standardization of production of the Punta Ycacos salt-making vessels was used as an index of the level of economic specialization. For this study,

I included ceramics from the four Punta Ycacos salt-making sites, as well as a control sample from the nearby contemporary settlement at Wild Cane Cay, where economic specialization was not expected. Attribute analysis was carried out to examine variability of the pottery vessels within and between types. Variability in temper material provided information on the local or imported origin of the pottery. Variability in vessel form within types indicated the level of standardization of the vessels, in terms of specialized production and trade. In this study, I examine orifice diameter for the pottery vessel rims and diameter of the solid clay cylinders. Cylinder diameter was the only measurable index of standardization in the collection of fragmentary vessel supports. Apart from the single complete cylinder, all other cylinders were broken into midsections, fragments with a socket or base, or an end-section without a socket or base attached. The diameter of the end-fragments was selected as the best index of the degree of variability.

The statistics presented are mean, standard deviation, median, range, coefficient of variation, and average median variation. To interpret the data, I selected average median variation instead of coefficient of variation because some of the samples have distributions significantly different from normal. For the average median variation, each value is subtracted from the median. The absolute value of this number is divided by the median. The average of this number is then multiplied by 100. It is important to note that the average median variation reduces the effect of outlying values in a distribution, which is not the case with the coefficient of variation. The average median variation statistic may be more powerful in discerning variability.

Results

Measurement of the pottery rim sherds indicated that the salt-making vessels were standardized in contrast to the vessels from Wild Cane Cay (table 4.1). The control sample of 245 Bedford Unslipped vessel rims from Wild Cane Cay had an average median variation of 20.6. The 132 Punta Ycacos Unslipped jar rims from the salt sites were twice as standardized in rim diameter than the other sherds in the sample, with an average median variation of 9.5. Similarly, the Punta Ycacos Unslipped cylinders are standardized, with an average median variation of 11.9.

In contrast, the Mangrove Unslipped jars from Stingray Lagoon are not standardized, as indicated by an average median variation of 20.9

Table 4.1. Comparison of Orifice Diameters of Punta Ycacos Salt-Making Vessels with Control of Bedford Unslipped from Wild Cane Cay

Sample	N	Diameter of Vessel Orifices (cm)					
		Mean	SD	Median	Range	CV	AMV
Bedford Unslipped	245	31.8	8.0	32	12–50	25.2	20.6
Punta Ycacos jars	132	21.9	3.4	22	14–38	15.6	9.5
Punta Ycacos cylinders	155	3.52	0.55	3.5	1.9–5.1	15.7	11.9

N = number of vessels; SD = standard deviation; CV = coefficient of variation; AMV = average median variation

(table 4.2). The Mangrove Unslipped jars are not significantly different from the control sample of Bedford Unslipped vessels from Wild Cane Cay, with an average median variation of 20.6. Mangrove Unslipped may be interpreted as a general purpose unslipped jar for the region.

The Warrie Red jars from Stingray Lagoon were more standardized than the Mangrove Unslipped water jars and the salt-making vessels (table 4.3). The sample of 15 measurable Warrie Red jars from Stingray Lagoon had an average median variation of 8.2. Warrie Red jars were more highly crafted, including stamped decorations, which may contribute to standardization. Standardization, in this case, reflects care in the manufacture of a limited set of ceramics, in contrast to the standardization of mass-produced objects for salt-making. In addition, the Warrie Red unit-stamped vessels were likely also trade pieces, along with the Lubaantun-style figurine whistles. The whistles were standardized by definition, since they were mold-made.

Table 4.2. Comparison of Orifice Diameters of Mangrove Unslipped Water Jars from the Salt Sites with Control of Bedford Unslipped from Wild Cane Cay

Sample	N	Diameter of Vessel Orifices (cm)					
		Mean	SD	Median	Range	CV	AMV
Mangrove Unslipped	41	24.2	6.3	24	14–44	26.2	20.9
Bedford Unslipped	245	31.8	8.0	32	12–50	25.2	20.6

N = number of vessels; SD = standard deviation; CV = coefficient of variation; AMV = average median variation

Table 4.3. Comparison of Orifice Diameters of Water Jars and Salt-Making Vessels from the Salt Sites

Sample	N	Diameters of Vessel Orifices/Cylinders (cm)					
		Mean	SD	Median	Range	CV	AMV
Warrie Red jars	15	12.9	1.2	13	10–14	9.5	8.2
Mangrove Unslipped jars	41	24.2	6.3	24	14–44	26.2	20.9
Punta Ycacos jars	132	21.9	3.4	22	14–38	15.6	9.5
Punta Ycacos cylinders	155	3.52	0.55	3.5	1.9–5.1	15.7	11.9

N = number of vessels; SD = standard deviation; CV = coefficient of variation; AMV = average median variation

There is evidence of intersite variability in salt production (table 4.4). For the Punta Ycacos Unslipped jar rims, 99 sherds from Stingray Lagoon have an average median variation of 10.5. This value is similar to the 11 sherds from David Westby, which have an average median variation of 10.9. In contrast, the 22 sherds from Orlando's Jewfish have an average median variation of 2.1, indicating low variability. This is also shown by a standard deviation of 1.1 and a diameter range of 18 to 24 cm. Killer Bee was excluded from the intersite analysis because there were few rim sherds.

Eight percent of the Punta Ycacos salt-making vessels from Stingray Lagoon were open bowls (table 4.5). They have significant variability, as shown by the average median variation of 19.6. This value is similar to the unspecialized vessels in the control sample of Bedford Unslipped from Wild Cane Cay, which has an average median variation of 20.6.

Table 4.4. Intersite Variability in Standardization of Punta Ycacos Unslipped Jars

Sample	N	Diameters of Vessel Orifices (cm)					
		Mean	SD	Median	Range	CV	AMV
Stingray Lagoon	99	22.3	3.7	22	14–38	16.6	10.5
David Westby	11	18.9	3.1	20	14–24	16.8	10.9
Orlando's Jewfish	22	21.7	1.1	22	18–24	5.1	2.1

N = number of vessels; SD = standard deviation; CV = coefficient of variation; AMV = average median variation

Table 4.5. Comparison of Punta Ycacos Unslipped Bowls and Jars with the Control Sample of Bedford Unslipped

Sample	N	Diameter of Vessel Orifices (cm)					
		Mean	SD	Median	Range	CV	AMV
Punta Ycacos							
Unslipped bowls	12	27.2	6.4	28	16–36	23.5	19.6
Bedford Unslipped	245	31.8	8.0	32	12–50	25.2	20.6

N = number of vessels; SD = standard deviation; CV = coefficient of variation; AMV = average median variation

There is no evidence of intersite variability in the clay cylinder vessel supports (table 4.6). The 64 cylinder ends from Stingray Lagoon have an average median variation of 11.5. For 27 cylinder ends from David Westby, the average median variation is 13.5. The 60 cylinder ends from Orlando's Jewfish have an average median variation of 11.0. The average median variation was not calculated for Killer Bee, since only four end cylinders were recovered.

As a group, using the average median variation, the Punta Ycacos jars and cylinders from the salt sites are both more standardized than and significantly different from the control sample of Bedford Unslipped vessels from Wild Cane Cay and the Mangrove Unslipped water jars from the salt sites. The salt-making jars and cylinders are equally standardized, having nonsignificant differences in the average median variation.

Discussion

Vessels used in the production of salt at the Punta Ycacos sites were standardized in their manufacture. Standardization is evident both in the jars used to boil the brine and the vessel supports used to hold the vessels over the fire. One of the four sites, Orlando's Jewfish, has significantly higher standardization of salt artifacts, suggesting the existence of separate work shops or work parties in the lagoon area. In contrast to the salt-making vessels, water jars used to fill the salt pots and a control sample of vessels from Wild Cane Cay were not standardized.

If standardization is used as a measure of economic specialization, the salt-making activity was twice as specialized as household ceramic use at Wild Cane Cay. The higher standardization of salt-making artifacts at

Table 4.6. Intersite Variability in Standardization of Punta Ycacos Cylinders

Sample	N	Diameter of Cylinders (cm)					
		Mean	SD	Median	Range	CV	AMV
Stingray Lagoon	64	3.56	0.50	3.40	2.3–5.1	14.1	11.5
David Westby	27	3.57	0.59	3.50	2.5–4.9	16.7	13.5
Orlando's Jewfish	60	3.50	0.55	3.55	1.9–4.7	15.8	11.0
Killer Bee	4	2.70	0.39	2.65	2.3–3.2	—	—

N = number of cylinders; SD = standard deviation; CV = coefficient of variation; AMV = average median variation

Orlando's Jewfish site compared with the other sites may indicate there were separate work groups. Whether they lived at the nearby trading port settlement of Wild Cane Cay or elsewhere in the Port Honduras region, salt was produced by people who did not live at the salt work shops. Inland consumers of salt from the Punta Ycacos salt works are suggested by the presence of Lubaantun-style figurine whistles, unit-stamped water jars, and Moho Red volcanic ash–tempered serving bowls—artifacts presumably made at inland communities. These artifacts, along with trade goods such as obsidian, were found at Wild Cane Cay and Lubaantun. Since Wild Cane Cay figured prominently in coastal canoe trade and in coastal-inland trade, the Maya at that community may also have controlled the salt trade.

Could the salt produced along the coast of Belize by the sal cocida method of boiling brine in pots over fires have replaced or reduced the need for long-distance import of salt from the north coast of the Yucatan? Research in Punta Ycacos Lagoon documents not only that salt-making sites did occur, but that they were specialized beyond the household level. The extent of production may have been limited by availability of nearby sources of wood fuel. Preliminary analysis of wood charcoal indicates a diversity of species was used (Baker 1999): this diversity may be interpreted as indiscriminate use of trees for fuel, in contrast to selection of high-quality woods that may have been overexploited.

While each Maya household clearly produced goods for its own use, many items were made by craft workers who made things for use by others. Kings and other Maya royalty procured highly crafted items made by attached specialists who worked for the throne. Elite burial vessels painted with mortuary ritual themes certainly constitute work by attached specialists (Reents-Budet 1998). Other work by attached specialists includes highly crafted objects made from imported, scarce material such as jade. In addition, there were craft workers producing chert tools at Colha, utilitarian pottery vessels in the outskirts of Maya cities, and salt along the coast of Belize. These craft workers were intermediate in their level of specialization between unspecialized household production and the attached specialists working for royal Maya households. In this chapter, I presented evidence that salt production at the Punta Ycacos salt works was carried out by independent specialists. That salt production was specialized is indicated by the standardization of the salt-making vessels in contrast to pottery from a nearby Maya settlement, where a diverse assemblage of domestic pottery was recovered. Implications of the specialized salt production are that the salt workers lived elsewhere and traveled daily to the lagoon salt works.

The salt produced in Punta Ycacos Lagoon and elsewhere along the Belizean coast conforms to a model of independent production of utilitarian goods and their short-distance transport within the Maya lowlands. Interestingly, this coastal-inland trade was linked to the long-distance trade of exotics and highly crafted goods for the inland elite. That some elite goods reached the salt works attests to the vertical alliances maintained by the powerful inland Maya royal lords to ensure their supply of salt—either for need or "appetite"—by tying the coastal Maya into their rituals, ceremonies, and marriages.

5

ЛЛЛЛ

Salt Production and Sea-Level Rise

The Punta Ycacos salt work shops were submerged by a sea-level rise that inundated the Yucatan coasts of Belize and Mexico. The excavation of 10 inundated sites dating to the Classic period in the Port Honduras region documents this late Holocene sea-level rise for the first time in southern Belize. The evidence has far-reaching implications for Classic Maya salt production and coastal settlement elsewhere along the Yucatan coast. Radiocarbon dating the submerged deposits, along with identification of associated plant remains, provides a compelling view of a more hospitable landscape during the Classic period than is suggested by the low-lying, flooded ground and red mangroves (*Rhizophora mangle*) that dominate the coastline and offshore islands of the Port Honduras—and indeed of much of the Belizean coastline—today.

Despite documentation of inundated archaeological sites along the Belizean coast, dating from Preclassic through Postclassic times, there have been few studies aimed at examining the processes of inundation. There are submerged archaeological deposits at Moho Cay near Belize City (McKillop 1980, 1984), Colson Point in the Stann Creek District (Graham 1989), Marco Gonzalez on southern Ambergris Cay (Graham 1994; Graham and Pendergast 1989), Wild Cane Cay and elsewhere in southern Belize (McKillop 1995a), and Cerros in the far northern mainland (Freidel and Scarborough 1982; map 5.1). Inundated sites are also reported on the west and north coasts of the Yucatan (Andrews and Corletta 1995; Dahlin 1983; Dahlin et al. 1998; Folan et al. 1983; Gunn and

Map 5.1. Inundated Archaeological Sites in the Southern Maya Lowlands. By Mary Lee Eggart.

Adams 1981). Only at Marco Gonzalez and at Canbalam off the north coast of the Yucatan has sea level been investigated in relation to ancient Maya settlement (Dahlin et al. 1998; Dunn 1990; Dunn and Mazzullo 1993; Graham 1989).

The Impact of Sea-Level Rise on Maya Settlement and Trade

With the current underwater location of the Punta Ycacos salt-making sites, one could argue that they were abandoned either because of sea-level rise or because of cultural changes at the end of the Classic period. The first model gives environmental agents some causal role in cultural change, attributing the abandonment of the Punta Ycacos salt works to sea-level rise. This scenario follows other research in the Maya area and beyond suggesting cultural changes due to environmental agents (Gunn and Adams 1981; Curtis et al. 1996; Dahlin 1983; Folan et al. 1983; Hodell et al. 1995). For example, shifts in the water balance in the southern Andes coincided with the rise, intensification, and abandonment of intensive agriculture, which had profound effects on the ancient Tiwanaka civilization (Binford et al. 1997). In the second model, site abandonment is unrelated to the sea-level rise but instead due to diminution of settlement in the Maya lowlands at the end of the Classic period and in particular to abandonment of nearby inland cities. These include Late Classic cities in southern Belize and the Pasion region of Guatemala, notably Lubaantun, Nim li punit, Uxbenka, Pusilha, Altar de Sacrificios, and Seibal (Adams 1971; Hammond 1975; Leventhal 1990; Dunham et al. 1989; Sabloff 1975). In the second model, the absence of inland consumers for coastal salt led to abandonment of the coastal salt sites. This alternative scenario gives the environment little direct role in cultural change.

In order to evaluate these contrasting models, information is needed on the timing and rate of sea-level rise and its impact on the maritime landscape during the late Holocene along the coast of Belize. Sea-level data from 10 years of fieldwork on inundated sites in the Port Honduras region, including the salt-making sites, are presented and evaluated with existing sea-level data from other archaeological, geological, and geographic studies. The Port Honduras data provide an explanation for the current underwater setting of the Punta Ycacos salt work shops and contribute new information on sea-level rise in the late Holocene: geologists and geographers have used the depths of dated mangrove peat deposits and shallow-water coral (*Acropora palmata*) below modern sea level to reconstruct ancient sea levels and produce sea-level curves. The current study follows research elsewhere by using the depth of dated archaeological deposits below sea level to extend the regional sea-level curve to more recent times. Other evidence includes the accumulation of mangrove peat above dated sites and the recovery from submerged deposits of ancient remains of plant species that do not grow in inundated settings. These data are pertinent to understanding the complex relationship between cultural factors (population change) and environmental factors (sea-level rise). In particular, the discussion pertains to the timing and abandonment of the Punta Ycacos salt works. In general, the discussion contributes to our knowledge of the place of environmental factors as agents in cultural change.

Coastal Geology of Belize

The coastline of Belize is protected by the Belize Barrier Reef, whose distance from shore lies between 15 km, in the north, to 50 km, in the south (map 5.2). The reef height drops off precipitously on the eastward, ocean-facing side. Inside the reef, the barrier lagoon includes hundreds of islands or cays and shoals. Two atolls are located outside the reef, Turneffe Atoll and Glover's Reef. The third atoll, Ambergris Cay, abuts the reef in the north.

It is generally believed that the cays within the barrier lagoon developed on submarine ridges and places of higher elevation that were colonized by mangroves or coral. The reef and a series of parallel ridges within the lagoon formed by block-faulting of a carbonate shelf in the late Pliocene or early Pleistocene (Esker et al. 1998; Macintyre et al. 1995; Purdy 1974; Purdy et al. 1975; Wantland and Pusey 1971). The orientation of the reef is northeast to southwest. Another explanation of the the location and shape of the reef and barrier lagoon cays, namely, that they follow the ancient Victoria River and other rivers (Choi and Ginsburg 1982; Choi and Holmes 1982), is not supported by recent seismic and core data (Esker et al. 1998). However, there continues to be discussion among geologists about the timing, extent, and impact of tectonic activity before the Pleistocene (Lara 1993, 1997; Precht 1997).

Different geological settings on the land and coastal shelf between the south and the north (with the division at Belize City) indicate that identi-

cal paleocoastal landscape reconstructions should not be expected along
the entire coast of Belize. Geologically, the northern Belize mainland is a
carbonate platform of Mesozoic and Cenozoic origin. In contrast, the
southern mainland consists of Tertiary and later intrusions forming the
Maya Mountains, which feed the rivers that flow into the southern marine shelf (Lara 1993; Purdy et al. 1975; Wright et al. 1959). These differences are reflected in carbonate versus terrigenous sediments in the
northern and southern shelves, respectively. Rainfall in the north aver-
ages 124 cm annually; in the south it is over 380 cm annually (Purdy et al.
1975). The southern shelf is much deeper, with depths of 26 m, whereas
the northern shelf is generally less than 5.5 m deep (Purdy et al. 1975:fig-
ure 4). Tide records for Ambergris Cay in the north and Carrie Bow Cay in
the south indicate a microtidal environment within the coastal shelf, with
a maximum of 0.5 and 0.15 m, respectively (Purdy et al. 1975:12–13;
Kjerfve et al. 1982). Tides are lowered by strong northerly winds ("north-
ers") up to 0.8 m from October to January. Differences in mollusks (Robertson 1975), ostracods (Teeter 1975), Foraminifera (Wantland 1975),
and sediments (Purdy et al. 1975; High 1975) also distinguish the southern shelf from the northern.

In the Port Honduras study area, the Rio Grande and Deep River
bracket a coastal bight called (as noted in chapter 1) Port Honduras, into
which flow several rivers that together deposit silt and a freshwater surface lens in a wide coastal area (map 5.3). The area is generally less than
5.5 m in depth, with high turbidity and mixing of surface freshwater
deeper (Purdy et al. 1975). Some 200 offshore islands form a barrier in
front of the Port Honduras. To the north of the Deep River, the geology
includes metamorphic rocks that support pine savanna and scattered
clumps of palmettos and Caribbean pine. To the south of the Deep River,
the underlying geology is sandstone, mud stone, and silt stone that support tropical rainforest (Wright et al. 1959; Dixon 1929; High 1975; Johnson and Chaffey 1974). The coastal area delineated by the Port Honduras
is a Holocene development, with near-shore marine facies described as
terrigenous sandy mud and transitional marl (dominated by *Halimeda*)
beginning 1–2 km offshore, containing selected carbonate (coral) islands
(Purdy et al. 1975:figure 15). The landscape is dominated by mangroves
along the coastline and the offshore islands, with shallow coastal lagoon-
barrier systems, marshes, and forelands with beach ridges. The area is
characterized by the mangrove association of *Rhizophora mangle*, with
Avicennia germinans and *Laguncularia racemosa* landward, along with

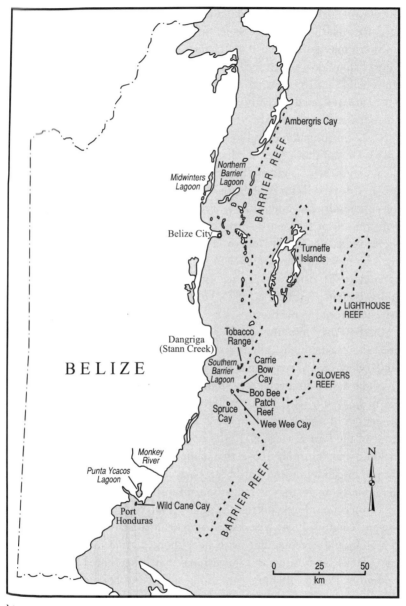

Map 5.2. Belize Barrier Reef System. By Mary Lee Eggart.

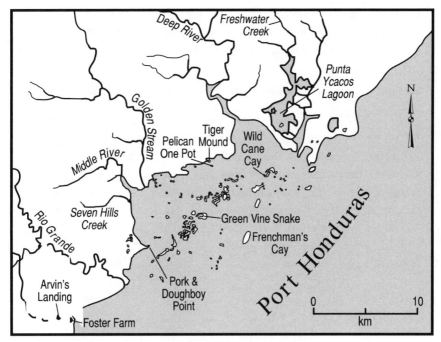

Map 5.3. Port Honduras. By Mary Lee Eggart

coconut woodland on some islands, dominated by *Cocos nucifera* (Fosberg et al. 1982; McKillop 1987, 1994a).

Punta Ycacos Lagoon is a large, shallow lagoon bordered on the seaward side by a barrier spit, similar to others along the coastline of Belize. The lagoon is fed on the landward side by Freshwater Creek, which originates on the pine savanna. The lagoon has a north arm and a south arm. Access to the sea is indirect, along either of two winding channels from the south arm through *Rhizophora* mangroves to a main channel which borders the main lagoon along its east side. The main channel and lagoon connect again farther inland, where they form an amorphous area of shallow water, *Rhizophora* mangroves, and mud flats, grading into the savanna.

Air photo interpretation suggests that Freshwater Creek, which now flows into Punta Ycacos Lagoon along a fault line (Esker et al. 1998; Purdy 1974), was likely once a tributary of Monkey River to the north. With a change in the course of Monkey River, Freshwater Creek was cut off, slowing the flow of water and sediment and facilitating the growth of a barrier spit across Punta Ycacos Lagoon (perhaps on an area of high Pleistocene relief) along the north side of Deep River to the south. The depth of mangrove mud deposits in Punta Ycacos Lagoon, as attested by soil probing, indicates the area has a long Holocene history as a lagoon.

Previous Evidence of Sea-Level Rise in Belize

Globally, sea level has been rising since the last glacial maximum at 18,000 B.P., when sea levels were 60–80 m or more below present levels (Bird 1993; Fairbanks 1989; Pirazzoli 1991). Cores into the seafloor in the western Atlantic indicate that there was rapid post-Pleistocene marine transgression after 10,000 B.P. and that the rate slackened after 6000 B.P. (Lighty et al. 1982:figure 2). Overall, sea level rose about 30 m since 10,000 B.P. in the western Atlantic (Bird 1993:14; Bloom 1979, 1983; Fairbanks 1989; Fairbridge 1987; Lighty et al. 1982; Pirazzoli 1991). Since an apparent rise in sea level can result not only from actual rise of the sea surface (i.e., eustatically) but also from a lowering of coastal areas (i.e., isostatically), subsidence of the earth's surface due to tectonic activity, earthquakes, or compaction of marine sediments (Bird 1993:17; Bloom 1983; Ellison and Stoddart 1991; Parkinson 1989; Scholl et al. 1969) needs to be evaluated when examining marine transgression of the coast of Belize. In addition, geoidal variations up to 180 m in sea-surface topography related to gravity, tides, the Earth's rotation, climate, and ocean circulation preclude a single global eustatic sea-level curve (Morner 1976). However, similar sea-level data from Florida to the Caribbean to Panama indicate there was a general eustatic sea-level rise in the region (Lighty et al. 1982).

The Belizean barrier lagoon system became submerged during global eustatic post-Pleistocene sea-level rise. At the beginning of the Holocene, sea level was 32–35 m lower than today. Structurally, the southern barrier lagoon is deeper, thus this area became inundated earlier in the Holocene than the northern lagoon (Burke 1993; Purdy 1974). Dating of sediments from geological cores indicates that the southern lagoon (south of Belize City) was flooded by 7000 B.P. (Shinn et al. 1982:74) and perhaps as early as 9000 B.P. in the Tobacco Range area (Macintyre et al. 1995:10). The northern lagoon was flooded by 6000 B.P. (Dunn 1990:76; Lowe 1995; Mazzullo et al. 1992). There are no dates for the initial Holocene marine transgression in the far south in the Port Honduras study area.

Most researchers describe a eustatic sea-level rise on a stable platform during the Holocene for the Belizean continental shelf (Esker et al. 1998; High 1975:93). Burke (1993:17) suggests that sea-level dates that are higher than expected for Ambergris Cay "indicate uplift during the Holocene of the northern reef province along the Ambergris ridge." Researchers working in the southern barrier lagoon suggest that tectonic activity predates the Holocene and had no impact on sea levels during the Holocene (Esker et al. 1998; Macintyre et al. 1995).

Research on sea-level rise and the Holocene development of the coastal landscape has been carried out in the northern and southern barrier lagoons, with limited work in the far south in the Port Honduras study area (map 5.2). Research has been carried out in the north on Ambergris Cay (Dunn 1990; Dunn and Mazzullo 1993; Eubanks 1975; High 1975; Mazzullo et al. 1987; Mazzullo and Reid 1988; Mazzullo et al. 1992; Purdy et al. 1975), Midwinter's Lagoon (Lowe 1995), Midwinter's and other lagoons (High 1975), and the Blue Hole (Drill et al. 1998). In addition, several studies on the mainland in northern Belize have provided insight into sea-level rise (Alcara-Herrera et al. 1994; Jacob 1992; Jones 1994; Pohl 1990). Research in the southern barrier lagoon has been carried out southwest of Dangriga, at Carrie Bow Cay (Rützler and Macintyre 1982), Boo Bee Patch Reef (Halley et al. 1977), Tobacco Range (Macintyre et al. 1995), and the surrounding continental shelf (Burke 1993; Choi and Ginsburg 1982; Choi and Holmes 1982; Esker et al. 1998: Lara 1993, 1997; Precht 1997). Limited geological fieldwork has been carried out farther south (Purdy et al. 1975; Wantland and Pusey 1971), with Esker et al.'s (1998) research just north of Port Honduras, as far south as Monkey River and the Snake Cays.

The coral and mangrove landscape of the Belizean barrier lagoon system is a Holocene development. Coral built up on the Pleistocene ridges during the Holocene marine transgression, while terrigenous and calcareous marine sediment accumulated in the valleys between the ridges and other low-lying areas of the shelf (Macintyre et al. 1995; Purdy 1974; Wantland and Pusey 1971:figure 1.13). In many cases, the coral growth kept pace with eustatic sea-level rise, resulting in up to 10 m of Holocene coral growth, as at Boo Bee Patch Reef (Halley et al. 1977:34). The persistence of Holocene coral growth on submarine limestone ridges was most pronounced in the northern lagoon, where the continental shelf is shallow. In the southern lagoon, where the Port Honduras study area is located, areas of raised Pleistocene surface relief were more rapidly and thoroughly submerged than in the northern lagoon. Nowhere in the southern lagoon, for example, is Pleistocene limestone exposed at the surface, as it is on Ambergris Cay or on the mainland, such as at Midwinter's Lagoon (Lowe 1995). Purdy (1974; Wantland and Pusey 1971:figure 1.10) shows a profile across the Port Honduras from Golden Stream, through Wild Cane Cay and the Snake Cays to the barrier reef, where Holocene coral built up on Pleistocene limestone ridges and mud filled in low-lying areas.

Red mangroves attached to shallow shoals, accumulating mangrove peat as sea level rose in the Holocene. *Rhizophora mangle* is an intertidal species, only rarely growing above high tide, so it is a good marker of sea-level fluctuations (Cameron and Palmer 1995; Stoddart 1990; Woodroffe 1988, 1995). Mangrove peat has been recovered more often in the southern than in the northern barrier lagoon, so it has proved a useful marker to date the inception of early Holocene marine transgression in the south in particular. In some places, such as Midwinter's Lagoon in northern Belize, mangrove peat was rarely encountered in sediment cores (Lowe 1995). In some places in the southern barrier lagoon, such as Tobacco Range, mangroves have persisted, keeping pace with rising sea levels for the past 7,000 to 9,000 years (Macintyre et al. 1995). There is up to 10 m of mangrove peat on the Pleistocene surface at Tobacco Range (Cameron and Palmer 1995). In other places, such as Boo Bee Patch Reef (Halley et al. 1977:figure 10), Carrie Bow Cay, and Spruce Cay (Burke 1993:figure 5), the mangrove communities were drowned and later buried by calcareous marine and/or terrigenous sediments (Halley et al. 1977; Macintyre et al. 1995; Shinn et al. 1982). In those places, there is a thin layer of mangrove peat radiocarbon-dated to about 9,000 years ago (8780 ± 100 B.P. at Boo Bee Patch Reef, Halley et al. 1977:figure 10), marking the inception of rapid marine transgression and flooding of the shelf.

Rate of Sea-Level Rise

The rate of sea-level rise for Belize and the western Atlantic has been estimated from the depth of dated *Acropora palmata* coral and *Rhizophora mangle* mangrove peat below present sea level. Since *Acropora palmata* coral must grow below water, sea-level curves, based on the depth of dated corals below sea level, provide minimum positions for sea level. Red mangroves normally grow within a narrow tidal range, so they also are good indicators of sea-level fluctuations. The sediment which accumulates under the mangroves over time consists of varying percentages of peat (decayed plant matter) and ash (minerals), mirroring fluctuations in sea level (Cameron and Palmer 1995:8– 12). Higher peat content reflects optimal growth conditions at the water's edge; a thick layer of peat may be produced. Higher ash content reflects an inland area of mud flat or ponding; typically only a thin layer of peat is left. Mangroves grow faster, and therefore peat accumulates faster, within the optimal range of nutrients governed by the tidal range. Mangroves are good indicators of sea-level rise during rapid transgression, as in the early Holocene. In the late Holocene, where mangrove growth slowed, mangroves are not as clear indicators of minor sea-level fluctuations.

Lighty et al.'s (1982) sea-level curve based on radiocarbon-dating *Acropora palmata* coral has tracked the Holocene marine transgression in the western Atlantic from 16 reefs in a broad geographic area. The discovery of similar sea-level rise throughout the region indicated a eustatic sea-level rise. In their curve, there was a gradual sea-level rise, slowing about 6000 B.P. Sea level is about 1 m above what it was a thousand years ago (Lighty et al. 1982:figure 2).

The reported rates of sea-level rise and the sea-level curves in the late Holocene are different for the northern and southern Belizean barrier lagoons, respectively. Clearly, the greater depth of the shelf in the southern lagoon impacted on the initial marine transgression and on subsequent flooding. Generally, sea level is plotted at higher levels in the northern barrier lagoon than in the south. Mazzullo and colleagues' (Mazzullo et al. 1987, 1992; Dunn and Mazzullo 1993) research on Ambergris Cay shows sea level was 2 m lower at 4500 B.P., 1 m lower at 3500 B.P., and 0.3 m lower at 2500 B.P. Mazzullo and colleagues report a stepping rise in sea level in the last 3,000 years, with three periods of relative standstill punctuated by sea-level rise (Mazzullo et al. 1987; Mazzullo and Reid 1988). Of particular interest to the present study is their correlation of sea-level rise with the occupation of the prehistoric Maya settlement of Marco Gonzalez, on the southern end of Ambergris Cay. They report a eustatic rise in sea level from 1 m below present at 3500 B.P., to 30 cm at 2000 B.P. (when the site was first occupied), to 15 cm below present at 750 B.P. Using sediment cores and probes, the landscape was reconstructed as an open marine environment throughout this time sequence, with mangroves prograding into the site area only in recent times (see also Graham 1989). Lowe (1995:74, figures 22–25) used the same sea-level curve to date changes in the ancient landscape at Midwinter's Lagoon evident from analysis of sediment cores. The initial flooding of the lagoon was estimated at 5,200 years ago, when sea level was about 3 m lower.

Sea-level data for the southern Belize barrier lagoon conform better to Lighty et al.'s (1982) sea-level curve, in which sea level was about 1 m lower a thousand years ago. At Tobacco Range, where the Pleistocene shelf is less than 10 m below present sea level, mangrove communities became established about 7000 B.P. and accumulated peat at 4.3 m/1,000 years (Macintyre et al. 1995:10). However, the rate of peat accumulation was variable (Cameron and Palmer 1995:3). At about 3000 B.P., there was a decrease in sea-level rise to less than 1 m/1,000 years, and peat deposits became more stabilized and mature deposits subsided (Macintyre et al. 1995:13). At Boo Bee Patch Reef, a submerged coral cay southeast of Dangriga, the patch reef accumulated at a rate of 1.6 m/1,000 years, whereas the lime silt and mud of the surrounding lagoon floor accumulated at a rate of 0.4 to 0.5 m/1,000 years (Halley et al. 1977:figure 10). At Boo Bee Patch Reef, which is in the deeper lagoon south of Tobacco Range, where the Pleistocene shelf is about 15 m below sea level, the accumulation of peat in the early Holocene could not keep pace with rising seas. The knoll became submerged by 8000 B.P. and coral became established in areas of high relief. Carrie Bow Cay, which is located beside the barrier reef southeast of Dangriga, consists of over 15 m of coral accumulated over leached calcite limestone of Pleistocene origin, with no early Holocene mangrove evident (Shinn et al. 1982:63–74, figure 64). Esker et al.'s (1998:figure 14) core and seismic study of the southern lagoon north of the Port Honduras has no data later than 4000 B.P.

Late Holocene Sea-Level Rise in the Port Honduras, Belize

New evidence documents a late Holocene rise in sea level in the Port Honduras. This extends current sea-level curves for Belize and elsewhere in the Caribbean to more recent times in the very late Holocene. Documentation of the sea-level rise allows reconstruction of late Holocene landscape, particularly in terms of availability of dry land for Maya settlement and availability of salt flats for solar evaporation of sea water. Finally, evidence of sea-level rise about A.D. 900, which also is the time of the collapse of the Classic Maya civilization, allows an examination of the relationship between cultural and natural factors in cultural changes: specifically, did the rise in sea level cause the abandonment of Classic Maya settlements or salt work shops? The evidence for sea-level rise and its implications are presented below.

The evidence for sea-level rise in the Port Honduras includes the location of dated archaeological sites below modern sea level, the accumulation of mangrove peat above dated archaeological sites, and the recovery of well-preserved plant remains of species that do not grow in inundated or saline deposits. These lines of evidence are standard markers for sea-level rise used by geographers, geologists, and archaeologists elsewhere. The stratigraphic location of prehistoric archaeological sites in relation to modern sea level is a common method for documenting ancient sea-level changes (DePratter and Howard 1977; Dunbar et al. 1992; Kraft et al.1977; McIntire 1954; Pearson et al. 1986; Winslow 1992). Accumulation of peat under mangroves has been used to establish Holocene sea-level records for various tropical areas (Ellison 1989; Ellison and Stoddart 1991; Woodroffe 1981, 1982, 1990, 1995). In a situation of rising sea levels, mangroves persist or continue to prograde where the rate of substrate accretion keeps pace with sea-level rise. Peat accumulation rates have been estimated for various sites. Plant remains from inundated deposits are used to reconstruct a former landscape, with charcoal used for radiocarbon-dating the sea-level changes (Alcara-Herrera et al. 1994).

Wild Cane Cay

Lower sea level during the Classic period was evident from archaeological excavations at Wild Cane Cay. The island, which measures about 80 × 300 m, was divided into six sampling areas for excavation, with a 2 × 2 m excavation unit randomly located in each area (figure 5.1). Excavations of 1 × 1 m subunits were by arbitrary 10 cm levels to a maximum depth of 190 cm. The continuity of archaeological deposits below the water table during our dry-season excavations was unexpected. In the search for sterile soil, excavations were continued up to 140 cm below the water table, which was about 50 cm below ground surface. The archaeological deposits were stratified midden deposits, with radiocarbon dates on wood charcoal confirming the age of the deposits assigned by ceramic analysis: Early Postclassic (A.D. 900–1200) deposits in soil layer A overlay Late and Terminal Classic (A.D. 600–900) deposits in soil layers B, C, and D. When Unit 3 was reopened in 1988 and excavated to the base of the archaeological deposits at 220 cm depth, the underlying sediment was coral sand. The

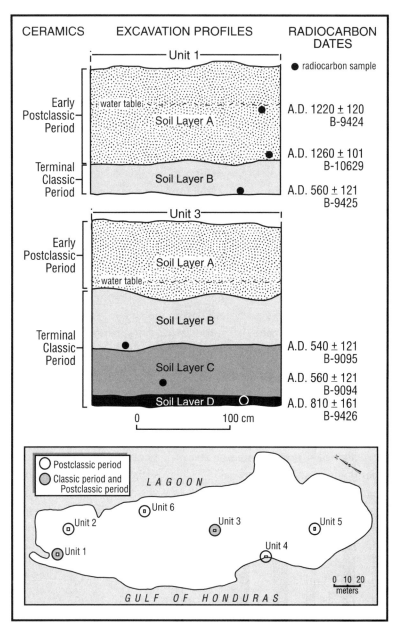

Fig. 5.1. Excavation Walls at Wild Cane Cay. Drawing by Mary Lee Eggart.

maximum depth of waterlogged deposits, which date to the Late Classic period, was 170 cm below the modern water table.

Dates provided from ceramic and radiocarbon analyses place all Classic and some Postclassic period archaeological deposits below present sea level (figure 5.1). Similar ceramics were recovered from layers B and C in Units 1 and 3. Calibrated dates to two standard deviations indicate deposition between cal A.D. 290 and 920. Two dates from Unit 3 coincide with the Unit 1 date. Lower deposits, in soil layer D, are from between cal A.D. 600 and 920. The dates overlap in the Late Classic period, between cal A.D. 439 and 660. Two dates on the Postclassic period layers from Unit 1 are in the Middle Postclassic, between cal A.D. 1100 and 1340 and cal A.D. 1160 and 1360, respectively (McKillop 1987:table 3.2). All dates are from samples below the present dry-season water table. When did the sea level submerge the deposits?

The recovery of abundant and well-preserved plant remains from the deeper inundated deposits is compelling evidence for a rapid submergence of the Classic period deposits soon after the deposition of the plant remains. Over 45 kg of plant remains were recovered, mostly from below 120 cm depth. Since the island must have been dry at the time of ancient Maya settlement, either the sea level rose after the abandonment of the island or the anthropogenic midden accumulation kept pace with sea-level rise. The recovery of abundant and well-preserved macrobotanical remains from the waterlogged anaerobic deposits dated to the Classic period argues for a rapid inundation soon after the Classic period settlement, as well as a later rise in sea level that submerged much of the Postclassic site. Since plant remains were well-preserved in the lower Postclassic levels, a sea-level rise likely submerged them soon after their deposition. The poor preservation of the upper Postclassic levels suggests that they were inundated either slowly during and after the Postclassic or even in more recent times.

Plant foods identified from the inundated deposits include species that are intolerant of saline or waterlogged conditions, indicating a drier landscape in the past (table 5.1). Apart from calabash, none of the species grows on Wild Cane Cay today or is considered native to the Belizean cays (Fosberg et al. 1982). Of a total of 134 samples, 74 percent of the Classic period samples contain plant food remains, whereas 64 percent of the Postclassic period remains contain plant food remains. The species include native palms, other fruit trees, and corn, suggesting that tree-cropping was carried out on the island in ancient Maya times as it is today on Wild

Table 5.1. Number of Plant Food Remains from Classic and Postclassic Middens at Wild Cane Cay[1]

Species/Family (common name)	Late Classic	Postclassic
Zea mays (corn)	2	0
Acrocomia mexicana (coyol palm)	363	155
Bactris major (poknoboy palm)	41	176
Orbignya cohune (cohune palm)	3,736	1,287
Byrsonima crassifolia (craboo)	251	4
Pouteria mammosum (mamey apple)	21	0
Crescentia cujete (calabash)	14	15
Ficus spp. (fig)	*	—
Persea americana (avocado)	*	—
Sapotaceae	*	—
Spondias spp. (hogplum)	1	17

1. For minimum number of individual (MNI) and ubiquity (percentage of samples from which each species was recovered) data, see McKillop 1994a.
* denotes identification from wood charcoal.

Cane Cay, although today's trees are dominated by European-introduced coconut, mango, and breadfruit.

The reduction in the size of the site due to sea-level rise was evident from offshore excavations in 1989 and 1990 at Wild Cane Cay supervised by Andrea Freudenberger (Butler) and the author. The presence of artifacts in a shallow offshore area was perplexing. Were they eroded from the island's surface or shoreline and deposited there by storms (such as hurricanes) or the redistribution of shoreline deposits from sea-level rise? Or were they submerged, buried deposits? Using a transit from the main datum on the island, stakes were set out in transects every 10 m around the island in the water. The objective was to determine the presence and abundance of artifacts buried beneath the seafloor. Teams excavated shovel tests by arbitrary levels and screened all soil (figures 5.2–5.3). Shovel testing continued from the shore out to sea off the western part of the island and into the mangroves off the eastern part of the island until no artifacts were recovered in an excavation. The presence of artifacts in excavations was used to create a map of the ancient size of the site on Wild Cane Cay, which would have been dry land (map 5.4). Offshore excavations revealed deep archaeological deposits below the seafloor. A cross-section view of the island from the land into the lagoon shows the archaeological deposits revealed by offshore shovel-testing (figure 5.4). The

Fig. 5.2. Offshore Excavation Area at Wild Cane Cay. Photo by H. McKillop.

Fig. 5.3. Offshore Excavation at Wild Cane Cay. Photo by H. McKillop.

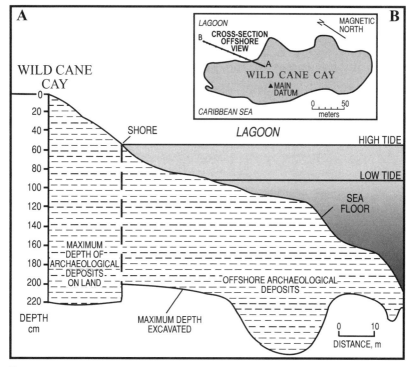

Fig. 5.4. Cross-section of Wild Cane Cay. Drawing by Mary Lee Eggart.

depth of the offshore archaeological deposits is comparable to that of the midden deposits on the island. Sterile soil was not always reached offshore because of the difficulty of excavating in deep water.

Other indications that the offshore deposits are in situ include the nature and distribution of the offshore material. The deposits are deep and stratified. Shoreline erosion would have produced mixed or reversed stratigraphy. Some of the offshore deposits farthest from shore include reduced quantities of eroded artifacts that likely do represent shoreline erosion. Botanical material, which would have floated away from eroded shorelines, was preserved in the offshore deposits.

A bathymetric map was prepared from transit data to evaluate whether the spatial distribution of artifacts from the excavations was correlated with depth, which would suggest shoreline erosion (map 5.5). The weight of ceramics in the offshore excavations was used to create a density distribution map with three contour intervals to compare with the bathymetry (map 5.6). The overlay of the bathymetry and artifact densities shows the

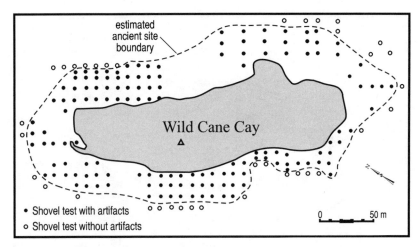

Map 5.4. Offshore Shovel Test Locations at Wild Cane Cay. By Mary Lee Eggart from transit map by H. McKillop.

highest artifact concentrations are closest to shore and the lowest artifact concentrations are farthest from shore. However, most of the artifacts are in the > 101 g density contour, which extends from the shore to 125 cm depth, indicating no correlation between density of artifacts and depth. The results of the spatial analysis, together with the excavation data, indicate the site was significantly larger, as indicated by the 1–100 g contour

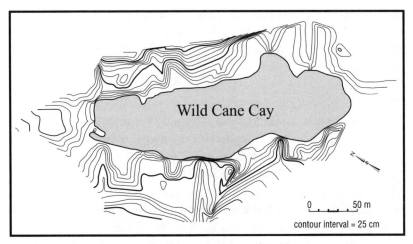

Map 5.5. Bathymetric Map of Offshore Area around Wild Cane Cay. By Mary Lee Eggart from GIS Intergraph MGE Map by H. McKillop.

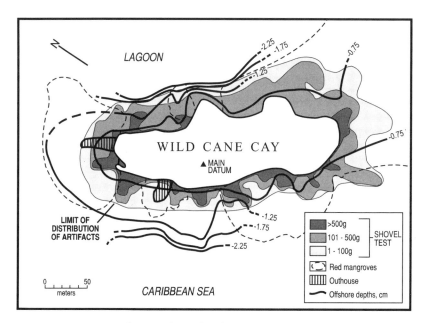

Map 5.6. Density Distribution of Weight of Ceramics from Offshore Excavations at Wild Cane Cay. By Mary Lee Eggart from GIS Intergraph MGE Map by H. McKillop.

line. Shoreline erosion and redeposition of Postclassic artifacts in the coastal waters account for the diminution of ceramics in the excavations farthest from shore and must account for some of the deposition closer to shore as well. Although shoreline erosion can make significant changes in the landscape (Stoddart 1963), in the case of Wild Cane Cay, most of the offshore deposits are intact buried remains that were submerged from eustatic sea-level rise.

Frenchman's Cay

Excavations at Frenchman's Cay in 1994 and 1997 revealed inundation of Late Classic stone building foundations and household middens (maps 5.3 and 5.7; Magnoni 1999; McKillop 1995c, 1997, 2001; McKillop and Wine-miller 2001; Watson 1999). The bases of the building foundations in Mounds 2 and 3 were 80 cm below the water table, indicating submergence after their Late Classic use. Sterile mangrove mud devoid of cultural remains was recovered below the buildings. Excavations of Mound 3, Crown Conch Mound, supervised by Aline Magnoni (1999) indicated two building sequences, with a lower coral rock foundation and its dirt floor submerged. Analysis of artifacts by the author found Late Classic ceramics and chert tools, with no artifacts postdating the Late Classic. Excavations of Mound 2, Great White Lucine Mound, directed by the author also revealed two building sequences, with the lower coral rock foundation and associated dirt floor submerged below the water table. The upper foundation was above the water table. Artifacts from the lower building foundation and floor date to the Late Classic. Excavations of Mound 1, Spondylus Mound, supervised by Rachel Watson (1999) indicate the coral rock foundation was not submerged, but that the midden accumulation below the foundation was submerged. Only one building phase was revealed, which remains undated owing to paucity of ceramics from the foundations.

Settlement evidence in the nonmound areas of Frenchman's Cay was investigated by placing four transects to maximize coverage of the southwest part of the island where artifacts had been noticed on the ground surface. The ground surface is seasonally inundated. Even during the dry season, the ground surface is wet along the northeast transect. Excavations were continued along each transect until no artifacts were found. A total of 36 shovel tests was carried out along the transects at 10 m intervals. Excavations were by arbitrary 20 cm levels to a maximum depth of 100 cm and screened through quarter-inch mesh.

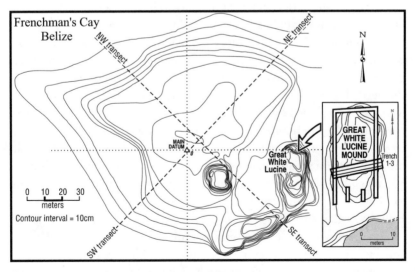

Map 5.7. Frenchman's Cay. By Mary Lee Eggart from transit map by H. McKillop.

Although the distribution of artifacts indicates the ancient settlement size, mollusk analysis provides clues about the paleolandscape. The spatial distribution of mollusk genera by habitat along the transects provides a picture of a changing environment (McKillop and Winemiller 2001). The dry land needed for the initial settlement is indicated by shallow-water marine genera with a few mangrove genera that would have characterized the adjacent seascape. By way of contrast, mangrove genera were more common later, as indicated by their presence in upper levels and along the northeast transect (which is flooded today). Evidently mangroves began encroaching on the site margins. Shallow-water marine mollusks were common in both building phases at Great White Lucine, indicating a dry landscape. The occurrence of mangrove mollusks in the upper layers of Great White Lucine points to a drier landscape during the construction of the building and more recent encroachment of mangroves due to rising seas.

Pelican One Pot

Pelican One Pot is a Classic period site buried under 40 cm of mangrove peat. The site is located on a small mangrove island off the mainland coast north of Golden Stream (map 5.3; figure 5.5). The island is covered with red mangroves, and the entire ground surface is slightly below the modern water table. Since buried cultural horizons had been discovered at nearby Tiger Mound and at Wild Cane Cay, a shovel test was carried out at Pelican One Pot. The only surface indication of a Maya site was an eroded pottery sherd, which seemed more likely to have been redeposited from elsewhere. The subsequent recovery of pottery sherds in a shovel test prompted a 1 × 1 m excavation unit to recover pottery and charcoal to date the deposit and to investigate the site's inundated location. Excavations were carried out by arbitrary 20 cm levels from the ground surface, with constant bailing to remove water during the excavations. Excavation was by shovel into buckets, with the contents screened through quarter-inch-mesh excavation screens in the sea. At the base of the cultural deposits, at 80 cm depth, a soil probe was extended deeper, to a depth of 125 cm depth, to examine the stratigraphy. Excavations were completed in one day in January 1992.

Excavations revealed the natural and cultural stratigraphy of the island and documented the sea-level rise (figure 5.6). The upper soil layer consists of mangrove peat to 40 cm depth. Below is located a layer of mixed

Fig. 5.5. Pelican Cay. Photo by H. McKillop.

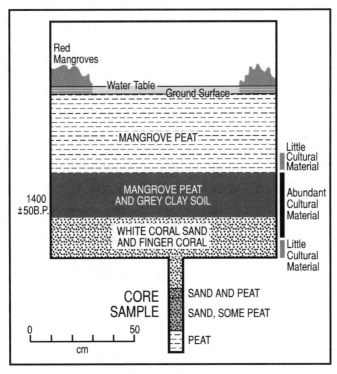

Fig. 5.6. Excavation Wall at Pelican. Drawing by Mary Lee Eggart.

mangrove peat and gray mud to a depth of 60 cm. The next soil layer is white coral sand and finger coral (*Porites* spp.) between 60 and 115 cm depth. The evidence of cultural activity is pottery sherds, charcoal, and other plant remains, concentrated between 40 and 70 cm depth in the mangrove peat–mud layer and the sand–finger coral layer. Some pottery sherds were also recovered 10 cm above in the mangrove peat layer and 10 cm below in the sand–finger coral layer. The lowest layer encountered by our excavations was a peat layer, below 115 cm depth. No artifacts were recovered above 30 cm depth or below 80 cm depth.

The sequence of habitation and sea-level rise is interpreted as follows: The mangrove peat below 115 cm depth indicates a sea-level rise before the ancient occupation of the island. The mangrove peat was accumulating as the sea level rose. In order to accumulate sediment, the mangrove peat must have been resting on a ridge or coral patch reef that was somewhat higher than the surrounding waters. Once sea level became more stable, coral invaded the shallow waters of the submerged ridge, building the island. The patch reef became exposed above sea level from a lowering of sea level, and the coral began to erode and weather, building coral sand. The ancient Maya established a settlement on the island in the Classic period, when it was dry land. The site is radiocarbon-dated to cal A.D. 450–650, which places it at the beginning of the Late Classic (A.D. 600–900). The living surface of the site was coral sand, as indicated in the excavation below 60 cm depth. The maximum depth of settlement is 80 cm depth. Sea level must have been lower at that time for settlement and for the cohune and coyol palms and the craboo to have grown on the island. Plant food remains recovered from the cultural deposits indicate a drier land surface if the cohune and coyol palms and craboo fruit trees were growing on the island (table 5.2). The plant foods were abundant between 40 and 60 cm depth, with few remains between 60 and 70 cm depth. The sea level began rising again, as indicated by the mangrove peat accumulation. Some of the

Table 5.2. Plant Food Remains from Classical Deposits (40–80 cm Depth) at Pelican One Pot

Species (common name)	# Fragments	MNI	Weight (g)
Orbignya cohune (cohune)	39	9	124.9
Acrocomia mexicana (coyol)	33	13	45.05
Byrsonima crassifolia (craboo)	30	4	2.94

MNI = minimum number of individuals

mangrove peat infiltrated into the clayey soil of the habitation layer. The mangroves have kept pace with sea-level rise to the present day, with sea level just above the ground surface. The accumulation of 40 cm of mangrove peat after the Classic period site was abandoned provides 1,400 years for 40 cm of peat deposition. This rate translates as 2.8 cm/100 years, or 0.28 m/1,000 years.

Tiger Mound

Tiger Mound site is located on a small island between Pelican One Pot and the mainland, north of Golden Stream (map 5.3). This uninhabited mangrove cay has a clearing in the center with salt-enriched soil that may have killed black and white mangrove trees whose dried trunks stand among black mangrove shoots. The ground surface is slightly below the water table at high tide. Discovered during routine searching of mangrove cays by the author and her dog, Tiger, the only surface evidence of the Maya site is a small earthen mound in the clearing. A 2 × 2 m excavation unit placed south of the mound revealed buried archaeological deposits. A radiocarbon date of cal A.D. 560–800 was obtained from wood charcoal at 80 cm depth in the unit. Systematic shovel-testing in cardinal directions at 10 m intervals across the island revealed an extensive and deeply buried archaeological horizon (map 5.8).

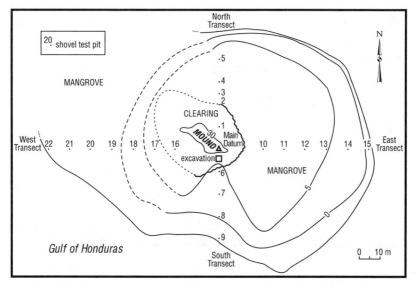

Map 5.8. Shovel Tests at Tiger Mound Site. By Mary Lee Eggart from transit map by H. McKillop.

Pork and Doughboy Point

A rise in sea level also is evident at Pork and Doughboy Point. Artifacts were abundant on the seafloor. They are distributed in an offshore area both north and east of the site (map 5.9; figure 5.7). Artifacts were recovered at 40 m north of the point of land. An underwater excavation 22 m off the eastern point demonstrated the presence of in situ Classic period deposits (Brandehoff-Pracht 1995). A radiocarbon date of cal A.D. 665–885 was obtained from wood charcoal from the excavations, corroborating the age assigned based on ceramic analysis. The offshore excavation was 47 cm below the water table. An experiment by Jodi Brandehoff-Pracht and the author was carried out in the Louisiana State University wave tank, to simulate conditions of wood charcoal eroding from a bank. Since the charcoal in the wave tank dispersed widely with wave action, we estimated that the charcoal in the offshore excavations was in situ. Otherwise, it would have dispersed and floated away as in the experiment.

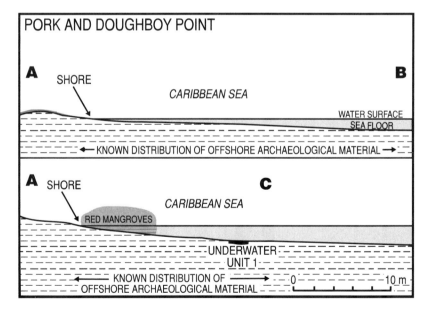

Fig. 5.7. Cross-section of Pork and Doughboy Site. Drawing by Mary Lee Eggart from Transit Map by H. McKillop.

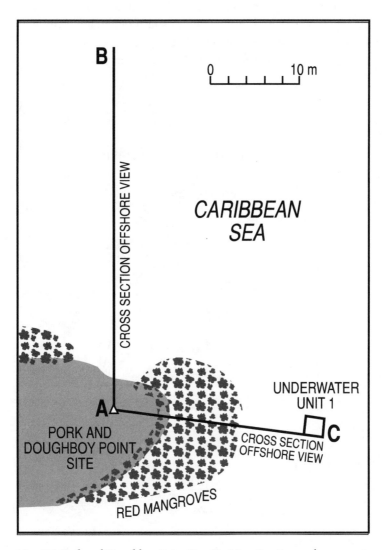

Map 5.9. Pork and Doughboy Point Site. By Mary Lee Eggart from transit map by H. McKillop.

Green Vine Snake

A site of unknown size and age, Green Vine Snake is marked by three mounds of coral rock (map 5.3 and 5.10). The ground surface is inundated between the mounds. A shovel test 11 m south of Mound 1 revealed fibrous peat with mangrove mud devoid of artifacts to 30 cm depth—similar to Pelican site. There were few artifacts between 30 and 60 cm depth.

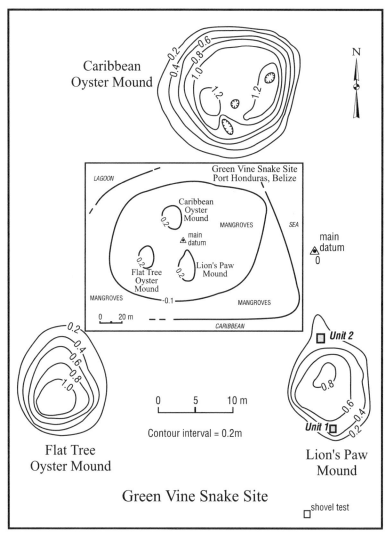

Map 5.10. Green Vine Snake Site. By Mary Lee Eggart from transit map by H. McKillop.

Artifacts, conch shells, and coral rocks were abundant between 60 and 80 cm depth. Boulder coral was encountered at 70 cm depth. A probe to 140 cm depth revealed continuation of mangrove peat and mud below the cultural deposits. Although of unknown age, the deposition of the site resembles Pelican, so Green Vine Snake is relevant to the discussion of sea-level rise and ancient Maya settlement.

Discussion

Sea-level rise submerged the Punta Ycacos and other Classic period settlements in the Port Honduras region (table 5.3). Radiocarbon dating of five inundated sites, along with ceramic analysis dating of other inundated sites, provides evidence of widespread submergence of Classic Maya sites in the region. Inundated sites in the Port Honduras that are not yet radiocarbon dated include Green Vine Snake (McKillop 1996a), Foster Farm and Arvin's Landing (Steiner 1994), Frenchman's Cay, Orlando's Jewfish, Killer Bee, and David Westby.

The sequence of sea-level rise in relation to ancient Maya settlement was complicated by anthropogenic factors, specifically the accumulation of ancient middens. At the beginning of this chapter, two models were introduced to evaluate the role of environmental factors (sea-level rise) versus cultural factors (population change) in the abandonment of the Punta Ycacos Lagoon salt work shops at the end of the Classic period. In order to evaluate these models, the timing of sea-level rise was investigated at the salt work shops and elsewhere in the Port Honduras coastal region by examining the depth of dated archaeological deposits below modern sea level. Then the impact of sea-level rise on subsequent settlement in the Postclassic was examined by the settlement history of the region. However, it is important to remember that the potential for continued settlement in the Postclassic does not necessarily explain the reason for the cessation of salt production in Punta Ycacos Lagoon: even if specific locations were inundated by rising seas, given a demand for salt, producers may have found alternative, drier locations to continue the production.

The Port Honduras fieldwork reveals three models for sea-level and settlement changes, exemplified by the Punta Ycacos Lagoon sites, Pelican Cay, and Wild Cane Cay, respectively. The models of settlement in reaction to sea-level rise are abandonment and marine transgression, abandonment and mangrove accumulation, and continued settlement with

Table 5.3. Depth and Dates of Late Classic Archaeological Sites below Sea Level in Port Honduras

Site (Laboratory Number)	Maximum Depth below Sea Level (cm)	Cultural Context	Environmental Context	Uncalibrated Radiocarbon Age (± 1 sigma)	2 sigma Calibrated Age (95% Probability)
Stingray Lagoon (B-69869)	100	work shop	underwater	1180±50 B.P.	cal A.D. 670–870
David Westby		work shop	underwater		
Orlando's Jewfish		work shop	underwater		
Pelican (B-69905)	80	midden	below peat inundated	1400±50 B.P.	cal A.D. 450–650
Green Vine Snake	unknown*	midden	inundated		
Tiger Mound (B-37037)	80	midden	inundated	1270±60 B.P.	cal A.D. 560–800
Killer Bee	unknown*	work shop	inundated		
Wild Cane Cay (B-9095)	140	midden	inundated	1200±80 B.P.	cal A.D. 600–920
Wild Cane Cay (B-9426)	80	midden	inundated	1540±60 B.P.	cal A.D. 290–530
Wild Cane Cay (B-9425)	80	midden	inundated	1510±60 B.P.	cal A.D. 439–660
Wild Cane Cay (B-9094)	120	midden	inundated	1510±60 B.P.	cal A.D. 439–660
Frenchman's Cay	80	building foundations	inundated		
Pork and Doughboy** (B-87007)	57	midden	underwater	1270±50 B.P.	cal A.D. 665–885

* The base of the archaeological deposits was not reached in the excavations.

** The calibrated radiocarbon date for Pork and Doughboy was provided by Beta Analytic. Other dates were calibrated using the calibration curves in Stuiver and Pearson 1986.

anthropogenic soil buildup (figures 5.8–5.9). In the first model, low-lying sites that were abandoned at the end of the Classic period were submerged by a sea-level rise and are now underwater. The salt-making sites in Punta Ycacos Lagoon fit this model (figure 5.8). In the second model, mangroves were able to keep pace with the rise in sea level, resulting in

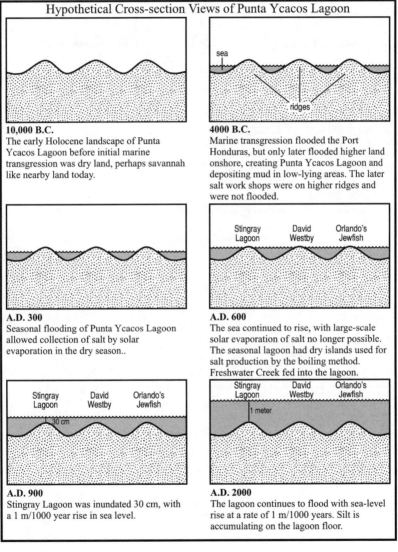

Hypothetical Cross-section Views of Punta Ycacos Lagoon

10,000 B.C.
The early Holocene landscape of Punta Ycacos Lagoon before initial marine transgression was dry land, perhaps savannah like nearby land today.

4000 B.C.
Marine transgression flooded the Port Honduras, but only later flooded higher land onshore, creating Punta Ycacos Lagoon and depositing mud in low-lying areas. The later salt work shops were on higher ridges and were not flooded.

A.D. 300
Seasonal flooding of Punta Ycacos Lagoon allowed collection of salt by solar evaporation in the dry season..

A.D. 600
The sea continued to rise, with large-scale solar evaporation of salt no longer possible. The seasonal lagoon had dry islands used for salt production by the boiling method. Freshwater Creek fed into the lagoon.

A.D. 900
Stingray Lagoon was inundated 30 cm, with a 1 m/1000 year rise in sea level.

A.D. 2000
The lagoon continues to flood with sea-level rise at a rate of 1 m/1000 years. Silt is accumulating on the lagoon floor.

Fig. 5.8. Hypothetical Temporal Sequence of Sea-Level Rise in Punta Ycacos Lagoon. Drawing by Mary Lee Eggart from Sketches by H. McKillop.

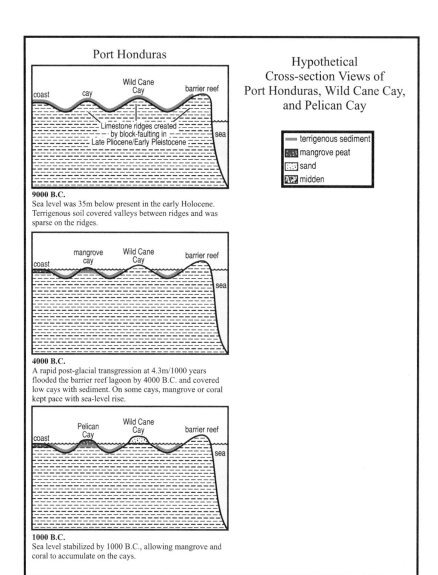

Fig. 5.9. Hypothetical Temporal Sequence of Sea-Level Rise in Port Honduras, Wild Cane Cay, and Pelican Cay. Drawing by Mary Lee Eggart from sketches by H. McKillop.

Port Honduras	Wild Cane Cay
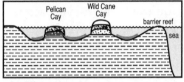	

A.D. 400

Sea level rose during the Classic Period occupation, with anthropogenic midden accumulation keeping pace with sea-level rise on Pelican and Wild Cane Cay.

The lowest Classic Period middens were dry at the time of initial settlement.

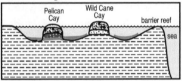	

A.D. 900

Sea level rose rapidly at 4.3m/1000 years during the Classic Period occupation, resulting in complete submergence of Classic period deposits and Pelican and reclamation by the sea. Land was higher at Wild Cane Cay, where anthropogenic soil helped keep the land above rising seas.

Middens and other remains were submerged during the Classic Period. Postclassic architecture was built on stone foundations on Wild Cane Cay

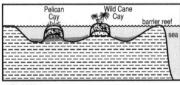	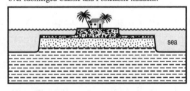

A.D. 1500

The rate of sea-level rise slowed to 1m or less per 1000 years.

Sea level continued to rise at Wild Cane Cay, submerging some Postclassic deposits. The shoreline was eroded by wave action, redepositing Postclassic midden offshore over submerged Classic and Postclassic middens.

A.D. 2000

Sea level continues to rise at 1m/1000 years, reclaiming more of Wild Cane Cay. Mangrove peat keeps pace with sea level rise at Pelican Cay.

Sea level continues to rise at Wild Cane Cay at 1m /1000 years, submerging more Postclassic period deposits and eroding the shoreline.

the accumulation of mangrove peat. For example, after the abandonment of the Classic period site on Pelican One Pot, mangroves became established in the submerged tidal environment, keeping pace with rising seas and accumulating mangrove peat to the present day (figure 5.9). This model may characterize many of the mangrove cays in the Port Honduras. Many Classic Maya sites may be buried and invisible from the ground surface. In the last model, settlement continued on the largest and driest cays, such as Wild Cane Cay, during the Postclassic, where anthropogenic soil accumulation in the Classic period created a buffer from the rising seas (figure 5.9). Settlement on offshore islands may have been expanded to take advantage of the abandonment of nearby inland cities and the increased Postclassic circum-Yucatan trade associated with the rise of Chichen Itza (McKillop 1989). Although sea level continued to rise in the Postclassic, midden accumulation also continued, resulting today in sites that remain dry, either seasonally (Green Vine Snake and Frenchman's Cay) or year round (Wild Cane Cay). Anthropogenic midden accumulation may have kept pace with sea-level rise. The sea-level rise may even have been gradual, with little impact on ancient settlement. Their Classic period midden (Wild Cane Cay) or architectural remains (Frenchman's Cay) are submerged and their shorelines are eroding. At Wild Cane Cay, much of the ancient settlement is offshore, with the cut bank eroding over intact, submerged deposits around the island. Historic settlement on Wild Cane Cay and Frenchman's Cay may also have contributed to the physical continuity of the islands, but with the abandonment of these sites, and the lack of continuing anthropogenic soil buildup, the fate of these islands lies with the rising seas.

The "permissive" role of the environment in cultural change is similar to the concept of "environmental threshold" introduced to explain the role of environmental changes related to the Tiwanaka civilization of the southern Andes (Binford et al. 1997). Changes in the availability of water in the southern Andes created environmental thresholds of "climatic extremes that limit the complexity of cultural development" (Binford et al. 1997:235). Initially, there was insufficient water for intensive agriculture, so the human population was small. Increase in water availability facilitated intensive raised-field agriculture, leading to high populations. A third threshold was the drop in water availability that choked agricultural production and led to a dramatic diminution in population, resulting in the collapse of the Tiwanaka civilization.

In a similar model, fluctuations in oxygen isotopes and in the proportion of calcite and gypsum in sediment cores from Chichanacanab, Yucatan, Mexico, were used as indicators of a wet or dry climate. The driest climate was between A.D. 800 and 1000, coinciding with the collapse of the Classic Maya civilization (Hodell et al. 1995). This drying trend is attributed as the main factor in the collapse. These findings were corroborated by data from another sediment core in Lake Punta Laguna, near Coba, Quintana Roo, Mexico (Curtis et al. 1996). A drier climate was indicated at

A.D. 585, 862, 986, and 1051 ± 50 years. The first dry period coincided with the Maya hiatus, while the next two dates coincided with the collapse. Opposite findings were reported from pollen analysis of sediment from a core in Lake Salpeten (Leyden 1987; Messenger 1990). The Lake Salpeten pollen core data indicated increased rainfall and global warming during the Late and Terminal Classic period (A.D. 800–1000). Curtis et al. (1996) suggest regional variation in the Maya lowlands meant that the ancient Maya response to climate change may have varied. Whether or not there was a drier climate—that is, less rainfall—in the Port Honduras, the ground became wetter due to eustatic sea-level rise at the end of the Classic period.

The ancient Maya use of coasts in general needs to be reevaluated according to the complex interplay of cultural and environmental factors. Variability is to be expected due to local conditions, both cultural and environmental. The duration and intensity of Maya use of coastal communities is reflected in the amount of anthropogenic midden accumulation, a point well articulated by Graham (1989, 1998). Depending on their depth, anthropogenic soil buildup would have been a buffer against natural forces of sea-level rise and shoreline erosion.

Localized environmental factors, such as the abundance of rivers feeding into the Port Honduras in contrast to their absence in many areas of the Yucatan coast of Mexico, impacted on the degree of loading of nearshore waters with river water, which would have seasonally raised sea level. Even the rarer occurrence of hurricanes in the Port Honduras in contrast to their more common trajectory across northern Belize and the Yucatan affects the amount of shoreline and surface erosion of coasts. Stoddart (1963) reported on the dramatic effects of Hurricane Hattie farther north on the offshore cays in Belize, for example. Southward-moving coastal currents in addition to sedimentation by rivers resulted in sediment deposition in sheltered coastal settings along the coast of Belize. The ephemeral existence of sandy beaches on the windward side of Frenchman's Cay and Moho Cay in the Port Honduras is a function of currents and wave action: a beach on the northeast corner of Frenchman's Cay in 1994 had disappeared by 1997. At nearby Moho Cay, the beach was washed from the southern shore to the windward shore during the same time.

In some areas, coastal accretion is evident by the extension of mangroves into shallow offshore waters or by the ancient Maya sites trapped within mangrove swamps. Watson's Island and Kakalche at Colson Point, as well as Marco Gonzalez, are surrounded by mangroves, which postdate the ancient Maya use of the sites (Graham 1989, 1994:137; Graham and Pendergast 1989). The Late Preclassic to Protoclassic shell midden at Butterfly Wing site on the south side of the Deep River is approachable only through inundated mangrove swamp, which was not likely the case during the site's use. Ongoing growth of mangroves around Wild Cane Cay and Frenchman's Cay, not only on the relatively sheltered leeward shores but also on the windward side of the cays, attests to the transitional nature of coastal landscapes and suggests that significant variability existed along the Maya coasts of Belize and the Yucatan peninsula of Mexico.

Predictive Modeling of the Classic Period Landscape

The Classic period view of the Port Honduras region would be limited without knowledge of the submerged and underwater sites. First, there would be very few sites. Second, the salt work shops would be missed. Third, there would be minimal indication of Classic period coastal trade. The trading port at Wild Cane Cay would become a Postclassic trading site, as would Frenchman's Cay. Specialized salt production communities would be unknown, since Stingray Lagoon, David Westby, and Orlando's Jewfish are underwater and Killer Bee is located in a mangrove swamp. Sites such as Tiger Mound and Pelican One Pot would remain invisible in mangrove swamps.

The dry view of south-coastal Belize would provide a false picture of limited Classic period coastal settlement in contrast to the more extensive settlement inland at Lubaantun, Nim li punit, and Pusilha, among others. The false reconstruction would continue into the Postclassic period, with the apparent increase in coastal settlement following the abandonment of the Classic period inland settlements.

The archaeological evidence was used for predictive modeling of the Classic period landscape. Topographic maps, air photos, Landsat imagery, bathymetric maps, and modern vegetation maps were used to digitize shoreline and vegetation patterns in the GIS Intergraph MGE. Based on evidence of sea-level rise from excavations, the 90 cm contour on a bathymetric map was used to estimate the Late Classic period coastline (map 5.11). The water depths around the offshore islands are not recorded well in the bathymetric map. Landsat imagery and air photos depict tonal

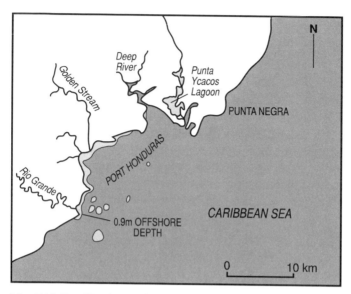

Map 5.11. Port Honduras, Showing 0.9 m Bathymetric Line. By Mary Lee Eggart from sketch by H. McKillop.

variation that in some cases has been documented by fieldwork as indicating a shallow offshore area, as at Wild Cane Cay.

The mainland coast and cays of Port Honduras, which contain many archaeological sites, are currently designated "problem soils" because of flooded, saline conditions (map 5.12; Wright et al. 1959). The location of sites in this zone and the plant remains recovered from those sites indicate that the offshore islands and the coastal strip along the mainland that are now mangroves would have supported plants adapted to dry, nonsaline soils. The mangrove zone would have been farther offshore beyond the area of dry land, in an intertidal zone, reflecting processes of coastal accretion of mangroves (see Cameron and Palmer 1995; Woodroffe 1995). Both the coastline that is currently mangrove swamp and the shallow offshore area comprise a substantial area of potential Classic period settlement (map 5.13). What did this land look like? The discovery and excavation of Classic period sites in this zone indicates that the land was indeed dry. The recovery of palm and other fruit remains from Classic period sites indicates that the soil was not saline or inundated.

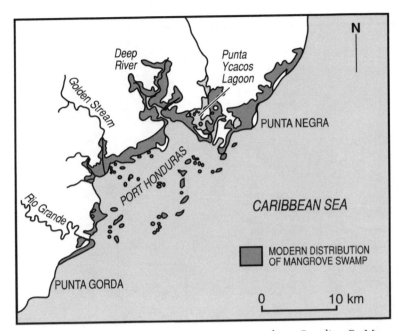

Map 5.12. Distribution of Mangroves along Port Honduras Coastline. By Mary Lee Eggart.

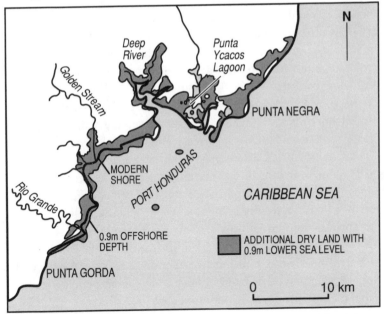

Map 5.13. Additional Dry Land during Late Classic along Port Honduras Coastline. By Mary Lee Eggart.

Summary

The underwater location of the Punta Ycacos salt-making sites is explained by a eustatic sea-level rise documented by archaeological excavations at 10 Classic period sites in the Port Honduras. The production of salt in Punta Ycacos Lagoon is related to the Late Classic surge in settlement in the Port Honduras region, as well as the adjacent inland region of southern Belize, where several large Maya cities are known. With the collapse of the southern Maya civilization and abandonment of inland cities in southern Belize and the Pasion region of Guatemala, the inland demand for the Punta Ycacos salt waned. That rising seas submerged the salt work shops soon after their abandonment is attested by the excellent preservation of plant remains and the lack of postdepositional site trampling, particularly at Stingray Lagoon. Sea level continued to rise during the Postclassic, as evidenced by submerged Postclassic deposits at Wild Cane Cay. At some point during the early part of the Postclassic, the salt work shops were inundated, becoming no longer usable for salt production.

Sea-level rise played an important role in the availability of resources and habitable land for the ancient coastal Maya. Three models presented describing the relationship between sea-level rise and ancient Maya settlement indicate that both environmental and cultural factors contributed to changes in settlement in the Port Honduras (figures 5.8–5.9). The first model, site abandonment and marine transgression, characterizes the Punta Ycacos salt works. In this case, the environmental agent, sea-level rise, caused the flooding of the sites and precluded their use during the Postclassic period for salt production. However, cultural rather than environmental factors likely were responsible for the abandonment of salt works in Punta Ycacos Lagoon, since they could have been relocated to drier land, as happens along coastlines elsewhere (Adshead 1992). That the salt works were not relocated was due to the abandonment of the inland Maya cities in southern Belize and adjacent Guatemala, resulting in a drop in the market for the Punta Ycacos salt. There was a limited coastal clientele for salt during the Postclassic in the Port Honduras. The occurrence of salt pots and associated vessel supports on Wild Cane Cay during the Postclassic indicates that salt-making continued after the abandonment of the Punta Ycacos salt works. The Postclassic salt-making likely was carried out as an incidental part of household activities instead of at specialized work shops.

The second model, site abandonment and mangrove accumulation, characterized Pelican Cay, whose Classic period settlement is deeply buried under mangrove peat that is today slightly below sea level. The widespread occurrence of similar mangrove cays in the Port Honduras and elsewhere along the coast of Belize begs the question as to whether they contain buried Classic Maya sites. In this model, Postclassic settlement was precluded owing to environmental agents. However, Pelican Cay may have been abandoned before the mangroves and the sea reclaimed the island.

The third model, in which anthropogenic soil accumulation kept pace with sea level, characterized Wild Cane Cay. In this case, cultural factors—either active raised-stone-building efforts or passive accumulation of household refuse—served to keep the land above the rising seas. The dry state of the cay made continued settlement possible on Wild Cane during the Postclassic. Generally, settlement shifted to higher and drier places in the Port Honduras. The islanders' participation in circum-Yucatan canoe trade provided a reason for the florescence of the community during the Postclassic.

This examination of the responses of the ancient coastal Maya to sea-level rise shows that there was a complex interplay between cultural and environmental factors. Although sea-level rise did not cause the abandonment of the salt work shops, sea-level rise did obviate their use during the Postclassic. The choices for settlement locations for the Postclassic Maya were diminished. Today, the widespread occurrence of mangrove swamps and shallow, inundated land hides most of the evidence for the ancient Maya in the Port Honduras and indeed elsewhere along the coast of Belize. This is a sobering reminder of the fate of modern low-lying coastal areas worldwide subject to global warming and sea-level rise.

6

ЛЛЛЛЛ

Salt Production, Trade,
and Late Classic Maya Society

Seasonal salt works were set up along the coast of Belize during the Late
Classic period to meet the growing inland demand for salt. At these salt
works, lagoon water was preprocessed by pouring it through salty soil in
large wooden containers. This process enriched the salt content of the
brine before the brine was boiled to evaporate the water. An alternative
method of obtaining salt, through solar evaporation, may have been used
in the coastal lagoons earlier in the Classic period, but the rise in sea level
drowned the salt flats, making only limited solar evaporation possible
during the Late Classic. Because of the unpredictable and relatively short
dry season in southern Belize, solar evaporation was less reliable than it
was farther north. After the abandonment of many inland cities in the
southern Maya lowlands at the end of the Classic period, there were few
inland consumers for coastal Belizean salt. Most salt works were abandoned, including those in Punta Ycacos Lagoon.

The salt works in Punta Ycacos Lagoon supplied the coastal settlements
in the Port Honduras region and the inland Maya at large cities in southern Belize and the Pasion region of Guatemala. Salt work shops were located on high ground in the seasonally flooded lagoon. The work shops
were used in the dry season to take advantage of solar evaporation and to
avoid the frequent rains of the rainy season. Salt pots were produced locally by each salt work shop, resulting in slight differences in dimensions
of the vessels. Still, the vessels and the salt cakes produced at the Punta

Ycacos salt works were standardized for bulk export to the interior. The specialized production of salt suggests salt production for coastal use and inland trade.

The lack of food remains contrasts with the abundance of charcoal associated with salt-making, and indicates that these sites were focused on salt production with limited, if any, settlement. The lack of settlement is corroborated by the absence of burials or house mounds. Moreover, the specialized nature of the ceramics did not include the full complement of vessel forms or ceramic types characteristic of other Port Honduras communities. The absence of fish bones indicates that salt production was not focused on salt-drying fish to feed the growing Classic period population. Indeed, the remains of relatively few saltwater fish have been recovered from inland Maya sites (McKillop 1984, 1985).

Wild Cane Cay, as a coastal trading port, was the bulking point for inland trade of salt and other marine resources, such as stingray spines, dried fish, manatee bone carvings, and shells. In return, figurine whistles, unit-stamped ceramics, and other goods were traded from inland cities to the coast. These elite goods mark the inclusion of the coastal leaders into high society—a good strategy to maintain the flow of coastal resources, notably stingray spines, fish, and salt, as well as goods such as obsidian, transported along the coast by seagoing canoe traders from more distant places. Some goods were used in salt ceremonies at the work shops at the beginning of each salt season and perhaps each workday to propitiate the gods in order to maintain the supply of salt. The whistles, for example, have several holes allowing a tune to be played.

There is no evidence of trade between the Port Honduras and the north coast of the Yucatan during the Late Classic period, arguing against import of salt from that area. Evidence of northern Maya lowland influence in terms of round structures and ceramics (Chase and Chase 1982) in northern Belize occurs later, during the Terminal Classic period. By way of contrast, extensive evidence points to coastal-inland trade and trade between the Maya highlands of Guatemala and the southern Maya lowlands in the Late Classic period contemporary with the Punta Ycacos salt works. Direct participation in exotic trade evident from material remains at the Punta Ycacos salt works is limited, in contrast to their greater abundance at the nearby trading ports of Wild Cane Cay and Frenchman's Cay. A single obsidian blade recovered from Orlando's Jewfish site was visually sourced to the El Chayal outcrop near modern Guatemala City. Volcanic ash-tempered serving vessels assigned to Moho Red variety from Orlando's Jewfish and Stingray Lagoon may be imported Belize Red dishes, providing a trade tie with the Belize River–area Maya. In any event, the volcanic ash used as the tempering agent was imported (Simmons and Brem 1979).

Evidence for coastal-inland trade is more extensive. Figurine whistles, unit-stamped pottery, and a granite mano and metate tie the salt works with inland cities in southern Belize and adjacent Guatemala, although the trade likely was via Wild Cane Cay. Both the lack of settlement at the salt work shops and the evidence for coastal-inland trade at nearby Wild Cane Cay argue for trade via that community. Production of salt in Punta Ycacos Lagoon was for local coastal use and inland trade to supply nearby Classic period cities. The lack of evidence for trade with the northern Yucatan, together with the local availability of salt from Punta Ycacos Lagoon, support a model of regional production and trade of Belizean salt during the Late Classic period in the southern Maya lowlands.

With the abandonment of the inland cities in southern Belize and the Pasion region at the end of the Late Classic period, the salt production in Punta Ycacos Lagoon was reduced for lack of customers. Sea level rose to submerge the workshops. Trading ports reoriented their commercial ties to deal with the emerging polities in the northern Yucatan, particularly Chichen Itza and its coastal port of Isla Cerritos. Wild Cane Cay figured prominently in this long-distance sea trade. With obsidian from six outcrops from central Mexico to highland Guatemala and Honduras, the Wild Cane Cay Maya participated in sea trade from the north and south along the Yucatan. Tohil Plumbate and Tulum Red ceramics, and gold, copper, basalt, and green stone artifacts as well, completed the inventory of exotic goods. In sharp contrast to the Late Classic period, the Postclassic period in the Port Honduras witnessed extensive trade with the Yucatan coast. Tulum Red pottery in burials and household middens at Wild Cane Cay indicate ties with the north, either through import of exotic ware or local copy of an exotic style. Central Mexican obsidian artifacts from Pachuca and Ucareo likely were transported around the Yucatan coast, as evidenced by their popularity at Chichen Itza and Isla Cerritos on the north coast and Ambergris Cay off the coast of northern Belize (McKillop 1995b). Although salt was produced at Wild Cane Cay and Frenchman's Cay to meet family needs, there was no significant demand for salt in the area during the Postclassic. The nearby inland cities in Belize and the

Pasion region of Guatemala had been abandoned, as had some coastal communities in the Port Honduras. The trade contacts with the Yucatan involved distribution of limited quantities of exotic resources, notably Mexican obsidian artifacts.

Artifactual and radiocarbon evidence limits the use of the Punta Ycacos Lagoon salt works to the Late Classic period. This time corresponds with the time of the height of the Maya civilization, when the highest population levels were reached and when the highest demands for salt would have existed. In addition, inland Maya settlement in southern Belize is concentrated in the Late Classic period, with only limited earlier settlement at Uxbenka. McAnany (1989b) notes that ethnographically there is an increase in specialized production of nonfood goods at times of high population and decreasing availability of arable land. That coastal settlement continued on the coast during the Postclassic period meant that salt needs had to be met from other sources. The distribution of limited quantities of brine-boiling artifacts at Frenchman's Cay and Wild Cane Cay suggests household production for immediate use may have been characteristic of the Postclassic along the coast. Previously I suggested that solar evaporation may have been utilized in Punta Ycacos Lagoon prior to the Late Classic, when sea level was lower. While possible, there is currently no archaeological evidence.

The Punta Ycacos salt works were abandoned at the end of the Classic period, when the inland consumers of salt left such cities as Lubaantun, Nim li punit, Uxbenka, and Pusilha (map 6.1). Subsequently, the salt works were inundated by a rise in sea level. Whether there was an actual rise in sea level or a relative rise caused by subsidence of the land, or both, the salt sites were permanently waterlogged soon after the salt works were abandoned. This interpretation is based on two factors. First, there is little evidence of postdepositional site trampling. The discarded sherds are larger than those at other sites in the coastal region, such as Wild Cane Cay, which witnessed uninterrupted settlement into the Postclassic period (McKillop 1987, 1996a, 2001). Second, the good preservation of organic remains, notably plant foods and wood charcoal, resembles the good preservation at other waterlogged sites in the region and contrasts with the poor preservation of organic remains at nearby drier sites.

How specialized was salt production along the coast of Belize during the Late Classic? Several lines of evidence from the Punta Ycacos salt works indicate salt production was specialized beyond the household level into work shops focused on production for export to nearby inland Maya

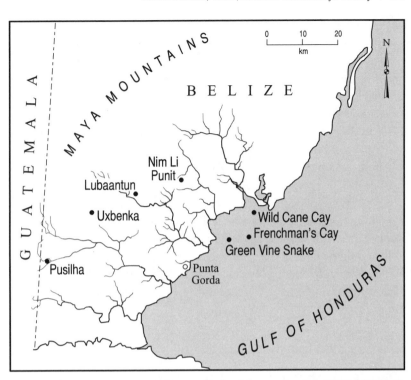

Map 6.1. Elite Maya at Port Honduras and Inland Sites in Southern Belize. By Mary Lee Eggart.

cities. The production was geographically localized near the raw material source. Production was spatially segregated from households and settlements. In fact, production was spatially segregated from other activities, such as eating, sleeping, and burial and from the royal and other elite Maya at inland cities.

The nature of the artifact assemblages at the salt work shops indicates low variability, arguing for a specific task. Most of the artifacts are remains of Punta Ycacos Unslipped pots and their vessel supports used in the brine-boiling process. A secondary group of artifacts are the Mangrove Unslipped and Warrie Red water jars used to store the brine and perhaps also the processed salt before it was hardened into salt cakes. A few sherds are from a fourth ceramic type, Moho Red, which were probably the remains of serving dishes used in salt festivals. This is a low diversity for a ceramic assemblage. Furthermore, there is not the variety of vessel forms and vessel quality—everyday to ceremonial—found at settlements in the area, such as Wild Cane Cay. The few stone tools do not constitute standard lithic assemblages at other settlements in the area.

How intensive was the salt production? It was likely seasonal, coinciding with the dry season for maximum solar evaporation, ease of boiling the brine, and the off-season for agricultural work. Salt production was twice as specialized as household production at Wild Cane Cay, as measured by standardization of the salt-making vessels used to make the salt cakes and a control sample of vessels from Wild Cane Cay.

These parameters indicate seasonal salt production by independent specialists. The specialized salt-making supplied coastal communities in the Port Honduras and nearby inland communities, whose trade goods were found at the salt work shops. The discovery and excavation of the Punta Ycacos salt work shops and the analyses of their artifacts indicates bulk resources, such as salt, were produced near lowland consumers. At least for the Late Classic Maya of southern Belize and the Pasion region of adjacent Guatemala, long-distance import of salt from the northern Yucatan salt flats was economically unnecessary.

Salt Production along the Belizean Coast

Salt works established along the coast of Belize during the Late Classic period provided a significant source of salt for the Late Classic Maya at the time of greatest demand in the southern lowlands. A variety of technologies was used in these coastal lagoon settings. The Placencia, Watson's Island, and Punta Ycacos salt works used the sal cocida technique, which was a good strategy in southern Belize, which had a long and unpredictable rainy season. Farther north, solar evaporation may have been more important. The dry season is longer and drier in the north. Salt production in the north relied on large plates that may have combined solar evaporation with boiling. Salt pans were noted historically on Ambergris Cay and may have been more widespread in the north prehistorically.

The Belizean salt works supplied salt to adjacent inland cities, linking coastal-inland exchange with existing sea transportation systems between the southern Maya highlands and the southern Maya lowlands during the Late Classic period. Trade between the southern and northern Maya lowlands developed in the Postclassic, with the rise to eminence of the northern lowland city of Chichen Itza. At that time, a thriving circum-Yucatan canoe trade route linked Chichen Itza, via its coastal trading port of Isla Cerritos, with Ambergris Cay, Wild Cane Cay, and other coastal ports. The emergence of trade between the northern and southern Maya lowlands can be traced to the Terminal Classic, with round structures in northern Belize (Chase and Chase 1982). With local Belizean salt and a paucity of evidence of trade between the northern and southern Maya lowlands during the Late Classic, salt from the vast salt flats on the north coast of the Yucatan played a minor if any role in supply the southern Maya lowlands. Belizean salt was closer at hand to the southern Maya lowlands cities.

Sea-Level Rise and Salt Production

The rise in sea level after the Classic period meant that many sites along the Yucatan coasts of Belize and Mexico, in addition to the Punta Ycacos salt works, were inundated and hidden from modern view. Moreover, coastal accretion of red mangroves in the near-shore waters along the mainland coast and offshore islands served to further hide ancient coastal sites. In some cases, such as Watson's Island, Kakalche, and Butterfly Wing, the ancient sites are noticeable in the mangroves by distinctive vegetation. In other cases, such as Pelican site in the Port Honduras, the sites are invisible from the ground surface and lie buried under modern mangroves and mangrove peat.

Excavation and dating of 10 submerged sites in the Port Honduras region indicates the sea rose about 1 m, which dramatically altered the land forms and vegetation patterns and buried Classic Maya sites. The traditional indicators of well-drained uplands desirable to the Classic Maya for settlement are not useful when searching for traces of Maya settlement along the Yucatan coast. The problem of "invisible sites" (Chase 1990; McKillop 1994b; Pyburn 1990; Steiner 1994) obscuring evidence of Maya settlement on dry ground in the Maya lowlands has the effect of underrepresenting ancient population. The submerged locations and the difficulty of excavating underwater or below the water table on land has limited the settlement data for the Late Classic Maya along the Belizean coast. The Punta Ycacos salt works provide a new dimension to our understanding of Late Classic Maya craft production using independent specialists working in work shops geographically separated from Maya settlements. What more lies buried beneath the sea?

Craft Specialization

The Late Classic Maya elite of the southern lowlands used exotic and well-crafted goods as gifts to other elite to forge political ties. Production and distribution of many everyday goods and resources occurred outside the city core and was beyond elite control. Still, Maya cities were the focus of procurement of exotic resources, production of some of the most highly crafted goods, and some degree of centralized distribution of everyday goods and resources. Evidence is difficult to find. In contrast to other ancient civilizations, Maya hieroglyphs do not record economic transactions, although they are a record of political and historical events and provide secondary evidence of the use of artifacts, through their pictorial display on pottery vessels and sometimes hieroglyphs identifying the owner, painter, or contents of vessels. Nor is there evidence of workshops of attached specialists making bulk goods, as elsewhere in Mesoamerica. Plazas could have been marketplaces, but we lack supporting epigraphic or artifactual evidence. Even bulk intraregional transport of food by tribute or taxation to feed the city folk or construction laborers is not evidenced by storehouses, although some bulk food must have been transported at least short distances to the cities. Fortunately, there is evidence of ancient Maya craft specialization.

The Classic Maya economy included both attached specialists producing highly crafted goods for the upper echelon of urban Maya society, as well as independent specialists making a variety of other goods for wider distribution among the Maya populace. The attached specialists worked in cities for royal and noble families, producing a limited number of elite ceramics, jade objects, and other goods from local and exotic resources that required high levels of skill. The independent specialists worked near sources of raw materials, according to resource availability, rather than concentrated in urban areas. Often this work was limited to the agricultural off-season. In some cases, production was on the scale of a cottage industry carried out in households, as in Janusek's (1999) "embedded specialization." The noncentralized organization of independent specialists reflects Classic Maya political economy, which contrasts with the centralized political economy of the Inca, Chimu, and Moche.

Maya kings and other urban royalty established and maintained alliances with the local elite in areas of independent specialization in order to ensure a supply of their goods and resources, as well as to maintain political control. If precious goods were used to maintain and solidify power relationships by horizontal exchange among the Classic Maya elite, then these same goods could be used to forge ties vertically with elite of lesser rank, including those in outlying communities. Political ties forged with elite of lower rank at minor centers within the city's region resulted in a downward distribution of exotics and highly crafted goods. Political alliances with lesser elite are recorded in hieroglyphic texts. One purpose or benefit from such a vertical alliance is economic: certainly we have evidence of political alliances later in time among the Aztecs, who variously created alliances or conquered new lands in part in order to obtain desired goods and resources.

The powerful Maya at inland cities in southern Belize forged political ties with their coastal neighbors through marriage alliances into the coastal lineages in order to ensure a supply of coastal resources and access to goods from farther away transported along coastal canoe trade routes. The impact of inland Maya on the coast is indicated by the Lubaantun-style figurine whistles and "unit-stamped" pottery that were recovered at coastal sites, in addition to other goods, such as polychrome vases, that may have been offered as gifts by the inland Maya. However, the bottom line is that the coast was the source of stingray spines and other ritual paraphernalia of marine origin, seafood, and salt, as well as a link to the sea trade for obsidian and other goods and resources obtained from more distant locations. Production and distribution of obsidian, salt, and marine resources were focused on the coastal area, in the "periphery" of the region. The coastal Maya on Wild Cane Cay received obsidian on a direct trade route from the Ixtepeque and El Chayal obsidian sources during the Classic period and not via the inland cities of southern Belize (McKillop et al. 1988). It has been suggested that "precious items entered the system at the top and gradually worked their way down through society" (Leventhal 1990). In the Port Honduras, at least some exotic items did not enter the region at the political seat of power in the major city, but instead on the coast—away from the political seat of power. Together with the control of production and distribution of salt on the coast, the only way for the inland Maya leaders to maintain access to coastal resources as well as exotic goods from the sea trade route was through alliances with the coastal Maya.

Production and distribution outside the city core weakened the centralized economic control of the Maya city-state. Trading ports on the periphery of regions, such as Wild Cane Cay, also weakened the elite economic control of procurement of goods and resources from farther away, including obsidian. It was politically and economically advantageous for the elite at major cities to forge ties with elite in peripheries who controlled local economic production and distribution.

The separation of Maya economy and power can be seen in the production of resources and products within the Maya lowlands, notably chert, salt, and utilitarian and serving vessels. Production occurred near localized abundance of the resource and spatially separated from elite control at major cities (see also Potter and King 1995). These and other resources were traded limited distances, but constituted the bulk of Maya trade. Vertical reciprocal exchanges between elite at major cities and those at lower-order communities, such as the situation described for Wild Cane Cay in southern Belize, certainly would have helped maintain access to economically important resources.

Production versus Trade and the Development of the Classic Maya

How important was production and distribution within the southern Maya lowlands to the Late Classic economy and society? What was the role of trade with the Maya highlands in the development of the Classic Maya civilization? Prestige items desired by the royal and other noble Maya at lowland Maya cities during the Classic period included finely crafted painted pots, elaborate clothing, and feather work made in royal work shops in the cities, but also some materials and goods acquired from within their realm or from farther away, including stingray spines and other marine resources from Maya coasts, granite and chert from within the southern lowlands, and jade, obsidian, and other materials from outside the southern Maya lowlands. Transport costs varied, with Ixtepeque and El Chayal obsidian, as well as Motagua River jade, less "exotic" to the Port Honduras Maya than to the Maya farther north in Belize. Similarly, Maya Mountain granite used for metates or Colha chert for stone tools were transported beyond the source areas, yet were not necessarily considered "long-distance" trade goods, even though their transport costs were greater than for local materials.

Trade goods included raw materials such as stingray spines that required no modification and others such as jade brought to lowland cities for manufacture into "highly crafted" goods. Tourtellot and Sabloff's (1972) interpretation of reciprocal elite trade in precious goods was that it was "not critical to bringing about changes in the level of social-cultural integration from ranked to state society and also has only secondary significance." By way of contrast, Freidel's (1979) "interaction model" sees the development of the Classic civilization derived from interregional communication and trade among elites. Trade was manifested by elite goods, public architecture with painted and stuccoed facades, and shared iconography. World systems theory applied to the Maya area, with the substitution of precious goods for the bulk items in Wallerstein's (1974) original model, also ties the exchange of goods and resources to the elite and economy to power. Blanton and Feinman (1984) noted the importance of controlling the flow of precious goods, and they argued for the movement of these goods from the periphery to the core as a stimulus in cultural development elsewhere in Mesoamerica.

Rathje's (1971; Rathje et al. 1978) theory, namely, that the Classic Maya civilization developed from the organizational skills the central lowland Maya needed to procure the basic resources of salt, obsidian, and basalt, implies bulk transport of goods over long distances. Various researchers have pointed out that Rathje's resources were not imported in bulk (McKillop 1980, 1987). Certainly bulk transport in preindustrial societies does occur, as with the overland salt trade across the Sahara, but not if there are local sources of the basic resource. The Punta Ycacos salt works and similar salt works elsewhere along the Belizean coast demonstrate that long-distance transport of salt was unnecessary during the Late Classic period for the supply zone of the Belizean salt.

Could it be that production and distribution of basic resources such as salt at a local and intraregional level helped foster the development of Late Classic Maya society, as elsewhere, such as Mesopotamia (Johnson 1973) or highland Mesoamerica (Sanders and Price 1968)? Certainly the non-centralized nature of Late Classic Maya production and distribution systems, as evidenced by salt, chert, and some classes of pottery, required both horizontal alliances among Maya royalty and vertical alliances with lesser lords, to maintain political integrity and a supply of desired goods and resources. In the case of the Port Honduras, vertical alliances were critical to maintaining access to exotic materials from distant lands traded by sea, ritual paraphernalia such as stingray spines for their royal ceremonies, and basic resources such as salt produced by independent specialists.

If salt was transported by sea in canoes from the north coast of the Yucatan throughout ancient Maya prehistory, then there should be evidence of continuous communication between people in the southern and northern Maya lowlands. This is not the case for the Late Classic period. Moreover, any disruptions in the supply of salt would have met with an effort—even militaristic—to reopen the flow the salt to the Late Classic Maya of the southern lowlands. The lack of consistent and close communication between people in the southern and northern Maya lowlands, particularly during the Late Classic, when the salt needs were the greatest in the southern lowlands, demonstrates that the southern Maya lowlanders were not dependent on the salt from the north coast of the Yucatan at this time. Salt from the coast of Belize was closer. The Belize salt was traded within existing regional trade networks. It was integrated into the coastal-inland trade of luxury and everyday maritime resources. Furthermore, the coastal-inland salt trade was integrated into the trade networks from the southern Maya highland obsidian sources that transported obsidian, jade, and other exotics along the coast of Belize and then inland to Late Classic cities. The coastal-inland trade took place within friendly political and economic territory. The trade of salt between the Belizean coast and the interior of the southern Maya lowlands fits within models of ancient trade in complex societies in which long-distance trade is limited to relatively few high-value items, whereas the supply of everyday goods and resources—such as salt—was from nearby sources.

Lessons from the Coastal Maya

The evidence of specialized salt production on the southern coast of Belize lies buried beneath the sea in Punta Ycacos Lagoon. The discovery and excavations of the salt work shops in the lagoon and the interpretation of the artifactual remains underscore the existence of specialized, nondomestic production geographically separated from Late Classic Maya cities. The research also points out the complex interplay of cultural and environmental forces in ancient Maya settlement choices. Finally, we are reminded of the ephemeral nature of life along low-lying coastlines subject to sea-level rise. Some places, such as Wild Cane Cay, were able for a time to coexist with rising sea levels, in part owing to anthropogenic soil buildup from ancient garbage heaps and stone building foundations. Without continued settlement, other places, such as Pelican Cay, were reclaimed by mangrove swamps, with no visible traces of the buried Classic period Maya settlement from the ground surface. Still other low-lying coasts, such as the Punta Ycacos Lagoon salt work shops, were submerged by rising seas, hiding the evidence of the production of salt, the white gold of the ancient Maya (Mosnier 1994).

Appendix 1. Catalog (Location) Numbers for Artifacts from the Salt Work Shops

Table 1. Catalog (Location) Numbers for Stingray Lagoon Site

Site	Location	Description
3218091	1	General Surface Collection
3218091	2	Cluster A
3218091	3	Cluster A South
3218091	4	Cluster A North
3218091	5	Northwest Hole
3218091	6	Southwest Corner
3218091	7	Cluster 1
3218091	8	Cluster 2
3218091	9	Cluster 3
3218091	10	Cluster 4
3218091	11	Cluster 5
3218091	12	Cluster 6
3218091	13	Cluster 7
3218091	14	Cluster 8
3218091	15	Cluster 9
3218091	16	Cluster 17
3218091	17	Cluster 18
3218091	18	Cluster 19
3218091	19	Other Cluster
3218091	20	Unit 1a, 0–10 cm depth
3218091	21	Unit 1b, 0–10 cm depth
3218091	22	Unit 1c, 0–10 cm depth
3218091	23	Unit 1d, 0–10 cm depth
3218091	24	General Surface Collection, 1992

Table 2. Catalog (Location) Numbers for Orlando's Jewfish Site

Site	Location	Description
3218010	1	General Surface Collection
3218010	2	Unit 1A, 0–10 cm depth
3218010	3	Unit 1A, 10–20 cm depth
3218010	4	Unit 1C, 10–20 cm depth
3218010	5	Unit 2A, 0–10 cm depth
3218010	6	Unit 2A, 10–20 cm depth
3218010	7	Unit 2A, 20–30 cm depth
3218010	8	Unit 2C, 0–10 cm depth
3218010	9	Unit 1C, 0–10 cm depth

Table 3. Catalog (Location) Numbers for David Westby Site

Site	Location	Description
3218011	1	Surface Collection
3218011	2	Shovel Test 1, 0–20 cm depth
3218011	3	Shovel Test 1, 10–20 cm depth
3218011	4	Shovel Test 2, 0–20 cm depth
3218011	5	Shovel Test 3, 0–20 cm depth
3218011	6	Shovel Test 4, surface
3218011	7	Shovel Test 4, 0–20 cm depth
3218011	8	Shovel Test 5, surface
3218011	9	Shovel Test 5, 0–20 cm depth
3218011	10	Shovel Test 5, 20–40 cm depth
3218011	11	Excavation Unit 1a, 0–10 cm depth
3218011	12	Excavation Unit 1a, 10–20 cm depth
3218011	13	Excavation Unit 1d, 0–10 cm depth

Table 4. Catalog (Location) Numbers for Killer Bee Site

Site	Location	Description
331801	1	Surface Collection
331801	2	Mound 1, Unit 1, 0–20 cm depth
331801	3	Mound 1, Unit 1, 20–40 cm depth
331801	4	Mound 1, Unit 1, 40–60 cm depth
331801	5	Shovel Test 1, 0–20 cm depth
331801	6	Shovel Test 1, 20–40 cm depth
331801	7	Shovel Test 1, 40–60 cm depth
331801	8	Shovel Test 1, 60–80 cm depth

Appendix 2. Weights and Counts of Fired Clay from Salt Work Shops

Table 1. Weights and Counts of Fired Clay from Stingray Lagoon Excavations

Site	Unit	Level (cm)	Weight (g)	Count (#)
321809	1a	0–10	13,946.9	5,101+
321809	1b	0–10	10,694.4	6,597
321809	1c	0–10	15,223.8	14,968
321809	1d	0–10	5,758.0	1,547
Total			45,623.1	28,213

Table 2. Counts and Weights of Fired Clay from Orlando's Jewfish Excavations

Unit	Level (cm)	Weight (g)	Count (#)
2a	0–10	4,571.5	2,079
2a	10–20	77.6	72
2a	20–30	108.7	78
2c	0–10	1,606.1	988
2c	10–20	616.8	346
Total		6,980.7	3,563

Table 3. Counts and Weights of Fired Clay from David Westby Excavations

Location	Unit	Depth (cm)	Weight (g)	Count (#)
11	1a	0–10	617.57	822
12	1d	10–20	unknown	unknown
13	1d	0–10	unknown	unknown
Total			6,837.59	822

Table 4. Counts and Weights of Fired Clay from Killer Bee Excavations

Site	Location (cm)	Unit (g)	Depth (#)	Weight	Count
331801	2	Mound 1, Unit 1	0–20	230.6	65
331801	3	Mound 1, Unit 1	20–40	1,163.5	120
331801	4	Mound 1, Unit 1	40–60	360.9	42
331801	5	Shovel Test 1	0–20	1,262.4	755
331801	6	Shovel Test 1	20–40	495.9	182
331801	7	Shovel Test 1	40–60	456.1	606
331801	8	Shovel Test 1	60–80	3,424.4	415
Total				9,226.2	2,828

Appendix 3. Catalog Numbers for Artifacts Illustrated in the Text

Figure 3.3   (*a*) 32/180-9-1/1-28, (*b*) 32/180-9-4/1-51

Figure 3.4   (*a*) 32/180-9-1/1-38, (*b*) 32/180-9-4/1-47, (*c*) 32/180-9-1/1-1, (*d*) 32/180-9-4/1-37, (*e*) 32/180-9-4/1-70

Figure 3.5   (*a*) 32/180-9-4/1-48, (*b*) 32/180-9-6/1-1, (*c*) 32/180-9-4/1-69

Figure 3.6   (*a*) 32/180-9-2/1-14, (*b*) 32/180-9-4/1-49, (*c*) 32/180-9-4/1-46

Figure 3.7   (*a*) 32/180-9-2/1-23, (*b*) 32/180-9-2/1-71, (*c*) 32/180-9-4/1-3

Figure 3.8   (*a*) 32/180-9-3/1-22, (*b*) 32/180-9-2/1-70, (*c*) 32/180-9-2/1-5

Figure 3.10   32/180-9-15/1-9

Figure 3.11   *top:* 32/180-9-1/1-56; *middle:* 32/180-9-23/1-32; *bottom:* 32/180-9-23/1-5

Figure 3.12   *top:* 32/180-11-12/1-9; *bottom:* 32/180-11-1/1-89

Figure 3.13   *from left to right:* 32/180-9-3/1-34, 32/180-9-19/1-8, 32/180-9-4/1-204, 32/180-9-3/1-33

Figure 3.14   *from left to right:* 33/180-1-1/1-27, 33/180-1-1/1-28, 33/180-1-1/1-29, 33/180-1-1/1-30

Figure 3.15   32/180-9/1-55

Figure 3.16   Killer Bee vessel supports with attached socket or base fragments: (*a*) 33/180-1-3/1-28, (*b*) 33/180-1-3/1-29, (*c*) 33/180-1-1/1-14, (*d*) 33/180-1-1/1-12, (*e*) 33/180-1-1/1-99, (*f*) 33/180-1-1/1-95, (*g*) 33/180-1-2/1-2, (*h*) 33/180-1-9/1-99

Figure 3.17   Stingray Lagoon vessel supports with attached socket or base fragments: (*a*) 32/180-9-21/1-3, (*b*) 32/180-9-1/1-65, (*c*) 32/180-9-1/1-54

Figure 3.18   Vessel supports with attached socket or base fragments from Orlando's Jewfish, Killer Bee, and Stingray Lagoon: (*a*) 32/180-10-1/1-164, (*b*) 33/180-1-1/1-95, (*c*) 32/180-10-1/1-165, (*d*) 32/180-9-2/1-98

Figure 3.19   32/180-10-1/1-199

Figure 3.20   32/180-9-24/1-63

References Cited

Abrams, Elliot M.

1994 *How the Maya Built Their World: Energetics and Ancient Architecture.* University of Texas Press, Austin.

Adams, Richard E. W.

1970 "Suggested Classic Period Occupational Specialization in the Southern Maya Lowlands." In *Monographs and Papers in Maya Archaeology,* edited by William R. Bullard Jr., 487–502. Papers of the Peabody Museum of Archaeology and Ethnology 61. Harvard University, Cambridge, Mass.

1971 *The Ceramics of Altar de Sacrificios.* Papers of the Peabody Museum of Archaeology and Ethnology 63(1). Harvard University, Cambridge, Mass.

Adshead, S. A. M.

1992 *Salt and Civilization.* St. Martin's Press, New York.

Alcara-Herrera, Javier A., John S. Jacob, Maria Luisa Machain Castillo, and Raymond W. Neck

1994 "Holocene Palaeosalinity in a Maya Wetland, Belize, Inferred from the Microfaunal Assemblage." *Quaternary Research* 41:121–30.

Andrews, Anthony P.

1983 *Maya Salt Production and Trade.* University of Arizona Press, Tucson.

1984 "Long-Distance Exchange among the Maya: A Comment on Marcus." *American Antiquity* 49:826–28.

1990 "The Role of Trading Ports in Maya Civilization." In *Vision and Revision in Maya Studies,* edited by Flora Clancey and Peter D. Harrison, 159–67. University of New Mexico Press, Albuquerque.

1993 "Late Postclassic Lowland Maya Archaeology." *Journal of World Prehistory* 7:35–69.

Andrews, Anthony P., and Robert Corletta

1995 "A Brief History of Underwater Archaeology in the Maya Area." *Ancient Mesoamerica* 6:101–17.

Andrews, E. Wyllys, IV

1969 *The Archaeological Use and Distribution of Mollusca in the Maya Low-*

lands. Middle American Research Institute, Publication 34. Tulane University, New Orleans.

Andrews, E. Wyllys, IV, Michael P. Simmons, Elizabeth S. Wing, and E. Wyllys Andrews V

1975   "Excavations of an Early Shell Midden on Isla Cancun, Quintana Roo, Mexico." Middle American Research Institute, Publication 31, 147–97. Tulane University, New Orleans.

Arnold, Philip J., III

1991   "Dimensional Standardization and Production Scale in Mesoamerican Ceramics." *Latin American Antiquity* 2:363–70.

Arnold, Philip J., III, Christopher A. Pool, Ronald R. Kneebone, and Robert S. Santley

1993   "Intensive Ceramic Production and Classic Period Political Economy in the Sierra de los Tuxtlas, Veracruz, Mexico." *Ancient Mesoamerica* 4:175–91.

Baker, David B.

1999   "A Comparison of Burned Botanical Remains from Two Maya Sites in Belize: Stingray Lagoon and Pork and Doughboy Point." Unpublished manuscript, Department of Geography and Anthropology, Louisiana State University, Baton Rouge.

Balkansky, Andrew K., Gary M. Feinman, and Linda M. Nichols

1997   "Pottery Kilns of Ancient Ejutla, Oaxaca, Mexico." *Journal of Field Archaeology* 24:139–60.

Ball, Joseph W.

1977   "An Hypothetical Outline of Coastal Maya Prehistory: 300 B.C.–A.D. 1200." In *Social Process in Maya Prehistory,* edited by Norman Hammond, 167–96. Academic Press, New York.

1978   "Archaeological Pottery of the Yucatan-Campeche Coast." In *Studies in the Archaeology of Coastal Yucatan and Campeche, Mexico.* Middle American Research Institute, Publication 46(2). Tulane University, New Orleans.

Becker, Marshall J.

1973   "Archaeological Evidence for Occupational Specialization among the Classic Period Maya at Tikal, Guatemala. *American Antiquity* 38:396–406.

Binford, Michael W., Alan L. Kolata, Mark Brenner, John W. Janusek, Matthew T. Seddon, Mark Abbott, and Jason H. Curtis

1997   "Climate Variation and the Rise and Fall of an Andean Civilization." *Quaternary Research* 47:235–48.

Bird, E. C. F.

1993   *Submerging Coasts: The Effects of a Rising Sea Level on Coastal Environments.* John Wiley and Sons, New York.

Blanton, Richard, and Gary M. Feinman

1984   "The Mesoamerican World System." *American Anthropologist* 86:673–82.

Bloch, M. R.

1963   "The Social Influence of Salt." *Scientific American* 209(1):88–99.

Blom, Frans

1932   "Commerce, Trade, and Monetary Units of the Maya." In *Middle American Papers*, Middle American Research Series, Publication 4, 531–56. Tulane University, New Orleans.

Bloom, Arthur L.

1979   *Atlas of Sea Level Curves*. Cornell University Press, Ithaca, N.Y.

1983   "Sea Level and Coastal Changes." In *Late Quaternary Environments of the United States*, vol. 2: *The Holocene*, edited by Henry E. Wright Jr., 42–51. University of Minnesota Press, Minneapolis.

Boxt, Matthew A.

1989   "Initial Report of the 1986–87 Field Season at Sarteneja, Belize: A Coastal Site in Northern Belize." In *Coastal Maya Trade*, edited by Heather McKillop and Paul F. Healy, 29–42. Occasional Papers in Anthropology 8. Trent University, Peterborough, Ontario, Canada.

Brady, James E., Joseph W. Ball, Ronald L. Bishop, Duncan C. Pring, Norman Hammond, and Rupert A. Housley

1998   "The Lowland Maya 'Protoclassic': A Reconsideration of Its Nature and Significance." *Ancient Mesoamerica* 9:17–54.

Brandehoff-Pracht, Jodi

1995   "Test Excavation at Pork and Doughboy Point, Belize." Master's thesis, Department of Geography and Anthropology, Louisiana State University, Baton Rouge.

Braud, Melissa R.

1996   "Underwater Test Excavations at David Westby Site, South Coastal Belize." Master's thesis, Department of Geography and Anthropology, Louisiana State University, Baton Rouge.

Brumfiel, Elizabeth M.

1987   "Elite and Utilitarian Crafts in the Aztec State." In *Specialization, Exchange, and Complex Societies*, edited by Elizabeth M. Brumfiel and Timothy K. Earle, 102–18. Cambridge University Press, New York.

Brumfiel, Elizabeth M., and Timothy K. Earle

1987   "Specialization, Exchange, and Complex Societies: An Introduction." In *Specialization, Exchange, and Complex Societies*. Edited by Elizabeth M. Brumfiel and Timothy K. Earle, 1–9. Cambridge University Press, New York.

Burke, Randolf B.

1993   "How Have Holocene Sea Level Rise and Antecedent Topography Influenced Barrier Reef Development?" In *Proceedings of Colloquium on Global Aspects of Coral Reefs, Health, and History*, edited by Robert Ginsburg, 14–20. University of Miami, Coral Gables, Fla.

Cameron, Cornelia C., and Curtis A. Palmer

1995   *The Mangrove Peat of the Tobacco Range Islands, Belize*. Atoll Research Bulletin 431. Smithsonian Institution, Washington, D.C.

Carr, H. Sorayya

1986 "Preliminary Results of Analysis of Fauna." In *Archaeology at Cerros, Belize, Central America*, vol. 1, edited by Robin A. Robertson and David A. Freidel, 127–46. Southern Methodist University Press, Dallas.

Charlton, Thomas H.

1969 "Texcoco Fabric-Marked Pottery, Tlatelco, and Salt-Making." *American Antiquity* 34:73–76.

Charlton, Thomas H., Deborah L. Nichols, and Cynthia Otis Charlton

2000 "Otumba and Its Neighbors." *Ancient Mesoamerica* 11:247–65.

Chase, Diane Z.

1981 "The Maya Postclassic at Santa Rita Corozal." *Archaeology* 34:25–33.

1982 "Spatial and Temporal Variability in Postclassic Northern Belize." Ph.D. diss., University of Pennsylvania, University Microfilms, Ann Arbor.

1990 "The Invisible Maya: Population History and Archaeology at Santa Rita Corozal." In *Precolumbian Population History in the Maya Lowlands*, edited by T. Patrick Culbert and Don S. Rice, 199–213. University of New Mexico Press, Albuquerque.

Chase, Diane Z., and Arlen F. Chase

1982 "Yucatec Influence in Terminal Classic Northern Belize." *American Antiquity* 47:596–614.

1986 *Offerings to the Gods: Maya Archaeology at Santa Rita Corozal*. University of Central Florida, Orlando.

1989 "Routes of Trade and Communication and the Integration of Maya Society: The Vista from Santa Rita Corozal." In *Coastal Maya Trade*, edited by Heather McKillop and Paul F. Healy, 19–32. Occasional Papers in Anthropology 8. Trent University, Peterborough, Ontario, Canada.

1992 "An Archaeological Assessment of Mesoamerican Elites." In *Mesoamerican Elites*, edited by Diane Z. Chase and Arlen F. Chase, 303–17. University of Oklahoma Press, Norman.

Choi, Dong Ryong, and Robert N. Ginsburg

1982 "Siliclastic Foundations of Quaternary Reefs in the Southernmost Belize Lagoon, British Honduras." *Geological Society of America Bulletin* 93: 116–26.

Choi, Dong Ryong, and Charles W. Holmes

1982 "Foundations of Quaternary Reefs in South-Central Belize Lagoon, Central America." *American Association of Petroleum Geologists Bulletin* 66(12): 2663–81.

Clark, John E.

1986 "From Mountains to Molehills: A Critical Review of Teotihuacan's Obsidian Industry." In *Economic Aspects of Prehispanic Highland Mexico*, edited by Barry L. Isaac, 23–74. Supplement 2, JAI Press, Greenwich, Conn.

1995 "Craft Specialization as an Archaeological Category." *Research in Economic Anthropology* 16:267–94.

Clark, John E., and Stephen Houston

1998   "Craft Specialization, Gender, and Personhood among the Post-Conquest Maya of Yucatan, Mexico." In *Craft and Social Identity*, edited by Cathy Costin and Rita Wright, 31–46. Archeological Papers 8. American Anthropological Association, Washington, D.C.

Cobos, Raphael

1989   "Shelling In: Marine Mollusca at Chichen Itza." In *Coastal Maya Trade*, edited by Heather McKillop and Paul F. Healy, 49–58. Occasional Papers in Anthropology 8. Trent University, Peterborough, Ontario, Canada.

Coe, Michael D.

1978   *Lords of the Underworld: Masterpieces of Classic Maya Ceramics*. Art Museum, Princeton University/Princeton University Press, Princeton.

1982   *Old Gods and Young Heroes: The Pearlman Collection of Maya Ceramics*. Israel Museum, Jerusalem.

Coe, Michael D., and Kent V. Flannery

1967   *Early Cultures and Human Ecology in South Coastal Guatemala*. Smithsonian Contributions to Anthropology 3. Smithsonian Institution, Washington, D.C.

Costin, Cathy L.

1991   "Craft Specialization: Issues in Defining, Documenting, and Explaining the Organization of Production." *Archaeological Method and Theory* 3:1–56.

Cowgill, George L.

1993   "Comments on Andrew Sluyter's 'Long-Distance Staple Transport in Western Mesoamerica: Insights through Quantitative Modeling.'" *Ancient Mesoamerica* 4:201–3.

Coyston, Shannon, Christine D. White, and Henry P. Schwarcz

1999   "Dietary Carbonate Analysis of Bone and Enamel for Two Sites in Belize." In *Reconstructing Ancient Maya Diet*, edited by Christine D. White, 221–43. University of Utah Press, Salt Lake City.

Craig, Alan K.

1966   *Geography of Fishing in British Honduras and Adjacent Coastal Areas*. Coastal Studies Technical Report 28(66). Louisiana State University, Baton Rouge.

Culbert, T. Patrick

1991   "Maya Political History and Elite Interaction: A Summary View." In *Classic Maya Political History*, edited by T. Patrick Culbert, 311–46. Cambridge University Press, New York.

Culbert, T. Patrick, and Don S. Rice, editors

1990   *Precolumbian Population History in the Maya Lowlands*. University of New Mexico Press, Albuquerque.

Curtis, Jason H., David A. Hodell, and Mark Brenner

1996   "Climate Variability on the Yucatan Peninsula (Mexico) during the Past 3,500 Years, and Implications for Maya Cultural Evolution." *Quaternary Research* 46:37–47.

Dahlin, Bruce

1983   "Climate and Prehistory on the Yucatan Peninsula." *Climatic Change* 5:245–63.

2000   "The Barricade and Abandonment of Chunchucmil: Implications for Northern Maya Warfare." *Latin American Antiquity* 11:283–98.

Dahlin, Bruce H., Anthony P. Andrews, Timothy Beach, Clara Bezanilla, Patrice Farrell, Sheryl Luzzadder-Beach, and Valerie McCormick

1998   "Punta Canbalam in Context: A Peripatetic Coastal Site in Northwest Campeche, Mexico." *Ancient Mesoamerica* 9:1–15.

DePratter, C. B., and J. D. Howard

1977   "History of Shoreline Changes Determined by Archaeological Dating: Georgia Coast, U.S.A." *Transactions of the Gulf Coast Association of Geological Societies* 27:252–58.

Dillon, Brian D.

1977   "Salinas de los Nueve Cerros, Alta Verapaz, Guatemala." Ballena Press Studies in Mesoamerican Art, Archaeology, and Ethnohistory No. 2. Ballena Press, Socorro, N.M.

Dixon, C. G.

1929   *Geology of Southern British Honduras.* Government Printer, Belize City, Belize.

Dochstader, Frederick J.

1964   *Indian Art of Middle America.* American Museum of Natural History, New York.

Dockall, J. E., and Harry J. Shafer

1993   "Testing the Producer-Consumer Model for Santa Rita Corozal, Belize." *Latin American Antiquity* 4:158–79.

Drennan, Robert D.

1984a   "Long-Distance Transport Costs in Pre-Hispanic Mesoamerica." *American Anthropologist* 86:105–12.

1984b   "Long-Distance Movement of Goods in the Mesoamerican Formative and Classic." *American Antiquity* 49:27–43.

Drill, Robert F., Lynton S. Land, Larry E. Mack, and Henry P. Schwarcz

1998   "A Submerged Stalactite from Belize: Petrography, Geochemistry, and Geochronology of Massive Marine Cementation." *Carbonates and Evaporates* 13:189–97.

Druc, Isabelle C.

2000   "Ceramic Production in San Marcos Acteopan, Puebla, Mexico." *Ancient Mesoamerica* 11:77–89.

Dunbar, James S., S. David Webb, and Michael Faught

1992   "Inundated Prehistoric Sites in Apalachee Bay, Florida, and the Search for the Clovis Shoreline." In *Paleoshorelines and Prehistory,* edited by Lucille Johnson, 117–46. CRC Press, Boca Raton, Fla.

Dunham, Peter S., Thomas R. Jamison, and Richard M. Leventhal

1989   "Secondary Development and Settlement Economies: The Classic Maya of

Southern Belize." In *Prehistoric Maya Economies of Belize,* edited by Patricia McAnany and Barry Isaac, 255–92. Research in Economic Anthropology, Supplement 4. JAI Press, Greenwich, Conn.

Dunn, Richard K.
1990   "Holocene Paleocoastal Reconstruction of Southern Ambergris Cay, Belize: And Archaeological Geology of the Marco Gonzalez Maya Site." Master's thesis, Department of Geology, Wichita State University.

Dunn, Richard K., and S. J. Mazzullo
1993   "Holocene Paleocoastal Reconstruction and Its Relationship to Marco Gonzalez, Ambergris Cay, Belize." *Journal of Field Archaeology* 10:453–68.

Earle, Timothy K.
1981   "CA Comment on Evolution of Specialized Pottery Production: A Trial Model, by Prudence M. Rice." *Current Anthropology* 22:230–31.

Eaton, Jack D.
1978   "Archaeological Survey of the Yucatan-Campeche Coast." In *Studies in the Archaeology of Coastal Yucatan and Campeche, Mexico.* Middle American Research Institute, Publication 46(1). Tulane University, New Orleans.

Ellison, Joanna C.
1989   "Pollen Analysis of Mangrove Sediments as a Sea Level Indicator: Assessment from Tongatapu, Tonga." *Palaeogeography, Palaeoecology, Palaeoclimatology* 74:327–41.

Ellison, Joanna C., and David R. Stoddart
1991   "Mangrove Ecosystem Collapse during Predicted Sea-Level Rise: Holocene Analogues and Implications." *Journal of Coastal Research* 7:151–65.

Emery, Kitty F.
1999   "Continuity and Variability in Postclassic Animal Use at Lamanai and Tipu, Belize." In *Reconstructing Ancient Maya Diet,* edited by Christine D. White, 61–81. University of Utah Press, Salt Lake City.

Esker, Dominic, Gregor P. Eberli, and Donald F. McNeill
1998   "The Structural and Sedimentological Controls on the Reoccupation of Quaternary Incised Valleys, Belize Southern Lagoon." *American Association of Petroleum Geologists Bulletin* 82(11):2075–109.

Eubanks, W. J., Jr.
1975   "Holocene Carbonate Sedimentation and Diagenesis, Ambergris Cay, Belize," In *Belize Shelf-Carbonate Sediments, Clastic Sediments, and Ecology,* edited by K. F. Wantland and W. C. Pusey III, 234–96. Studies in Geology 2. American Association of Petroleum Geologists, Tulsa.

Ewald, Ursula
1985   *The Mexican Salt Industry: 1560–1980.* Gustav Fischer Verlag, New York.

Fairbanks, Richard G.
1989   "A 17,000–year Glacio-Eustatic Sea Level Record: Influence of Glacial Melting Rates on the Younger Dryas Event and Deep-Ocean Circulation." *Nature* 342:637–42.

Fairbridge, R. W.
1987 "The Spectra of Sea Level in a Holocene Time Frame." In *Climate, History, Periodicity, and Predictability,* edited by M. R. Rampino, J. E. Sanders, W. S. Newman, and L. K. Koningsson, 127–42. Van Nostrand, New York.

Fash, William L.
1991 *Scribes, Warriors, and Kings.* Thames and Hudson, New York.

Feinman, Gary
1999 "Rethinking Our Assumptions: Economic Specialization at the Household Scale in Ancient Ejutla, Oaxaca, Mexico," In *Pottery and People,* edited by James M. Skibo and Gary M. Feinman, 81–98. University of Utah Press, Salt Lake City.

Feldman, Lawrence
1971 "A Tumpline Economy: Production and Distribution Systems of Early Central-East Guatemala." Ph.D. diss., Department of Anthropology, Pennsylvania State University.
1974 "Shells from Afar: 'Panamic' Mollusca in Maya Sites." In *Mesoamerican Archaeology: New Approaches,* edited by Norman Hammond, 129–34. University of Texas Press, Austin.

Flannery, Kent V.
1968 "The Olmec and the Valley of Oaxaca: A Model for Inter-regional Interaction in Formative Times." In *Dumbarton Oaks Conference on the Olmec,* edited by Elizabeth P. Benson, 79–110. Dumbarton Oaks, Washington, D.C.

Foias, Antonia E., and Ronald L. Bishop
1997 "Changing Ceramic Production and Exchange in the Petexbatun Region, Guatemala: Reconsidering the Classic Maya Collapse." *Ancient Mesoamerica* 8:275–91.

Folan, William J., Joel Gunn, Jack D. Eaton, and Robert W. Patch
1983 "Paleoclimatological Patterning in Southern Mesoamerica." *Journal of Field Archaeology* 10:453–68.

Fosberg, F. Raymond, David R. Stoddart, M.-H. Sachet and D. L. Spellman
1982 *Plants of the Belize Cays.* Atoll Research Bulletin 258. Smithsonian Institution, Washington, D.C.

Freidel, David A.
1978 "Maritime Adaptation and the Rise of Maya Civilization: The View from Cerros, Belize." In *Prehistoric Coastal Adaptations: The Economy and Ecology of Maritime Middle America,* edited by Barbara L. Stark and Barbara Voorhies, 239–65. Academic Press, New York.
1979 "Culture Areas and Interaction Spheres: Contrasting Approaches to the Emergence of Civilization in the Maya Lowlands." *American Antiquity* 44:37–54.
1992 "Children of the First Father's Skull: Terminal Classic Warfare in the Northern Maya Lowlands and the Transformation of Kingship and Elite Hierarchies." In *Mesoamerican Elites,* edited by Diane Z. Chase and Arlen F. Chase, 99–117. University of Oklahoma Press, Norman.

Freidel, David A., and Vernon Scarborough
1982   "Subsistence, Trade, and Development of the Coastal Maya." In *Maya Subsistence*, edited by Kent V. Flannery, 131–55. Academic Press, New York.

Fried, Morton H.
1967   *The Evolution of Political Society.* Random House, New York.

Fry, Robert E.
1980   "Models of Exchange for Major Shape Classes of Lowland Maya Pottery." In *Models and Methods in Regional Exchange*, edited by Robert E. Fry, 3–18. Society for American Archaeology Papers 1. Society for American Archaeology, Washington, D.C.

Gann, Thomas W. F.
1918   *The Maya Indians of Southern Yucatan and Northern British Honduras.* Bureau of American Ethnology Bulletin 64. Smithsonian Institution, Washington, D.C.

Gifford, James C.
1976   *Prehistoric Pottery Analysis and the Ceramics of Barton Ramie in the Belize Valley.* Memoirs of the Peabody Museum of Archaeology and Ethnology 18. Harvard University, Cambridge, Mass.

Graham, Elizabeth
1987   "Resource Diversity in Belize and Its Implications for Models of Lowland Trade." *American Antiquity* 54:753–67.
1989   "Brief Synthesis of Coastal Site Data from Colson Point, Placencia, and Marco Gonzalez, Belize." In *Coastal Maya Trade*, edited by Heather McKillop and Paul F. Healy, 135–54. Occasional Papers in Anthropology 8. Trent University, Peterborough, Ontario, Canada.
1991   "Archaeological Insights into Colonial Period Life at Tipu, Belize." In *The Spanish Borderlands in Pan-American Perspective. Columbian Consequences*, vol. 3, edited by David Hurst Thomas, 319–35. Smithsonian Institution Press, Washington, D.C.
1994   *The Highlands of the Lowlands: Environment and Archaeology in the Stann Creek District, Belize, Central America.* Monographs in World Archaeology 19. Prehistory Press, Madison, Wis.
1998   "Metaphor and Metaphorism: Some Thoughts on Environmental Metahistory." In *Advances in Historical Ecology*, edited by William Balée, 119–37. Columbia University Press, New York.

Graham, Elizabeth A., and David M. Pendergast
1989   "Excavations at the Marco Gonzalez Site, Ambergris Cay, Belize, 1986." *Journal of Field Archaeology* 16:1–16.

Guderjan, Thomas H.
1988   "Maya Maritime Trade at San Juan, Ambergris Caye, Belize." Ph.D. diss., Department of Anthropology, Southern Methodist University, Dallas.

Guderjan, Thomas H., and James F. Garber, editors
1995   *Maya Maritime Trade, Settlement, and Population on Ambergris Caye, Belize.* Labyrinthos Press, Culver City, Calif.

Guderjan, Thomas H., James F. Garber, and Hermann A. Smith
1989   "Maritime Trade on Ambergris Cay, Belize." In *Coastal Maya Trade*, edited by Heather McKillop and Paul F. Healy, 123–33. Occasional Papers in Anthropology 8. Trent University, Peterborough, Ontario, Canada.

Gunn, Joel, and Richard E. W. Adams
1981   "Climate Change, Culture, and Civilization in North America." *World Archaeology* 13:87–100.

Guyton, Arthur C.
1987   *Human Physiology and Mechanisms of Disease*, 4th ed. W. B. Saunders, Philadelphia.

Halley, Robert B., Eugene A. Shinn, J. Harold Hudson, and Barbara Lidz
1977   "Recent and Relict Topography of Boo Bee Patch Reef, Belize." *Proceedings of the Third International Coral Reef Symposium*, vol. 2, 29–35. University of Miami, Coral Gables, Fla.

Hamblin, Nancy
1980   "Animal Utilization by the Cozumel Maya: Interpretation through Faunal Analysis." Ph.D. diss., Department of Anthropology, University of Arizona, Tucson.

Hammond, Norman
1975   *Lubaantun: A Classic Maya Realm*. Monographs of the Peabody Museum of Archaeology and Ethnology 2. Harvard University, Cambridge, Mass.

Harrison, Peter D.
1999   *The Lords of Tikal*. Thames and Hudson, New York.

Healy, Paul F., Heather I. McKillop, and Bernetta Walsh
1984   "Analysis of Obsidian from Moho Cay, Belize: New Evidence on Classic Maya Trade Routes." *Science* 225:414–17.

High, L. R., Jr.
1975   "Geomorphology and Sedimentology of Holocene Coastal Deposits, Belize." In *Belize Shelf—Carbonate Sediments, Clastic Sediments, and Ecology*, edited by K. F. Wantland and W. C. Pusey III, 1–40. Studies in Geology 2. American Association of Petroleum Geologists, Tulsa.

Hodell, David A., Jason H. Curtis, and Mark Brenner
1995   "Possible Role of Climate in the Collapse of Classic Maya Civilization." *Nature* 375:391–94.

Hult, Weston, and Thomas R. Hester
1995   "The Lithics of Ambergris Caye." In *Maya Maritime Trade, Settlement, and Population on Ambergris Caye, Belize*, edited by Thomas H. Guderjan and James F. Garber, 139–61. Labyrinthos Press, Culver City, Calif.

Jacob, John S.
1992   "The Agroecological Evolution of Cobweb Swamp, Belize." Ph.D. diss., Texas A & M University, College Station.

Janusek, John W.
1999   "Craft and Local Power: Embedded Specialization in Tiwanaka Cities." *Latin American Antiquity* 10:107–31.

Johnson, Gary A.
1973 *Local Exchange and Early State Development in Southwestern Iran.* Anthropological Papers 51. Museum of Anthropology, University of Michigan, Ann Arbor.

Johnson, M. S., and D. R. Chaffey
1974 *An Inventory of the Southern Coastal Plain Pine Forests, Belize.* Land Resource Study No. 15. Ministry of Overseas Development, Land Resources Division, Tolworth Tower, Surbiton, Surrey, England.

Jones, John
1994 "Pollen Evidence for Early Settlement and Agriculture in Northern Belize." *Palynology* 18:205–11.

Joyce, Rosemary A.
2000 *Gender and Power in Prehispanic Mesoamerica.* University of Texas Press, Austin.

Joyce, Thomas A.
1929 "Report on the British Museum Expedition to British Honduras, 1929." *Journal of the Royal Anthropological Institute* 59:439.

Joyce, Thomas A., J. Cooper-Clark, and J. Eric S. Thompson
1927 "Report on the British Museum Expedition to British Honduras, 1927." *Journal of the Royal Anthropological Institute* 57:295.

Joyce, Thomas A., Thomas W. F. Gann, E. C. Gruning, and R. C. E. Long
1928 "Report on the British Museum Expedition to British Honduras, 1928." *Journal of the Royal Anthropological Institute* 58:323.

Kidder, Alfred V.
1954 "Miscellaneous Archaeological Specimens from Mesoamerica." *Notes on Middle American Archaeology and Ethnology* 117:5–26. Carnegie Institute of Washington, Washington, D.C.

Kjerfve, Bjorn, Klaus Rutzler, and George H. Kierspe
1982 "Tides at Carrie Bow Cay, Belize." In *The Atlantic Barrier Reef Ecosystem at Carrie Bow Cay, Belize,* edited by Klaus Rutzler and Ian G. Macintyre, 47–51. Smithsonian Contributions to the Marine Sciences 12. Smithsonian Institution, Washington, D.C.

Kosakowsky, Laura J., and Duncan C. Pring
1998 "The Ceramics of Cuello, Belize: A New Evaluation." *Ancient Mesoamerica* 9:55–66.

Kraft, J. C., S. E. Aschenbrenner, and George Rapp Jr.
1977 "Paleogeographic Reconstructions of Coastal Aegean Sites." *Science* 195:941–47.

Lange, Frederick W.
1971 "Marine Resource: A Viable Subsistence Alternative for the Prehistoric Lowland Maya." *American Anthropologist* 73:610–39.

Lara, Maria E.
1993 "Divergent Wrench Faulting in the Belize Southern Lagoon: Implications for Tertiary Caribbean Plate Movements and Quaternary Reef Distribu-

tion." *American Association of Petroleum Geologists Bulletin* 77:1041–63.

1997   "Reply." *American Association of Petroleum Geologists Bulletin* 81:334–37.

Leventhal, Richard M.

1990   "Southern Belize: An Ancient Maya Region." In *Vision and Revision in Maya Studies,* edited by Flora S. Clancey and Peter D. Harrison, 125–41. University of New Mexico Press, Albuquerque.

Leyden, Barbara W.

1987   "Man and Climate in the Maya Lowlands." *Quaternary Research* 28:407–14.

Lighty, R. G., Ian G. Macintyre, and R. Stuckenrath

1982   "Acropora Palmata Reef Frameworks: A Reliable Indicator of Sea Level in the Western Atlantic for the Past 10,000 Years." *Coral Reefs* 1:125–30.

Longyear, John M., III

1952   *Copan Ceramics: A Study of Southeastern Maya Pottery.* Carnegie Institution of Washington Publication 597. Carnegie Institution, Washington, D.C.

Lowe, David B.

1995   "Sedimentology of Holocene Mixed Carbonate Siliclastic Deposits, Midwinter Lagoon, Belize, Central America." Master's thesis, Wichita State University.

Macintyre, Ian G., M. M. Littler, and D. S. Littler

1995   *Holocene History of Tobacco Range, Belize, Central America.* Atoll Research Bulletin 430. Smithsonian Institution, Washington, D.C.

MacKinnon, J. Jefferson

1989   "Coastal Maya Trade Routes in Southern Belize." In *Coastal Maya Trade,* edited by Heather McKillop and Paul F. Healy, 111–22. Occasional Papers in Anthropology 8. Trent University, Peterborough, Ontario, Canada.

MacKinnon, J. Jefferson, and Susan Kepecs

1989   "Prehispanic Salt-Making in Belize: New Evidence." *American Antiquity* 54:522–33.

Magnoni, Aline

1999   "Relative Sea-Level Rise and Excavations at Crown Conch Mound, a Partially-Submerged Ancient Maya Mound, Frenchman's Cay, Belize." Master's thesis, Department of Geography and Anthropology, Louisiana State University, Baton Rouge.

Mallory, John K.

1986   "'Workshops' and 'Specialized Production' in the Production of Maya Chert Tools: A Response to Shafer and Hester." *American Antiquity* 51:152–58.

Mannino, Joseph

1995   *Human Biology.* Mosby, New York.

Marcus, Joyce

1976   *Emblem and State in the Classic Maya Lowlands.* Dumbarton Oaks, Washington, D.C.

1983   "Lowland Maya Archaeology at the Crossroads." *American Antiquity* 48:454–88.

1984   "Reply to Hammond and Andrews." *American Antiquity* 49:829–33.

1991   "Another Pinch of Salt: A Comment on MacKinnon and Kepecs." *American Antiquity* 56:526–27.

1995   "Where Is Lowland Maya Archaeology Headed?" *Journal of Archaeological Research* 3:3–53.

Maxwell, David

2000   "Beyond Maritime Symbolism: Toxic Marine Objects from Ritual Contexts at Tikal." *Ancient Mesoamerica* 11:91–98.

Mazzullo, S. J., K. E. Anderson-Underwood, C. D. Burke, and W. D. Bischoff

1992   "Holocene Coral Patch Reef Ecology and Sedimentary Architecture, Northern Belize, Central America." *Palaios* 7:591–601.

Mazzullo, S. J., and A. M. Reid

1988   "Sedimentary Textures of Recent Belizean Peritidal Dolomite." *Journal of Sedimentary Petrology* 58:479–88.

Mazzullo, S. J., A. M. Reid, and S. M. Gregg

1987   "Dolomitization of Holocene Mg-Calcite Supratidal Deposits, Ambergris Cay, Belize." *Geological Society of America Bulletin* 98:224–31.

McAnany, Patricia A.

1989a "Stone-tool Production and Exchange in the Eastern Maya Lowlands: The Consumer Perspective from Pulltrouser Swamp." *American Antiquity* 54:332–46.

1989b "Economic Foundations of Prehistoric Maya Society: Paradigms and Concepts." In *Prehistoric Maya Economies of Belize*, edited by Patricia A. McAnany and Barry Isaac, 347–72. Research in Economic Anthropology, Supplement 4. JAI Press, Greenwich, Conn.

McIntire, W. G.

1954   *Correlation of Prehistoric Settlements and Delta Development.* Coastal Studies Institute, Technical Report 5. Louisiana State University, Baton Rouge.

McKillop, Heather

1980   "Moho Cay, Belize: Preliminary Investigations of Trade, Settlement, and Marine Resource Exploitation." Master's thesis, Department of Anthropology, Trent University, University Microfilms, Ann Arbor.

1984   "Prehistoric Maya Reliance on Marine Resources: Analysis of a Midden from Moho Cay, Belize." *Journal of Field Archaeology* 11:25–35.

1985   "Prehistoric Exploitation of the Manatee in the Maya and Circum-Caribbean Areas." *World Archaeology* 16:337–53.

1987   "Wild Cane Cay: An Insular Classic Period to Postclassic Period Maya Trading Station." Ph.D. diss., Department of Anthropology, University of California–Santa Barbara, University Microfilms, Ann Arbor.

1989   "Coastal Maya Trade: Obsidian Densities from Wild Cane Cay, Belize." In *Prehistoric Maya Economies of Belize*, edited by Patricia McAnany and

Barry Isaac, 17–56. Research in Economic Anthropology, Supplement 4. JAI Press, Greenwich, Conn.

1994a "Ancient Maya Tree-Cropping: A Viable Subsistence Alternative for the Island Maya." *Ancient Mesoamerica* 5:129–40.

1994b "Traders of the Maya Coast: Five Field Seasons in the Swamps of South Coastal Belize." *Mexicon* 16:115–19.

1995a "Underwater Archaeology, Salt Production, and Coastal Maya Trade at Stingray Lagoon, Belize." *Latin American Antiquity* 6:214–28.

1995b "The Role of Northern Ambergris Caye in Maya Obsidian Trade: Evidence from Visual Sourcing and Blade Technology," In *Maya Maritime Trade, Settlement, and Populations on Ambergris Caye, Belize,* edited by Thomas H. Guderjan and James F. Garber, 163–74. Labyrinthos Press, Culver City, Calif.

1995c "The 1994 Field Season in South-Coastal Belize." *LSU Maya Archaeology News* 1, Department of Geography and Anthropology, Louisiana State University. http://www.ga.lsu.edu/ArchaeologyNews95.htm/

1996a "Ancient Maya Trading Ports and the Integration of Long-Distance and Regional Economies: Wild Cane Cay in South-Coastal Belize." *Ancient Mesoamerica* 7:49–62.

1996b "Prehistoric Maya Use of Native Palms: Archaeobotanical and Ethnobotanical Evidence." In *The Managed Mosaic: Ancient Maya Agriculture and Resource Use,* edited by Scott L. Fedick, 278–94. University of Utah Press, Salt Lake City.

1997 Excavations in Coral Architecture at Frenchman's Cay, 1997. *LSU Maya Archaeology News* 2, Department of Geography and Anthropology, Louisiana State University. http://www.ga.lsu.edu/ArchaeologyNews97.htm/

2000 "Type-Variety Analysis of Maya Pottery from Port Honduras, Belize." Unpublished manuscript. Department of Geography and Anthropology, Louisiana State University, Baton Rouge.

2001 "In Search of Maya Sea Traders: Archaeology at Wild Cane Cay." Unpublished manuscript. Department of Geography and Anthropology, Louisiana State University, Baton Rouge.

McKillop, Heather, and Paul F. Healy, editors

1989 *Coastal Maya Trade.* Occasional Papers in Anthropology 8. Trent University, Peterborough, Ontario, Canada.

McKillop, Heather, and Stuart Herrmann

2000 "Intra-regional Distribution of Obsidian in the Port Honduras, Belize." Unpublished manuscript. Department of Geography and Anthropology, Louisiana State University, Baton Rouge.

McKillop, Heather, L. J. Jackson, Helen Michel, Fred Stross, and Frank Asaro

1988 "Chemical Sources Analysis of Maya Obsidian Artifacts: New Perspectives from Wild Cane Cay, Belize." In *Archaeometry 88,* edited by R. M. Farqhuar,

R. G. V. Hancock, and Larry A. Pavlish, 239–44. Department of Physics, University of Toronto, Toronto.

McKillop, Heather, and Terance Winemiller

2001   "Ancient Maya Environment, Settlement, and Diet: Quantitative and GIS Analyses of Mollusca from Frenchman's Cay, Belize." In *Maya Zooarchaeology*, edited by Kitty Emery. Institute of Archaeology, University of California, Los Angeles (in press).

McKillop, Heather, Terance Winemiller, and Farrell Jones

2000   "A GIS Analysis of Obsidian from the Surface at Wild Cane Cay." Paper presented at the Annual Meeting of the Society for American Archaeology, Philadelphia.

McSwain, R.

1991   "Chert and Chalcedony Tools." In *Cuello: An Early Maya Community in Belize*, edited by Norman Hammon, 160–73. Cambridge University Press, New York.

Meighan, Clement W., and John A. Bennyhoff

1952   "Excavations in British Honduras." Manuscript. Department of Archaeology, Government of Belize, Belmopan, Belize.

Messenger, Lewis C., Jr.

1990   "Ancient Winds of Change: Climate Settings and Prehistoric Social Complexity in Mesoamerica." *Ancient Mesoamerica* 1:21–40.

Miller, Arthur

1977   "The Maya and the Sea: Trade and Cult at Tancah and Tulum, Quintana Roo, Mexico." In *The Sea in the Pre-Columbian World*, edited by Elizabeth Benson, 97–140. Dumbarton Oaks, Washington, D.C.

Mitchum, Beverly A.

1991   "Lithic Artifacts from Cerros, Belize: Production, Consumption, and Trade." In *Maya Stone Tools, Selected Papers from the Second Maya Lithic Conference*, edited by Thomas R. Hester and Harry J. Shafer, 45–54. Prehistory Press, Madison, Wis.

Mock, Shirley B.

1994   "The Northern River Lagoon Site (NRL): Late to Terminal Classic Maya Settlement, Saltmaking, and Survival on the Northern Belize Coast." Ph.D. diss., Department of Anthropology, University of Texas, Austin.

Moholy-Nagy, Hattula

1990   "The Misidentification of Mesoamerican Lithic Workshops." *Latin American Antiquity* 1:268–79.

1997   "Middens, Construction Fill, and Offerings: Evidence for the Organization of Classic Period Craft Production at Tikal, Guatemala." *Journal of Field Archaeology* 24:293–313.

Morner, N. A.

1976   "Eustacy and Geoid Changes." *Journal of Geology* 84:123–51.

Mosnier, Serge
1994   "Le Sel, or blanc des Mayas." *Sciences et Avenir* 566:44–49.
Murra, John V.
1980   *The Economic Organization of the Inca State.* Research in Economic Anthropology, Supplement 1. JAI Press, Greenwich, Conn.
Nance, C. Roger
1992   "Guzman Mound: A Late Preclassic Salt Works on the South Coast of Guatemala." *Ancient Mesoamerica* 3:27–46.
Nenquin, Jacques
1961   *Salt: A Study in Economic Prehistory.* De Tempel, Brugge, Belgium.
Neumann, Thomas W.
1977   "The Biocultural Approach to Salt Taboos: The Case of the Southeastern United States." *Current Anthropology* 18:289–308.
Palka, Joel W.
1997   "Reconstructing Classic Maya Socioeconomic Differentiation at the Collapse of Dos Pilas, Peten, Guatemala." *Ancient Mesoamerica* 8:293–306.
Parkinson, Randall W.
1989   "Decelerating Holocene Sea-Level Rise and Its Influence on Southwest Florida Coastal Evolution: A Transgressive/ Regressive Stratigraphy." *Journal of Sedimentary Petrology* 59:960–72.
Parsons, Jeffrey R.
1989   "Una Etnografia Arquelogica de la Produccion Tradicional de Sal en Nexquipayac, Estado de Mexico." *Arqueologia* 2:69–80.
Peacock, D. P. S.
1982   *Pottery in the Roman World: An Ethnoarchaeological Approach.* Longman, London.
Pearson, Charles E., David B. Kelley, Richard A. Weinstein, and Sherwood M. Gagliano
1986   *Archaeological Investigations on the Outer Continental Shelf: A Study within the Sabine River Valley, Offshore Louisiana and Texas.* OCS Study. Service, Reston, Va.
Pendergast, David M.
1969a   *The Prehistory of Actun Balam, British Honduras.* Art and Archaeology Occasional Papers 16. Royal Ontario Museum, Toronto.
1969b   *Altun Ha, British Honduras (Belize): The Sun God's Tomb.* Art and Archaeology Occasional Papers 19. Royal Ontario Museum, Toronto.
1970   *A. H. Anderson's Excavations at Rio Frio Cave E, British Honduras (Belize).* Art and Archaeology Occasional Papers 20. Royal Ontario Museum, Toronto.
1971   *Excavations at Eduardo Quiroz Cave, British Honduras (Belize).* Art and Archaeology Occasional Papers 21. Royal Ontario Museum, Toronto.
1979   *Excavations at Altun Ha, Belize, 1964–1970. Volume 1.* Royal Ontario Museum, Toronto.
Pirazolli, P. A.
1991   *World Atlas of Holocene Sea-Level Changes.* Elsevier Oceanographic Series 58. Elsevier, Amsterdam.

Pohl, Mary D.
1976 "Ethnozoology of the Maya: An Analysis of Fauna from Five Sites in the Peten, Guatemala." Ph.D. diss., Department of Anthropology, Harvard University, Cambridge, Mass.

Pohl, Mary D., editor
1990 *Ancient Maya Wetland Agriculture.* Westview Press, Boulder.

Pool, Christopher A.
1990 "Ceramic Production, Distribution, and Resource Procurement at Matacapan, Veracruz, Mexico." Ph.D. diss., Department of Anthropology, Tulane University, New Orleans.

Potter, Daniel R., and Eleanor M. King
1995 "A Heterarchical Approach to Lowland Maya Socioeconomics." In *Heterarchy and the Analysis of Complex Societies,* edited by Robert M. Ehrenreich, Carole L. Crumley, and Janet E. Levy, 17–32. Archeological Papers 6. American Anthropological Association, Washington, D.C.

Precht, William F.
1997 "Divergent Wrench Faulting in the Belize Southern Lagoon: Implications for Tertiary Caribbean Plate Movements and Quaternary Reef Distribution: Discussion." *American Association of Petroleum Geologists Bulletin* 81: 329–33.

Price, Barbara J.
1978 "Commerce and Culture Process in Mesoamerica." In *Mesoamerican Communication Routes and Culture Contacts,* edited by Thomas A. Lee and Carlos Navarrete, 231–45. Papers of the New World Archaeological Foundation 40. Brigham Young University, Provo, Utah.

Purdy, E. G.
1974 "Karst Determined Facies Patterns in British Honduras: Holocene Carbonate Sedimentation Model." *American Association of Petroleum Geologists Bulletin* 58(5):825–55.

Purdy, E. G., Walter C. Pusey III, and K. F. Wantland
1975 "Continental Shelf of Belize—Regional Shelf Attributes." In *Belize Shelf—Carbonate Sediments, Clastic Sediments, and Ecology,* edited by K. F. Wantland and Walter C. Pusey III, 1–52. Studies in Geology 2. American Association of Petroleum Geologists, Tulsa.

Pyburn, K. Anne
1990 "Settlement Patterns at Nohmul: Preliminary Results of Four Excavation Seasons." In *Precolumbian Population History in the Maya Lowlands,* edited by T. Patrick Culbert and Don S. Rice, 183–97. University of New Mexico Press, Albuquerque.

Rands, Robert L., and Ronald L. Bishop
1980 "Resource Procurement Zones and Patterns of Ceramic Exchange in the Palenque Region, Mexico." In *Models and Methods in Regional Exchange,* edited by Robert E. Fry, 19–46. Society for American Archaeology Papers 1, Washington, D.C.

Rathje, William L.
1971 "The Origin and Development of Lowland Classic Maya Civilization." *American Antiquity* 36:275–85.

Rathje, William L., David A. Gregory, and Frederick M. Wiseman
1978 "Trade Models and Archaeological Problems: Classic Maya Examples." In *Mesoamerican Communication Routes and Cultural Contacts*, edited by Thomas A. Lee and Carlos Navarrete, 147–75. New World Archaeological Foundation Paper 40. Brigham Young University, Provo, Utah.

Reents-Budet, Dorie
1994 *Painting the Maya Universe: Royal Ceramics of the Classic Period.* Duke University Press, Durham.
1998 "Elite Maya Pottery and Artisans as Social Indicators." In *Craft and Social Identity*, edited by Cathy Costin and Rita Wright, 71–89. Archaeological Papers of the American Anthropological Association 8. American Anthropological Association, Washington, D.C.

Reents-Budet, Dorie, Ronald L. Bishop, Jennifer T. Taschek, and Joseph W. Ball
2000 "Out of the Palace Dumps: Ceramic Production and Use at Buenavista del Cayo." *Ancient Mesoamerica* 11:99–121.

Reina, Ruben E., and Robert M. Hill III
1978 *The Traditional Pottery of Guatemala.* University of Texas Press, Austin.

Reina, Ruben E., and John Monaghen
1981 "The Ways of the Maya: Salt Production in Sacapulas, Guatemala." *Expedition* 23:13–33.

Renfrew, Colin D.
1975 "Trade as Action at a Distance: Questions of Integration and Communication." In *Ancient Civilization and Trade*, edited by Jeremy A. Sabloff and C. C. Lamberg-Karlovsky, 3–59. University of New Mexico Press, Albuquerque.

Rice, Don S.
1978 "Population Growth and Subsistence Alternatives in a Tropical Lacustrine Environment." In *Prehispanic Maya Agriculture,* edited by Peter D. Harrison and B. L. Turner, 35–61. University of New Mexico Press, Albuquerque.

Rice, Don S., and T. Patrick Culbert
1990 "Historical Contexts for Population Reconstruction in the Maya Lowlands." In *Precolumbian Population History in the Maya Lowlands,* edited by T. Patrick Culbert and Don S. Rice, 1–36. University of New Mexico Press, Albuquerque.

Rice, Prudence M.
1981 "Evolution of Specialized Pottery Production: A Trial Model." *Current Anthropology* 22:219–40.
1987a "Economic Change in the Lowland Maya Late Classic Period." In *Specialization, Exchange, and Complex Societies,* edited by Elizabeth M. Brumfiel and Timothy K. Earle, 76–85. Cambridge University Press, New York.
1987b *Pottery Analysis: A Source Book.* University of Chicago Press, Chicago.

1989 "Ceramic Diversity, Production, and Use." In *Quantifying Diversity in Archaeology*, edited by Robert Leonard and George T. Jones, 109–17. Cambridge University Press, New York.

Riehm, K.
1961 "Prehistoric Salt Boiling." *Antiquity* 35:181–91.

Robertson, R. R.
1975 "Systematic List of Commonly Occurring Marine Mollusks of Belize." In *Belize Shelf—Carbonate Sediments, Clastic Sediments, and Ecology*, edited by K. F. Wantland and W. C. Pusey III, 40–52. Studies in Geology 2. American Association of Petroleum Geologists, Tulsa.

Roys, Ralph L.
1943 *The Indian Background of Colonial Yucatan*. Carnegie Institution of Washington, Publication 548. Carnegie Institution, Washington, D.C.

Rützler, Klaus, and Ian G. Macintyre, editors
1982 *The Atlantic Barrier Reef Ecosystem at Carrie Bow Cay, Belize*. Smithsonian Contributions to the Marine Sciences 12. Smithsonian Institution Press, Washington, D.C.

Rye, Owen S.
1976 *Pottery Technology: Principles and Reconstruction*. Manuals in Archeology 4. Taraxacum, Washington, D.C.

Sabloff, Jeremy A.
1975 *Excavations at Seibal, Department of the Peten, Guatemala: Ceramics*. Memoirs of the Peabody Museum of Archaeology and Ethnology 13(2). Harvard University, Cambridge, Mass.
1977 "Old Myths, New Myths: The Role of Sea Traders in the Development of Ancient Maya Civilization." In *The Sea in the Pre-Columbian World*, edited by Elizabeth Benson, 67–95. Dumbarton Oaks, Washington, D.C.

Sahlins, Marshall
1972 *Stone Age Economics*. Aldine, Chicago.

Sanders, William T.
1977 "Environmental Heterogeneity and the Evolution of Lowland Maya Civilization." In *The Origins of Maya Civilization*, edited by Richard E. W. Adams, 287–97. University of New Mexico Press, Albuquerque.

Sanders, William T., and Barbara Price
1968 *Mesoamerica: The Evolution of a Civilization*. Random House, New York.

Sanders, William T., and Robert S. Santley
1983 "A Tale of Three Cities: Energetics and Urbanism in Prehispanic Central Mexico." In *Prehistoric Settlement Patterns: Essays in Honor of Gordon R. Willey*, edited by Evon Z. Vogt and Richard M. Leventhal, 243–91. University of New Mexico Press, Albuquerque.

Santley, Robert S., Philip S. Arnold III, and Christopher A. Pool
1986 "The Ceramic Production System at Matacapan, Veracruz, Mexico." *Journal of Field Archaeology* 16:107–32.

Santley, Robert S., and R. R. Kneebone
1993 "Craft Specialization, Refuse Disposal, and the Creation of Spatial Archaeological Records in Prehispanic Mesoamerica." In *Prehispanic Domestic Units in Western Mesoamerica*, edited by Robert S. Santley and Kenneth G. Hirth, 37–63. CRC Press, Boca Raton, Fla.

Santone, Lenore
1997 "Transport Costs, Consumer Demand, and Patterns of Intraregional Exchange: A Perspective on Commodity Production and Distribution from Northern Belize." *Latin American Antiquity* 8:71–88.

Schele, Linda, and Peter Mathews
1991 "Royal Visits and Other Intersite Relationships among the Classic Maya." In *Classic Maya Political History*, edited by T. Patrick Culbert, 226–52. Cambridge University Press, New York.

Schele, Linda, and Mary Ellen Miller
1986 *The Blood of Kings: Dynasty and Ritual in Maya Art*. George Braziller, New York.

Scholl, D. W., F. C. Craighead, and M. Struiver
1969 "Florida Submergence Curve Revisited: Its Relations to Coastal Sedimentation Rates." *Science* 163:562–64.

Service, Elman R.
1975 *Origins of the State and Civilization: The Process of Cultural Evolution*. W. W. Norton, New York.

Shafer, Harry J., and Thomas R. Hester
1983 "Ancient Maya Chert Workshops in Northern Belize, Central America." *American Antiquity* 48:519–43.
1986 "Maya Tool Craft Specialization and Production at Colha, Belize: A Reply to Mallory." *American Antiquity* 51:158–66.

Shinn, Eugene A., J. Harold Hudson, Robert B. Halley, Barbara Lidz, Daniel M. Robbin, and Ian G. Macintyre
1982 "Geology and Sediment Accumulation Rates at Carrie Bow Cay, Belize." In *The Atlantic Barrier Reef Ecosystem at Carrie Bow Cay*, edited by Klaus Rützler and Ian G. Macintyre, 63–75. Smithsonian Institution, Washington, D.C.

Shipley, W. E., III, and Elizabeth Graham
1987 "Petrographic Analysis and Preliminary Source Identification of Selected Stone Artifacts from the Maya Sites of Seibal and Uaxactun, Guatemala." *Journal of Archaeological Science* 14:367–83.

Sidrys, Raymond V.
1983 *Archaeological Excavations in Northern Belize, Central America*. Monograph 17. Institute of Archaeology, University of California, Los Angeles.

Simmons, Michael P., and Gerald F. Brem
1979 "The Analysis and Distribution of Volcanic Ash-Tempered Pottery in the Lowland Maya Area." *American Antiquity* 44:79–91.

Sluyter, Andrew
1993 "Long-Distance Staple Transport in Western Mesoamerica: Insights through Quantitative Modeling." *Ancient Mesoamerica* 4:193–99.

Smith, Michael E.
1990 "Long-Distance Trade Under the Aztec Empire: The Archaeological Evidence." *Ancient Mesoamerica* 1:153–69.

Smith, Robert E.
1955 *Ceramic Sequence at Uaxactun, Guatemala*, vols. 1–2. Middle American Research Institute Publication 20. Tulane University, New Orleans.

Smith, Robert E., and James C. Gifford
1966 *Maya Ceramic Varieties, Types, and Wares at Uaxactun: "Supplement to Ceramic Sequence at Uaxactun, Guatemala."* Middle American Research Institute Publication, vol. 28 no. 4. Tulane University, New Orleans.

Spence, Michael W.
1981 "Obsidian Production and the State in Teotihuacan." *American Antiquity* 46:769–88.

Steiner, Edward P.
1994 "Prehistoric Maya Settlement along Joe Taylor Creek, Belize." Master's thesis, Department of Geography and Anthropology, Louisiana State University, Baton Rouge.

Stoddart, David R.
1963 *Effects of Hurricane Hattie on the British Honduras Reefs and Cays, October 30–31, 1961.* Atoll Research Bulletin 95. Smithsonian Institution, Washington, D.C.
1990 "The Impact of Sea-Level Rise on Mangrove Shorelines." *Progress in Physical Geography* 14:483–520.

Strong, William D.
1935 *Archaeological Investigations in the Bay Islands, Spanish Honduras.* Smithsonian Miscellaneous Collections 92(14). Smithsonian Institution, Washington, D.C.

Stuiver, Minze, and Gordon W. Pearson
1986 "High-Precision Calibration of the Radiocarbon Time Scale, A.D. 1950–500 B.C." *Radiocarbon* 28:805–38.

Taube, Karl A.
1989 "The Maize Tamale in Classic Maya Diet, Epigraphy, and Art." *American Antiquity* 54:31–51.

Teeter, J. W.
1975 "Distribution of Holocene Marine Ostracoda from Belize." In *Belize Shelf—Carbonate Sediments, Clastic Sediments, and Ecology,* edited by K. F. Wantland and W. C. Pusey III, 400–499. Studies in Geology 2. American Association of Petroleum Geologists, Tulsa.

Thompson, Sir J. Eric S.
1951 "Canoes and Navigation of the Maya and their Neighbours." *Journal of the Royal Anthropological Institute* 79:69–78.

1970   *Maya History and Religion.* University of Oklahoma Press, Norman.

Tourtellot, Gair, and Jeremy A. Sabloff

1972   "Exchange Systems among the Ancient Maya." *American Antiquity* 37: 126–35.

Trik, Aubrey S.

1963   "The Splendid Tomb of Temple 1 at Tikal, Guatemala." *Expedition* 6:2–18.

Valdez, Fred, Jr., and Shirley B. Mock

1991   "Additional Considerations for Prehispanic Saltmaking in Belize." *American Antiquity* 56:520–25.

Valdez, Fred, Jr., Lauren Sullivan, and Thomas H. Guderjan

1995   "Ceramics from Northern Ambergris Caye Sites." In *Maya Maritime Trade, Settlement, and Populations on Ambergris Caye, Belize,* edited by Thomas H. Guderjan and James F. Garber, 95–112. Labyrinthos Press, Culver City, Calif.

Van der Leeuw, S. E.

1976   *Studies in the Technology of Ancient Pottery.* Organization for the Advancement of Pure Research, Amsterdam.

Vermeer, Donald E.

1959   *The Cays of British Honduras. Report of Field Work Carried Out under ONR Contract 222(11).* Department of Geography, University of California, Berkeley.

Wallerstein, Immanuel

1974   *The Modern World System,* vol. 1. Academic Press, New York.

Wantland, Kenneth F.

1975   "Distribution of Holocene Benthonic Foraminifera on the Belize Shelf." In *Belize Shelf—Carbonate Sediments, Clastic Sediments, and Ecology,* edited by Kenneth F. Wantland and Walter C. Pusey III, 332–99. Studies in Geology 2. American Association of Petroleum Geologists, Tulsa.

Wantland, Kenneth F., and Walter C. Pusey III

1971   *The Southern Shelf of British Honduras.* New Orleans Geological Society, New Orleans.

Watson, Rachel M.

1999   "Excavations of Maya Coral Architecture, Spondylus Mound, Frenchman's Cay, Belize." Master's thesis, Department of Geography and Anthropology, Louisiana State University, Baton Rouge.

White, Christine D., and Henry P. Schwarcz

1989   "Ancient Maya Diet: As Inferred from Isotopic and Elemental Analysis of Human Bone." *Journal of Archaeological Science* 16:451–74.

Williams, Eduardo

1999   "The Ethnoarchaeology of Salt Production at Lake Cuitzo, Michoacan, Mexico." *Latin American Antiquity* 10:400–414.

Winemiller, Terance

1997   "Limestone Resource Exploitation by the Ancient Maya at Chichen Itza,

Yucatan, Mexico." Master's thesis, Department of Geography and Anthropology, Louisiana State University, Baton Rouge.

Wing, Elizabeth S.

1975 "Animal Remains from Lubaantun." In *Lubaantun: A Classic Maya Realm*, by Norman Hammond, 379–82. Monographs of the Peabody Museum of Archaeology and Ethnology 2. Harvard University, Cambridge, Mass.

1977 "Factors Influencing the Exploitation of Marine Resources." In *The Sea in the Pre-Columbian World*, edited by Elizabeth Benson, 47–66. Dumbarton Oaks, Washington, D.C.

Winslow, M. A.

1992 "Modeling Paleoshorelines in Geologically Active Regions: Applications to the Shumagin Islands, Southwest Alaska." In *Paleoshorelines and Prehistory*, edited by L. Johnson, 151–69. CRC Press, Bota Raton, Fla.

Woodroffe, Colin D.

1981 "Mangrove Swamp Stratigraphy and Holocene Transgression, Grand Cayman Island, West Indies." *Marine Geology* 41:271–94.

1982 "Geomorphology and Development of Mangrove Swamps, Grand Cayman Island, West Indies." *Bulletin of Marine Science* 32:381–98.

1988 "Mangroves and Sedimentation in Reef Environments: Indicators of Past Sea-Level Changes and Present Sea-Level Trends." *Proceedings of the Sixth International Coral Reef Symposium*, edited by J. H. Choat et al., 3:535–39. Sixth International Coral Reef Symposium Executive Committee, Townsville, Australia.

1990 "The Impact of Sea-Level Rise on Mangrove Shorelines." *Progress in Physical Geography* 14:483–520.

1995 *Mangrove Vegetation of Tobacco Range and Nearby Mangrove Ranges, Central Belize Barrier Reef.* Atoll Research Bulletin 427. Smithsonian Institution, Washington, D.C.

Woods, A. J.

1981 "Form, Fabric, and Function: Some Observations of the Cooking Pot in Antiquity." In *Ceramics and Civilization*, vol. 2, *Technique and Style*, edited by W. D. Kingery, 157–72. Ceramic Society, Columbus, Ohio.

Wright, A. Charles S., D. H. Romney, R. H. Arbuckle, and V. E. Vial

1959 *Land Use in British Honduras: Report of the British Land Use Survey Team.* Colonial Research Publication 24. Colonial Office, London.

Index

Page numbers for illustrations are in italics.

Heather McKillop is William G. Haag Professor of Archaeology in the Department of Geography and Anthropology at Louisiana State University. She has carried out fieldwork on the coast of Belize since 1979 and has published many articles on the ancient coastal Maya.